DATE DUE			

THE RED SEA
-TERROR-
TRIANGLE

THE RED SEA
–TERROR–
TRIANGLE

Sudan, Somalia, Yemen, and Islamic Terror

SHAUL SHAY

TRANSLATED BY RACHEL LIBERMAN

The Interdisciplinary Center, Herzliya

The International Policy Institute for Counter-Terrorism

TRANSACTION PUBLISHERS
NEW BRUNSWICK (U.S.A.) AND LONDON (U.K.)

First paperback printing 2007
Copyright © 2005 by The Interdisciplinary Center Herzliya Projects Ltd.

This book is printed on acid-free paper that meets the American National Standard for Permanence of Paper for Printed Library Materials.

Library of Congress Catalog Number: 2004051604
ISBN: 0-7658-0247-3 (cloth); 1-4128-0620-8 (paper)
Printed in the United States of America

Library of Congress Cataloging-in-Publication Data

Shai, Shaul.
    The Red Sea terror triangle : Sudan, Somalia, Yemen, and Islamic terror /
Shaul Shay.
    p. cm.
Includes bibliographical references and index.
ISBN 0-7658-0247-3 (cloth : alk. paper)— ISBN 1-4128-0620-8 (pbk: alk.
paper)
    1. Terrorism—Sudan—History. 2. Terrorism—Somalia—History. 3.
Terrorism—Yemen—History. 4. Islam and terrorism—Sudan. 5. Islam and
terrorism—Somalia. 6. Islam and terrorism—Yemen. 7. Sudan—History.
8. Somalia—History. 9. Yemen—History. I. Title.
HV6433.S73S43 2004
303.6'25'0953—dc22

2004051604

Contents

Introduction

In the wake of the terror attacks on September 11, 2001, the United States declared war against global terror and set Al Qaida and the Taliban regime in Afghanistan as the initial targets of the campaign. A short time after the "Coalition against Terror," with the US at its head, launched its offensive in Afghanistan, the question arose as to which country would serve as the next target in the counter-terror campaign. Politicians, security experts and academics indicated three countries that might be next in line in the war against terror; Sudan, Somalia and Yemen.

This assumption was not coincidental. It was based on the historical record of each of these countries, which was involved in some form or another in the provision of shelter and refuge to Islamic terror organizations, and in the case of Sudan—even in the direct support of these organizations and their operation.

The fear vis-à-vis the campaign waged by the United States and the "Coalition against Terror" prompted an "about face" in the Sudanese and Yemenite approaches, both of which hastened to denounce involvement in terror and aligned themselves alongside the United States in its war. In Somalia, which is defined as a "failing state" that lacks an effective central government, the various rival factions have declared that they support the war against terror, and cast accusations against each other regarding support and involvement in terror. The United States took vigorous steps to enlist these countries in the counter-terror campaign and demanded that the authorities take practical action against Islamic terror entities in their countries. Nevertheless, parallel to the growing cooperation, the United States and the coalition deployed air and sea forces in order to prevent the infiltration of Al Qaida activists and other radical Islamic terror organizations into countries in the region.

Sudan, Yemen and Somalia are located in a region of strategic importance, on both sides of the vital sea route linking the Arabian Sea (the Indian Ocean) and the Red Sea. All of the oil tankers from the Persian Gulf region pass through the Bab al-Mandab Straits, which are under the control of Eritrea and Yemen, on their way to Europe. The importance of the Horn of Africa and the Arabian Peninsula did not escape the attention of the colonial powers, which overtook this region and actively controlled it until the sixties of the twentieth century.

The three countries at the center of this study are Muslim states located at the periphery of the focal point of Islamic development and intensification (in the Arabian Peninsula, Egypt and the vicinity of the "Fertile Crescent"). These countries developed into national entities from within the reality of colonial government on the one hand, and the influence of the core Arab countries, on the other (for example, the Egyptian influence in Sudan or Saudi Arabian influence in Yemen).

Sudan and Somalia constitute an Islamic cultural bridgehead in the eastern and southern parts of the African continent. The geopolitical location of these countries attracted not only the colonial powers followed by the superpowers during the "Cold War," but also radical Islamic entities that grasped the innate potential of this region vis-à-vis the fortification and dissemination of radical Islam. The involvement of Iran following the Khomeini Revolution and that of radical Islamic entities from Saudi Arabia left its stamp on the nations of that area and turned them into a focal point for confrontation with the West (mainly the United States). Osama Bin Laden, Al Qaida and members of radical Islamic organizations discovered allies and refuge in these countries. The presence of radical Islamic entities in the area, alongside local problems and conflicts on a national, ethnic and tribal basis, turned the countries in that region into a focal point for nations both near and far.

The aim of this book is to study the three countries which I have dubbed "the terror triangle of the Red Sea," particularly the links that each of them maintains with Islamic terror and the reciprocal ties between them, based on the assumption that in the future all or some of them may constitute a basis for Islamic terror organizations.

The book contains five sections: The first three sections describe the historical, political and social developments in each of the countries and their involvement in Islamic terror. The fourth section describes the impact of Islamic terror that has developed in those three countries upon the entire region, as expressed in large terror attacks that were perpetrated in neighboring countries. The fifth section offers an integrative analysis of the characteristics of the three countries as well as the reasons for their involvement in terror. This section is also dedicated to an extensive discussion of cultural aspects that constitute the roots of Islamic terror, as well as the connection between Islamic terror and "failing countries," which represent its preferred arena for activity. At the end of this section I will present an assessment regarding the characteristics of future terror threats, as well as recommendations regarding ways to contend with them in this arena.

Part I

Sudan and Islamic Terror

1

Sudan—A Historical Review

The Beginning of Islam in Sudan (up to the al Mahdi Period)

From a historical perspective it would appear that Sudan was the natural candidate for the development of a Fundamentalist Islamic regime due to a variety of socioeconomic, geopolitical, ethnic, and other reasons. The infiltration of Islam into the areas where Sudan was established began in the fifteenth century with the influence of Muslim merchants and mainly stemmed from the activities of individual clerics (*faqaha*) who arrived from Saudi Arabia and Egypt, preaching Islam in the villages and among the nomad tribes in Sudan. Islamic influence during this period spread gradually alongside the traditions and beliefs that were prevalent among populations in that region.[1]

Alongside the Islamic activity of the *faqaha*, in the sixteenth century, Sudan witnessed the growth of a phenomenon (as the result of a process that had begun earlier in other Muslim focal points) known as the Sufi Orders.[2] The growth of the Sufi Orders came as a counter-reaction to the deterioration of the Islamic empire and reflected the search for mystical and spiritual answers as the result of the decreased power of Islam in the light of the disappointment with the orthodox religious establishment of the *Ulama* (religious clerics). The Sufi Orders extolled the preference for spiritual abstemiousness over material achievements, and preached simplicity and humility. They regarded themselves as a bridge between the simple individual and the spiritual world of faith and godliness. They offered the individual in the Sudanese society the possibility of winning a blessing (a spiritual blessing) by clinging to the commandments of Islam according to the Orders' instructions, which forged the link between the individual, the community, and the true faith.

3

In the sixteenth to eighteenth centuries, the Sufi Orders spread throughout northern Sudan. Among the many Orders, the "Khatamiya" was particularly prominent. This Order was established by Muhammad Otman al Marani, who came from Mecca, and became the largest and strongest Sufi Order in Sudan.

A significant shift in Islamic stature occurred in 1820 as a result of the invasion by Ottoman and Egyptian powers of the area called Balad el-Sudan (the Land of the Black). Muslim rulers in the area established a government and an administrative system that acted to expand the "Islamization" to other areas, including the southern districts of (modern-day) Sudan. The Ottoman-Egyptian regime founded an Islamic establishment headed by Ulama and many of the Sufi Orders were incorporated into the new religious structure, including the Khatamiya, which also developed into a central economic force due to its status as an ally of the Ottoman-Egyptian regime. On the other hand, there were Sufi Orders that opposed the Islamic establishment and constituted a core of opposition to the regime. One of the Orders included in this category was the Samania Order, among whose members was Muhammad Ahmad Abdallah, none other than "al Mahdi."

In 1881 the first attempt was made to establish an independent political and religious entity in Sudan. Muhammad Ahmad Abdallah declared himself "al Mahdi" (the messiah) and announced a Jihad to drive the foreign rule out of Sudan. In the beginning, the authorities in Cairo and Khartoum attached little significance to al Mahdi and his followers; however, al Mahdi gradually succeeded in recruiting more members to the ranks of his movement and united several tribes around him. At their head he set out on a Jihad against the Egyptian and Ottoman forces, and defeated them. As the result of his victories, al Mahdi's movement gained momentum and his forces took over large areas in the southern Nile Basin.

The British, who at that time encroached upon the Ottoman Empire's hold in Egypt, decided to deal with the problem of the uprising in Sudan. In 1883, a task force led by General Charles Gordon was sent to suppress the uprising and rescue the Egyptian forces trapped in Khartoum. Gordon's forces reached Khartoum but were then surrounded by al Mahdi's columns. Al Mahdi's siege on Khartoum went on for about a year until January 1885, when his forces breached the city and conquered it. General Gordon was killed in the battle over the city. The conquest of Khartoum was the pinnacle of al Mahdi's war, after which he then established an Islamic state as the result of the successful Jihad and enforced the Sharia as the state law. During the course of the war, Islamic suicide attacks[3] were initiated for the first time and the British forces found it difficult to contend with this phenomenon.

Six months after al Mahdi had captured Khartoum he succumbed to typhus, but his successor, the Calipha Abdallah, succeeded in fortifying his control, established his capital in Umdurman, and the Islamic state with him at the helm continued to thrive until the Battle of Umdurman in 1898, when his forces were defeated by a British-Egyptian task force under the command of General Kitchner. In the course of history, the Islamic state established by al Mahdi became a myth and a foundation stone in the Muslim religious annals of Sudan.[4] In 1899, a British-Egyptian agreement was signed regarding the establishment of a British-Egyptian Condominium (under British dominance) over Sudanese territory. This condominium existed until 1956, when Sudan won its independence.

Sudan's Road to Independence[5]

The joint Anglo-Egyptian authority was no more than a pretext; in reality the British controlled events in Sudan. However, this did not suffice to sever the connection between the political developments in Sudan and in Egypt.

The Egyptian national movement had not relinquished what it regarded as Egypt's historical and legal rights in Sudan, which it viewed as vital to Egyptian interests. It was clear to Egypt that from Sudan it would be possible to obstruct the country's source of water, and that cotton cultivation could be developed there that would compete with Egypt's industry. This is what led to their aspiration to rule Sudan or at the very least ensure that a friendly regime would be in control.

The importance of the Sudanese question to Egyptian policy and to Egyptian-British relations on the one hand, and Sudan's slow internal development on the other, resulted in a situation whereby up to the 1940s Sudan's political life was dependent mainly on the Anglo-Egyptian relations. Only in the 1940s did the buds of public organizations in Sudan begin to develop and burgeon into political parties. The unique character of these parties lay in their strong link with the main religious Orders in this country, particularly the "Mahdiya" (whose supporters are called "Antsar") and the Khatamiya (or "Mirgania.") The population, which predominantly remained organized in tribal frameworks, was dominated by these two Orders. The Mahdiya Order rallied around the leadership of Abd al Rahman, al Mahdi's son, who had considerable sway over the tribal population, mainly in central and western Sudan. The Khatamiya Order, led by the al-Mirgani family, represented a more orthodox approach from the religious aspect, and its support among the population was not as strong.

The leadership of the Mahdiya, which aspired to play a central role in Sudan, gradually reduced its hostile activities against the British, but persevered in its struggles against Egypt, which it regarded as an obstacle to Sudan's aspiration for independence. From the mid-1940s, the Umma party (Community of Islamic Believers), the political arm of the Mahdiya, amassed the entities that called for an independent Sudan, and relied in the elections mainly on the votes of the tribesmen who supported the Order.

In contrast, the Khatamiya Order adopted a clear pro-Egyptian policy, and its leadership under Sayyad Ali al Migrani aspired to unify Sudan and Egypt. The main support for the pro-Egyptian factions was based in the urban centers, where Egypt had influence, mainly over the intelligentsia. In contrast to the adversary's camp, in the pro-Egyptian camp there was no unanimity, and the attempt to unify the various factions under the leadership of the Khatamiya in the framework of the "National Unity Party" did not endure.

The 1940s also witnessed the development of strong professional unions in Sudan with clear leftist leanings. Although there was no developed industry in Sudan, the network of railroads built by the British represented a meeting place for thousands of workers and served as a kind of "hothouse" for the development of the unions. The combination of educated leftist elements and leadership of the professional unions led to the establishment of the Sudanese Communist party. In the 1940s, the struggle for independence in Sudan was placed at the top of the political agenda, pushing social problems aside.

Sudan's struggle for independence at the end of the 1940s was waged on two levels, featuring: the desire to overthrow the British custodianship, and at the same time, the desire to form some sort of link with Egypt, as opposed to aspiring to establish an independent Sudanese state. Britain, which supported an independent Sudanese state for its own reasons, initiated a gradual advancement of the country towards independence, while cooperating with anti-Egyptian Sudanese elements and entities that favored independence. The Egyptians and their lackeys attempted to put a stop to this process and in 1951 Farouk, the King of Egypt, declared an end to the Condominium and the annexation of Sudan to Egypt.

The Egyptian Revolutionary regime, which was established in 1952, believed that the approach of the previous regime would never help to realize its goals in Sudan and practiced different tactics. In February 1953, Egypt and Britain agreed that Sudan would be granted independence after a three-year transitional period, after which time the Sudanese would determine if they wanted an independent state or annexation to Egypt. Egypt's assessment came true, and at the beginning of the 1950s its supporters won the majority in all of the legislative bodies, but its leader, Ismail al Azhari, had second thoughts and began to support an independent Sudan. Al Azhari is an example of a series of leaders in the Arab world who believed in unification with Egypt, but at the last minute their nationalist feelings prevailed, as did their personal ambitions.

Al Azhari's "betrayal" caused a rift in his party, and the leadership of the Khatamiya began to support a new party—the Democratic Unionist Party—but it was powerless to prevent the establishment of an independent Sudanese state. Officially, Sudan became an independent republic on January 1, 1956; Egypt, however, continued to play a central role in its political life, albeit behind the scenes. In the general elections held prior to the declaration of independence, none of the large parties won a clear-cut majority. The first government, headed by Al Azhari, fell after a short period of time and was replaced by another coalition government led by Abdallah al Khalil, a member of the Umma. This government, which was made up of parties with conflicting approaches—the Umma and the Popular Democratic Party (which was pro-Egyptian)—was shaky and did not enable the survival of a stable government. The economic situation in Sudan deteriorated; the British development plants that operated the irrigation system and Sudan's cotton industry were neglected, and against this background the system's inefficiency and corruption became even more evident. Dissension grew, particularly within the urban population.

Sudan's Fundamental Problems

Sudan's southern regions, which were incorporated with the northern regions whose population was composed of Arabs due to the spread of Muhamad Ali's dynasty that controlled Egypt, constituted a stumbling block in the route followed by the independent Sudanese government. Due to various considerations, the British continued to maintain this unnatural framework although three of Sudan's southern districts were run by them separately. The activity of Christian missionaries in this area motivated some of the population to convert to Christianity, although the majority adhered to their ancient pagan religions.

Upon the approach of the deadline when independence was to be granted, the relationship between the two parts of the land deteriorated. The Muslim residents of the northern sector were unwilling to relinquish the inclusion of the southern regions in the framework of a centralized state, while the southerners demanded at least a certain degree of self-rule. An expression of the fear and resentment of the northerners towards them was apparent in the violent uprising that took place in the summer of 1955. The ruthless suppression of this uprising added another layer to the traditional animosity between the regions of the land. The government failed to establish a farseeing policy towards the south, and the fostering of a southern party connected to the Umma, which mainly represented the interests of the southerners living in the north, was for the sake of appearances only and did nothing to solve the problem. On the contrary, its roots actually deepened (see a detailed review of the conflict between the north and the south in Appendix A).

However, the main problem faced by the regime in Khartoum was the relationship between Sudan and Egypt. The regime of Abd al Nasser was not pleased with the Umma's rule in Sudan, and supported pro-Egyptian circles both overtly and covertly. The weak Sudanese government found it difficult to stand up to this pressure, which also relied on the active assistance of the Mirgania and the Popular Democratic Party, and the passive solidarity of many intellectuals who were educated in Egypt or in Egyptian institutions in Sudan.

The Egyptian pressure peaked during the border dispute in the Hala'ib-Shalatin region that erupted at the end of 1958, when Egypt (then—the United Arab Republic) was at the height of its power and prestige. The area of conflict was situated near the Red Sea and was rich in oil and other natural resources. Egypt demanded transfer of the area to its control. The Sudanese took a firm stand and refused to give in to pressure, but Sudanese nationalists feared that the weak government could not hold on to this position forever. This fear was one of the reasons for the toppling of the weak democratic government in Sudan.

The conflict between the north and south, the internal disputes (regarding the nature of the government), the lack of an organized political system as well as the lack of maturity necessary for the country to be run democratically—all of these aspects caused "chronic" instability in Sudanese governments, which rose and fell constantly. The corrupt politicians and the lack of an effective central government caused the deterioration of the Sudanese economy.

During this period two main parties stood out in the framework of the internal power struggles: The National Union Party, led by Ismayil al Azhari, was founded in 1952 but split up shortly after the declaration of Sudanese independence into the National Unionist Party and the Popular Democratic Party, which was actually the successor of the Khatamiya movement; and the Umma Party led by Sayed Abd al Rahman al Mahdi and established in 1945. Between the year 1953, when the first elections were held for the Sudanese Parliament (prior to its independence), and 1958, no less than four different coalitions came and went, causing internal rifts and shifts in the directions of the main movements. This political instability ultimately led to the seizure of power in Khartoum by General Ibrahim Abud (Abud's action was significantly influenced by the Young Officers' Revolution in Egypt in July 1952).

The Military Dictatorship of General Abud[6]

In a bloodless military coup d'état, the Chief-of-Staff General Abud seized control, together with a group of senior officers, and dissolved the civilian institutions. In Khartoum, there was a rumor that the revolution had been granted the blessing of the prime minister. The right wing, pro-Western and anti-Egyptian character of the uprising is what triggered these rumors, but over the years this opinion lost credibility and to this day there is no clear proof in this regard.

The Umma, which was the central civilian power in Sudan, declined in its twilight days, particularly after the demise of its leader Abd al Rahman al Mahdi. The military junta exploited this weakness in order to reinforce its regime in the state, but did not succeed in rallying support outside of the army. Already in the beginning of 1959 conflict arose within the junta itself between the right-wing majority and a small group of left-wing, pro-Egyptian officers who made two attempts to overthrow the regime that year. The clashes among the members of the military dictatorship continued during the following years, but the struggle took place behind the scenes.

The military dictatorship, which finally overcame the internal conflict among its ranks, was unsuccessful in its internal and foreign policies. Its policy did not deviate from the routine, and therefore failed in various areas (the relations with Egypt, economic development, improving the performance of the system, etc.), but the regime's most conspicuous failure was in its policy towards the south. General Abud attempted to eradicate the "problem of the southerners" via an extremist method of conversion to Islam, but as a result of this policy many southern leaders and residents fled the country. These refugees began organizing themselves in political movements in order to achieve autonomy for Sudan's southern regions. Influenced by the movements that were established outside of Sudan, the southern population in Sudan itself initiated organization in the framework of political-military movements. The most prominent southern military organization was called "Anya Niya," after a poisonous insect whose sting causes death. From 1964, guerrilla activities of the organization caused the Sudanese army increasing headaches. The terrain, which was covered with marshes and thick vegetation, in addition to the aid that the rebels received from the civilian population inside and outside of Sudan, made the Sudanese Army's task far from easy.

The prolonged but fruitless struggle had a detrimental effect on the army's morale, deepened public rancor, and caused a rift between Sudan and its African neighbors as well as the Vatican, which was accused by Sudan of aiding the Christian rebels in the south. In the summer of 1964, towards the end of his regime, Abud attempted to alter his policy towards the south and established a committee whose role was to try to find a solution to the problem. However, in October 1964, an uprising toppled his regime, so that the sincerity of his intentions was never put to the test. It is no coincidence that the first link in the chain of events that led to the Sudanese "October Revolution" was a student demonstration in Khartoum against the regime's ineffective policy vis-à-vis the south.

Similar failures characterized other military regimes in the region, but Sudan was the only country in which the military junta was replaced by a parliamentary civilian government. The explanation for this undoubtedly lies in Sudan's unique social structure. The military regime was unable to eradicate the influence of the large Sudanese parties, which relied on religious orders and various tribes, nor that of the communist party that relied on traditional and powerful trade unions. These forces, which were suppressed by the military dictatorship, preserved their dynamics and organizational structures while awaiting the right moment to take back control.

As noted, the students' demonstration, which was forcefully suppressed by the Khartoum police, was the "snowball" to trigger similar demonstrations that spread to other Sudanese cities. Police failed to suppress the demonstrations and the military refused to open fire at the demonstrators. Representatives of the veteran parties and other civilian groups (students, workers, farmers) established the United National Front, which demanded and received the government's resignation. Abud continued to serve as president for a while, but without the military's support he lacked real strength. He was ultimately forced to resign and was placed under house arrest.

The Strengthening of the Civil Government in Sudan[7]

The members of the United National Front came to an agreement that in March 1965 general elections would be held for a constituent assembly, and until then a temporary government would rule the country. The temporary government, made up of representatives of the parties and the trade unions, was headed by al Hatam Khalifa, a politically independent educationalist.

The main organizational power behind the establishment of the United National Front, was composed of the communists and their followers. The party's effective underground organization and its sophisticated techniques for bringing out the masses constituted important elements in the success of the uprising. The communist leaders, who were among the initiators of the uprising, became popular individuals in Sudan's urban centers. Moreover, it became evident that the trade unions, which were part of the United National Front, were chiefly controlled by the communists or at least sent leftist representatives to the government.

The large traditional parties constituted a minority in the government in comparison to the communist representatives and the left-wing ministers who cooperated with them. Naturally, the non-affiliated Khalifa followed the majority in the government. The most

important step that clearly reflected the government's leftist leanings was the permission that it granted to Egyptian and Algerian
arms carriers to fly over Sudan in aid of the leftist insurrection movement in the Congo. The city of Juba (in southern Sudan) served as a
forward supply base for the Congo rebels and contributed significantly to their successes at the end of 1964 and the beginning of
1965.

The left-wing government did not reflect the actual balance of
power in Sudan. In the capital of Khartoum and in other urban centers, the communist party and the Popular Democratic Party (the
pro-Egyptian party that cooperated with the communists) had their
fair share of supporters. However, in most other areas of the country
the majority supported the Umma Party, which was the political arm
of the Mahdiya. The fact that Ismail al Azhari and his party (the
National Union Party) leaned towards cooperation with the Umma
increased their force as well as the chances of the right-wing sector.
However, only in 1965 was the Umma organizationally prepared
for a struggle against the left, after its young and talented leader
Zadek al Mahdi, the original Mahdi's great grandson, shook up the
ranks in the Party. The left-wing leaders were aware of the true balance of power and therefore feared general elections. They demanded
a postponement of the elections set for March 1965, claiming that
the shaky situation in the south would hinder the election process.
In the interim, the leftist leaders hoped to exploit their power in the
government in order to expand their influence in the country and
perhaps even to change the electoral system, which enabled tribal
leaders to generate their influence in favor of the Umma.

Problems in the South following the October Revolution [8]

The ousting of the Abud government and the establishment of the
civilian government increased the chances of negotiations between
the north and the south. The temporary government included three
southern representatives who had the support of the residents of the
southern sectors, in contrast to their predecessors in the Abud government. The government demonstrated goodwill towards the
southerners in various ways, such as reinstating Sunday as the weekly
day of rest, as was customary prior to the Islamization crusade instigated by the Abud government, and a call to southern refugees to
return to Sudan.

Several political groups, which were divided into two main streams, were established among the southerners; the first stream consisted of the "Southern Front," most of whose members resided inside Sudan, as well as the SANU (the Sudan African National Union), most of whose leaders came from among the ranks of the refugees outside of Sudan. This stream aspired to achieve autonomy for the southern regions. The second stream, which was of lesser importance, was composed of several parties and groups that sided in co-operation with the north. Most of the leaders and members of these groups resided in the northern cities, and the most prominent individual in this stream was William Deng who split away from the SANU and founded his own party under the same name.

The northern leaders were willing to grant the south autonomy in various areas, but the southerners demanded a form of Home Rule, and agreed to leave to the central government authority only matters related to foreign and security affairs. The northern leaders were not willing to take such far-reaching steps and justifiably suspected that at least some of the southern leaders would exploit the Home Rule as a first step towards achieving full independence. Violent riots instigated by the southerners in Khartoum due to a false rumor that one of their representatives in the government had been assassinated by northerners proved that the element that was lacking in relations between the north and the south was the vital basis for the resolution of their problems—mutual trust.

Due to pressure applied by the right-wing parties, which aspired to hold the elections as soon as possible, a "round-table conference" was held in Khartoum in March 1965. It was attended by representatives of the north and the south as well as representatives of African countries. The conference's purpose was to arrive at an agreement that would pave the way to general elections in Sudan, in order to enable the achievement of a permanent resolution between the north and the south. No practical arrangement was achieved at the conference. The southerners, who had expected the support of African countries as part of the African movement's struggle for liberation from Arab rule, were severely disappointed. The African countries did indeed express sympathy for the struggle of the residents of southern Sudan but refrained from offering political support, fearing that the altering of borders on an ethnographic basis would create a precedent that might well destabilize the political map of Africa, whose distribution into countries had for the most part been irrational and achieved through the imposition of artificial borders.

The General Elections in May 1965[9]

The breakdown of the Khartoum conference did not prevent the scheduled elections from being held, which in the interim were postponed to May. In mid-January two camps had been formed in Sudan: (1) a right-wing camp, composed of the Umma, al Azhari's party, and the Muslim Brotherhood; and (2) a left-wing camp made up of the communists, the Popular Democratic Party, and several trade unions. Officially, the army took a neutral stand but it is logical to assume that it actively gave its support to the rightist camp. In the beginning, the left-wing parties controlled the government with the support of the members of the trade unions and leftist youth movements. The right, on the other hand, depended on the support of the Antsar, tribal members who supported the Mahdia. This source of power was spread across the districts, far from Khartoum the capital. In the beginning of February, prior to the visit of England's Queen Elizabeth to Sudan, the Umma's system began to amass its supporters in Khartoum. The power assembled by the Umma in the capital far exceeded the left-wing forces, and while the army stood on the sidelines, the right-wing parties forced the Khalifa government to resign. The new government, which was established on the basis of party representation, reflected the right wing's superior power throughout the country.

The rightists' clear advantage enabled the elections to be held at the beginning of May, almost without disruption. The Popular Democratic Party boycotted the elections and attempted to sabotage them, but without success. The Umma and its offshoots won more than half of the 173 seats that were reserved for the northerners in the constituent assembly (sixty seats were reserved for the southerners). Al Azhari's party won more than fifty seats, and the rest of the seats were distributed among the communists and the unaffiliated representatives. The Umma could have formed a government from its own members alone, but it preferred to establish a coalition with al Azhari's party. There were two apparent reasons for the Umma's decision; its desire to establish a stable and broad-based government, and the need to share responsibility with another entity.

The main problem related to the foundation of the coalition was the assignment of roles. Members of Azhari's party claimed that this distinguished statesman, with an impressive record of activity in Sudanese politics since the 1930s, should be prime minister. The Umma members insisted that this role should be granted to their party because they had won the elections. Ultimately, a compromise was reached: Ismail al Azhari was appointed permanent chairman of the presidential council while Muhammad Mahjub, an Umma personage, was appointed prime minister and this party held the main cabinet portfolios.

Nevertheless, the landslide victory of the right-wing parties did not ensure stability in Sudan's political life. One of the main obstacles was the problem regarding the south. It was impossible to ignore the failure of the Khartoum conference for any length of time. The fundamental demands of the southerners had not changed. In the meantime, a more extreme group had been formed among the southerners that opposed negotiations with the north and demanded that a civil war be launched. The conditions for launching an armed struggle were now favorable because the "Anya Niya" had seized a substantial amount of weaponry that had been dispatched to the Congo rebels via Sudan. In addition, the left-wing foreign policy adopted by the temporary Sudanese government triggered animosity in the Congo government and other regional entities, which were now willing to aid the southern rebels. Thus, in the summer of 1965 another war erupted in southern Sudan—a war that had a profound impact on the government's stability, the army's morale, the economic situation, and Sudan's foreign relations. Moreover, under these conditions it was hard to anticipate any sort of solution that might put an end to the conflict and enable Sudan to concentrate on constructive issues, which had been completely ignored in previous years.

But north Sudan had also failed to achieve stability and peace, and the right-wing government had many opponents among the leftists and the pro-Egyptian circles. Several times since the general elections these entities had demonstrated their ability to sabotage government activities by declaring strikes and staging riots. These entities were supported by primary foundations that were deeply involved in Sudanese society (the Khatamiya Order on the one hand, and the trade unions, on the other), which made it hard for the Umma to act against them. The House of Representatives decided to outlaw the communist party, but the party did not cease its activities, although it did go underground.

Relations between the coalition partners were also far from idyllic. Al-Azhari and his party did cooperate with the Umma against the left since the establishment of the renewed civilian government, but the profound hostility that had existed in the past had not changed. The dispute regarding al Azhari's actual status flared up every time the need arose to dispatch Sudanese delegations to international conferences, which illustrated the tension and conflict existing between the two parties. Al Azhari, who in practical terms served as prime minister, demanded to head these delegations, but Mahjub claimed that this was his right, as part of his role as the prime minister who was actively running the country. The coalition crises that erupted due to the disputes were settled one way or another, but the controversy between the two partners made it hard for the government to run the state.

As stated above, Sudan's second attempt to establish a democratic government also failed, and the years 1965-1968 were characterized by changing coalitions and splits within the ranks of the large parties (the Umma party splintered in 1966). During this period a new attempt was made to settle the dispute between the north and the south by convening another "round table conference" (in 1965), but this conference did not yield any real solution.

The Period of Jaafar al Numeiri's Administration (1969-1986)

On May 25, 1969 a coup d'état was instigated by a group of officers headed by Colonel Jaafar al Numeiri. The group of officers took over the government offices and established a revolutionary council that reinforced its control over the country, with the collaboration of the Sudanese communist party. Due to his alliance with the Sudanese communists, al Numeiri initially adopted a pro-Soviet foreign policy and a socialist approach in the handling of internal problems (economics, social issues). In the framework of his steps to strengthen his control, al Numeiri outlawed all of the Islamic movements, and many of their leaders and members fled the country. The protest movements and opposition activities were ruthlessly suppressed. For example, an insurrection initiated by the Antsar movement and staged on the Island of Aba on the Nile was suppressed by military forces and most of the insurgents were executed.

However, the alliance between al Numeiri and the communists ended in 1971 when a plan to overthrow the government was discovered in which members of the communist party were involved.[10] After foiling the attempted coup d'état, al Numeiri's policy underwent an abrupt turnabout and his regime actively suppressed the communist party and its followers, while adopting a pro-Western direction focused on a plea to the United States, the West, and moderate Arab countries for economic aid.[11]

In 1972, al Numeiri contacted the south in an effort to resolve the conflict. These contacts led to the Addis Ababa Conference, which was designated to stop the civil war and grant autonomous rule to the southern sectors. The agreements reached at the Addis Ababa Conference were also reflected in the 1973 constitution, which recognized Christianity and traditional religions in the south as state religions, but in practice the discrimination and prejudice against the south continued. Al Numeiri's inability to stabilize his government and his failure to solve the country's severe economic problems motivated him to formulate a new policy of national reconciliation.[12] In 1977, al Numeiri met secretly at Port-Sudan with Zadek al Mahdi, one of the main opposition leaders, and jointly with him established the principles for the new policy. In 1978, a public declaration was made in London by Sharif al Hindi, head of the National Union Party, regarding the new national reconciliation policy, in the framework of which political prisoners were released, political activity of previously outlawed parties and organizations was permitted, a neutral foreign policy was formulated and most of the opposition leaders returned to Sudan from their places of exile, including Zadek al Mahdi and Hassan al Turabi.

Hassan al Turabi, much like other opposition leaders, regarded the national reconciliation policy as an opportunity to fortify his movement (the Muslim Brotherhood), and to boost it under the sponsorship of the regime. Although the Muslim Brotherhood movement officially remained unlawful, the authorities actually turned a blind eye to its information and political activities, thus significantly enhancing its power.[13] The national reconciliation process temporarily strengthened al Numeiri's status and weakened the opposition, some of whose components became partners to the establishment while others preserved their hostile attitude towards the regime but became weaker and more divided.

During the years 1978-1980 al Numeiri reorganized the country's governmental system in order to boost his status and in this framework negated the unique autonomous status of the south and turned it into one of six districts (five of which were in the north). Al Numeiri granted considerable freedom to the districts by allowing them to nominate three candidates for the office of governor in each district, but the final choice from among the candidates was al Numeiri's. Thus, his influence and control in the district were maintained (particularly in the southern district).[14]

It would appear that al Numeiri introduced the above-mentioned comprehensive administrative steps also due to his desire to execute extensive economic projects in the south. The two central projects were the development of oil fields, due to the discovery of oil in the Benito area by Chevron, and the digging of the Jonglei Canal in order to form a lake of the Nile's water in the south. The weakening of the autonomy in the south was vital to al Numeiri in order to thwart anticipated opposition to the digging of the Jonglei Canal, which could have a detrimental effect on the agriculture in the south, and also to prevent demands by the south to claim oil profits.

However, the demoted status of the south quickly spurred the tension between the north and the south. In addition, starting from 1979, Sudan was immersed in a severe economic recession, which necessitated the introduction of unpopular emergency steps (the devaluation of the national currency, raised prices), which, in turn, caused riots and agitation. Al Numeiri's failure to resolve the economic problems, the political instability, and the attempts to overthrow his government motivated him to seek the support of Saudi Arabia (mainly for economic aid) and Egypt. Libya's invasion of neighboring Chad also fueled al Numeiri's fears, and at the end of brief political negotiations, in 1983, Sudan signed an alliance for political union with Egypt. Al Numeiri's reliance on Egypt increased his external security and enabled him to formulate a new plan in the area of domestic policy, the main goal of which was Islamization of the country (September 1983).

Al Numeiri's Islamic Turnabout

In contrast to the sudden and severe rift between al Numeiri and the communists in 1971, the Islamic turnabout in 1983 stemmed from an ongoing process that began with the "national reconciliation process" and led to discussions and the achievement of understandings between al Numeiri and the Islamic leadership, making the latter a member of the establishment. It would appear that during the years 1972-1983, al Numeiri underwent a personal process of Islamization, which affected his policy.[15] In the years 1972-1977, al Numeiri became the patron of Sufi Orders and legalized the activities of the Republic Brothers—a small rival faction to the Muslim Brotherhood. In 1980, a book was published in al Numeiri's name (*The Islamic Way Why?*), which discussed Islamic religious rulings.[16] Researchers like Peter Woodward believe that the book was not written by al Numeiri himself, but rather by his aides. In any case, the very fact that the book was published in Numeiri's name and dealt with the interpretation of Islamic religious rulings undoubtedly represented a significant milestone in Numeiri's intentional adoption of Islam.

In September 1983, al Numeiri imposed the "September Laws," which heralded the implementation of Islamic Law (Sharia) as the state law, in addition to a series of legal steps imposing the Sharia on the population's daily life, including punitive action based on Islamic Law, for example, amputating the hand of a thief, stoning adulterers to death and lashings for relatively minor misdemeanors. In addition, the supervision of and punishment for prostitution as well as for imbibing and for the sale of alcohol became more stringent, and the mandatory dress code for women also became more drastic.[17] Criticism against the September Laws and opposition to them came from almost all sections of the political spectrum in Sudan, each for its own reasons. Even Zadek al Mahdi, leader of the Umma with its Islamic leanings, expressed his opposition to the process, claiming that the economic and social conditions in Sudan were not ripe for the enforcement of the Sharia. Zadek al Mahdi was imprisoned for his public criticism of al-Numeiri.

Of course, the most adamant opposition to the imposition of the Sharia came from the southern districts. The enforcement of the Sharia as state law and the Islamization of the educational system was in practical terms a one-sided abolition of all of the understandings achieved at the Addis Ababa Conference, which had been ratified in the 1973 constitution by al Numeiri's government. In response to the Khartoum government's steps, Colonel John Garang established the SPLA—the Sudan People's Army, which was joined by commanders and soldiers from the south who had served in the Sudanese army, and initiated a widespread guerrilla war against government forces in the south. At the same time, the political leadership in the south established a political arm—the SPLM (Sudan People's Liberation Movement), which favored the concept of a new Sudan that would grant the south local autonomy, or alternatively establish a central federative government in cooperation with the south. Other demands made by this movement focused on replacing al Numeiri's one-party regime with a liberal and democratic government, as well as a just distribution and allocation of economic resources between the north and the south.

During 1984 and 1985, the southern rebels inflicted severe losses upon the government forces, causing the cessation of the excavation work on the Jonglei Canal and putting a halt to the development of the oil fields in Benito. The war in the south and the severe economic crisis, stemming from the attempt to base the economy upon the laws of the Sharia, and the loss of foreign investors and foreign currency in the country, triggered increasing resentment among wide circles (including Muslims) in northern Sudan. In contrast to Zadek al Mahdi, who criticized al Numeiri's regime from the opposition, Hassan al Turabi was an active partner in the government and at that time served as public prosecutor, responsible for the enforcement of Islamic law. But al Turabi quickly understood that al Numeiri's actions were bound to fail and therefore withdrew his support in 1984 and began criticizing the latter's policies openly. In the beginning of 1985, al Numeiri despaired of his alliance with the Islamic circles and instructed the military to conduct widespread arrests among the Muslim Brotherhood. Thus, al Numeiri was left without political allies, and his regime relied almost entirely on the army and the security forces.

In light of an additional deterioration in the country's economic plight, al Numeiri flew to the United States on March 27, 1986, in hopes of recruiting economic aid. The opposition took advantage of his absence and organized mass demonstrations and an economic strike that paralyzed the Sudanese economy.[18] In light of the anarchy that prevailed in the country, on April 6, 1986, a military junta led by Chief-of-Staff General al Rahman Sawar al-Dahab seized control, ousted al Numeiri, and declared the founding of a military provisionary-council until democratic elections could be held in the state. Thus, al Numeiri's administration, the longest in the history of Sudan (1969-198), came to an end. During the period of his rule, Sudan had undergone tremendous fluctuation between extreme ideological poles—from an alliance with the communists to enforcement of the Sharia as state law. These radical changes accurately reflect the polarity that exists in Sudan's society and political system; each of these elements awaits the right moment to realize its goals. Those inclined towards communism came up against the adamant opposition of the Islamic circles and some of the southern leaders, while Islamic leanings led to the steadfast opposition of the south (to the point of a civil war), and liberal and socialist circles in northern Sudan.

During the period in between the transition from communism to Islam, al Numeiri attempted to boost the concept of "national reconciliation," while establishing a broad-based coalition including the various movements, but this step was destined to fail due to the profound polarization in Sudanese society. An ineffectual and corrupt governmental system, in addition to the fortification of an economic and political nouveau riche class, deepened the gap and distrust between the masses and the government.

It would appear that al Numeiri's attempt to adopt Islamic ways came too late and without the proper educational and informational preparation. In the given political and economic situation, he was doomed to failure. Despite its Muslim roots and links with Islamic tradition, the population of northern Sudan was characteristically tolerant and moderate regarding the private individual's lifestyle. Thus, al Numeiri's radical policies aroused opposition even within large sectors of the population that hypothetically should have welcomed the "Laws of September." Moreover, in view of the critical basic conditions in which the country found itself in 1983, the presentation of the Islamic approach as a solution to all of Sudan's economic and social woes stimulated resistance even among many Islamic sectors that were fully aware that the failure of al Numeiri's regime would be interpreted by the general public as the inability of Islam to resolve Sudan's problems, and they therefore expressed their reservations regarding al Numeiri's acts, claiming that the conditions were not yet ripe for the enforcement of the Sharia in Sudan. In any event, the first attempt to establish an Islamic state in the spirit of the Sharia experienced dismal failure, which led to the fall of al Numeiri's regime.

The Regime of Zadek al Mahdi

Immediately after the coup d'état, General Sawar al Dahab established a provisional military council aimed at ensuring as smooth a transition as possible from the one-man regime of al Numeiri to a multi-party government. The provisional council fulfilled its role, but the short time span and the complexity of Sudan's political system did not enable any profound change in the composition and operational patterns of the political parties.

In 1986 democratic elections took place in Sudan and the Umma and the Democratic Unionist Party established a coalition that was joined by several smaller parties; they founded the National Front, a weak and artificial coalition headed by Zadek al Mahdi. The NIF (National Islamic Front), Hassan al Turabi's fundamentalist movement, won fifty-one seats in the Parliament (about 20 percent of all the seats),[19] but refused to join the coalition headed by al Mahdi because of what it considered the coalition's moderate and hesitant policy vis-à-vis the main issue of instituting the Sharia. Al Turabi maintained that the idea of enforcing the Sharia should not be abandoned, and argued that the fault lay in the flawed implementation by al Numeiri's regime, and not in the essential nature of these laws. Zadek al Mahdi preferred not to take an unequivocal stand in this regard and thus did not officially declare the annulment of the September Laws. On the other hand, no effort was made to enforce these laws.

Al Mahdi's period of government was characteristically unstable and indecisive throughout its existence, due to the attempt to satisfy all of the various powerbrokers and the phenomena of corruption that spread throughout the administration and further weakened the Sudanese economy.[20] Towards the end of his administration, al Mahdi agreed to al Turabi's demand to impose the Sharia in exchange for the latter's consent to join the weak coalition that he headed, and at the same time launched negotiations to end the war in the south, which constituted an onerous load upon the Sudanese economy and led it the brink of an abyss.[21] In June 1989, al Mahdi's government came to an end when Brigadier General Omar al Beshir, at the head of a military junta, seized power in a bloodless coup d'état.

Omar al Beshir's Rise to Power[22]

After Brigadier General Omar al Beshir carried out the coup d'état in Sudan and deposed Zadek al Mahdi, the new regime faced three main problems that required immediate attention: the severe economic crisis, the civil war in the south, and the country's political instability.

Immediately upon his ascendance to power, Omar al Beshir took vigorous action to consolidate his government as well as recruit political support and material aid for the state. Also, widespread arrests of individuals from all aspects of the political spectrum took place, and political activities were banned. Among those arrested was Hassan al Turabi, head of the NIF (National Islamic Front).

The new regime placed its own people in key positions, and on July 9, 1989, a new government was founded with chairman of the Revolutionary Council Omar al Beshir at its head. He also fulfilled the roles of Minister of Defense and Chief of Staff. Most of the ministerial positions (including that of Foreign Minister) were filled by technocrat civilians, generally unaffiliated individuals who were not tainted by scandals and had not served in previous governments. In practical terms, the Revolutionary Council governed the state because it set policy and held legislative authority while the government (which was essentially technocratic) constituted an element whose role was to execute policy formulated by the Revolutionary Council.

At the beginning of the road, al Beshir and his colleagues were not affiliated with any particular political trend. Al Beshir even defined himself as "a Sudanese patriot without political or tribal affiliation."[23] Nevertheless, already in 1989, there were rumors about al Beshir's identification with the radical Islamic point of view. On July 14, 1989 al Beshir declared a one-sided ceasefire in an effort to enter negotiations with the southern rebels, but the latter continued to view the new regime with suspicion.

In the economic sphere, the new regime enacted several steps aimed at alleviating the difficulties, even temporarily, via the provision of essential products at subsidized prices and fighting the black market, profiteering, and illegal commerce in foreign currency. At the same time, the new regime made efforts to strengthen foreign ties with the West as well as with Saudi Arabia and Egypt, in an attempt to recruit economic and political support. (Egypt was the first country to recognize the new government, and President Mubarak was the first foreign leader to visit Khartoum shortly after the coup d'état.)

In the beginning, the new regime enjoyed the support of the army and large sections of the population, due mainly to the profound disappointment and frustration with Zadek al Mahdi's leadership. However, quickly enough it became evident that the new regime was unable to resolve the state's fundamental problems in a short period of time, and al Beshir realized that he would have to form a wider political alliance in order to stabilize his government and acquire adequate public legitimization. As noted above, because he had Islamic leanings al Beshir appealed to the Islamic movement to expand the support base for his government. At the end of 1989, Hassan al Turabi was released from prison and from then on the ties and cooperation between Omar al Beshir and Hassan al Turabi intensified.

Al Turabi did not take on any formal role but in practical terms he became the state's religious authority. Under al Turabi's influence Sudan was declared an Islamic republic functioning on the basis of Islamic law (the Sharia), and the members of the National Islamic Front gradually reclaimed most of the powerful governmental and political positions in the country. In his writings and in interviews granted by al Turabi from 1990 onwards he made every effort to minimize the scope of influence which he and his party had over the regime, but it seems that his charismatic personality, qualifications, and education overshadowed the figure of the leader Omar al Beshir and he was actually the "strongman" in the country.

Al Turabi's movement—the National Islamic Front—was the main and strongest political movement in Sudan despite the fact that ostensibly its activity had been banned in the framework of the overall prohibition imposed by al Beshir vis-à-vis the activities of political parties. Upon the renewal of political activity in Sudan at the end of the 1990s the NIF split into two parties:[24]

1. The governmental party led by President al Beshir—the National Congress;
2. Hassan al Turabi's party—the Popular National Congress

Subsequently the two parties were united under the name "The National Congress": al Beshir was designated chairman, while al Turabi was defined as secretary-general of the movement.[25]

The Islamic movement's practical control was expressed via the following components:

1. Movement members held key positions in the "Revolutionary Council," in the government, the security mechanisms, the police, and the army.
2. The regime's ideological line in education and the media was dictated by the movement.

3.   "The Council of Forty"—a covert body responsible for securing the regime and preventing its deviation from the Islamic line—was controlled by the movement.

4.   Inspired by the Iranian Revolutionary Guards, a militia of the National Islamic movement ("The Popular Defense Forces") was founded in Sudan. This semi-military force was to ensure the movement's control and constituted a vanguard in the dissemination and enforcement of its ideological messages, including participation as the "forefront" in the war in the south.

During the years 1991-1992, the government's administrative structure underwent reorganization in order to reinforce the administration's hold and control, as well as al Turabi's movement. In this framework, in January 1991, Sudan was divided into nine districts (as opposed to six districts in the previous division). A governor was appointed in each district as well as a council of ministers selected by the Revolutionary Council in Khartoum, thus ensuring their loyalty to the regime.

In February 1992, the Provisional National Council was established to serve as a substitute for an elected Parliament until the election of a permanent Parliament by the national committees in the various districts and cities (similar to Kadafi's Libyan model). In the Provisional National Council a majority was also assured for members of the NIF. Under the influence of the NIF, Sudan began to adopt and practice Islamic foreign policy, whose aim was to export the radical Islamic message to the neighboring countries.

Omar al Beshir and Hassan al Turabi continue to rule Sudan as of 2004, but since 1999 adversity has developed between the two (elaboration to follow).

Notes

1.   Peter Woodward, *Sudan 1898-1989—The Unstable State*, Boulder CO: Lynne Rienner Publishers, 1990, p. 22.

2.   The meaning of the word *"suf"* in Arabic is "wool." The term was used to indicate the simple and rough clothing worn by members of the Sufi Order (the dervish), designated to reflect the worldview that preaches simplicity and humility in daily life and preference for spiritual purity over material achievements. Malisa Ruthven, *Islam in the World*, Harmondorst: Penguin, 1984, pp. 248-286.

3.   Peter Woodward, "Islam and Politics," in Muddathin, Badal, Hardallo, Woodward (eds.), *Sudan Since Independence*, Ipswich, Suffolk: The Ipswich Book Co. Ltd., 1986, pp. 1-3.

4.   Peter Woodward, *Sudan Since Independence*, pp. 130-199.

5.   Based on *Ma'archot*, Issue 171, December 1965.

6.   Based on *Ma'archot*, Issue 171, December 1965.

7.   Based on *Ma'archot*, Issue 171, December 1965.
8.   Based on *Ma'archot*, Issue 171, December 1965.
9.   Based on *Ma'archot*, Issue 171, December 1965.
10.   M. Wai Dunstam, "Revolution, Rhetoric and Reality in the Sudan," *Journal of Modern Africa Studies*, 17, No. 1, March 1979.
11.   Muhammad Beshir Hamid, *The Politics of National Reconciliation in the Sudan: The Numeiri Regime and the National Front Opposition*, Center for Contemporary Arab Studies, Georgetown University, Occ Papers Series, 1984.
12.   Alexander S. Cuds, "Islam and the Politics in Sudan," in P. Piscatory (ed.), *Islam in the Political Process*, London: Cambridge University Press, 1983, p. 49.
13.   Peter Woodward, *Sudan 1890-1989—The Unstable State*, p. 153.
14.   A. Al Ayub, "The Regional Government Act of 1980," in Peter Woodward (ed.), *Sudan since Numeiri*, London: SoAS, 1986.
15.   Peter Woodward, *Sudan 1890-1989—The Unstable State*, p. 157.
16.   Jaafar Muhammad Numeiri, *Al Nahjal al Islami il Madha* (The Islamic Way Why?), Cairo: Al Maktad Al Masri Al hadith, 1980.
17.   Muhammad Beshir Hamid, "Aspects of Sudan's Foreign Policy," in Muddathin, Badal, Hardallo, Woodward (eds.), *Sudan since Independence*, p. 162.
18.   *Quarterly Economic Review at Sudan*, No. 3, 1986, pp. 10-11.
19.   *Quarterly Economic Review at Sudan*, No. 2, 1986, p. 6.
20.   Al Raga (Sudan daily newspaper), May 16, 1987; *Al Jmana* (Sudan daily newspaper) May 16, 1987.
21.   *Al Sudan*, April 4, 1988; *Al Watan*, April 20, 1988.
22.   Graham F. Thomas, *Sudan's Struggle for Survival 1984-1993*, London: Darf Publishers Ltd., 1994, pp. 95-131.
23.   *Observer*, July 16, 1989.
24.   Randolph Martin, "Sudan's Perfect War," *Foreign Affairs*, March/April 2002.
25.   *Dawn*, May 25, 2002.

2

Sudan and Islam

Hassan al Turabi—Biographical Milestones[1]

Hassan al Turabi was born on February 1, 1932, in the village of Kassala near the Ethiopian border. He is the descendent of a religious family of distinguished lineage whose founder headed a Sufi Order 300 years ago, founded a school for the study of Islam and built the village of Turabi (whose name was adopted by the family). He has six sons, and his wife Vissal is among the direct descendents of al Mahdi. In 1955-1957, al Turabi studied Law in London, and upon graduating he returned to Sudan and taught Law at the University of Khartoum. During the years 1959-1964 he lived in Paris and completed his doctoral studies. During his stay in Europe he grew familiar with Western culture, customs and worldviews and became fluent in English, French, and German.

In 1964, al Turabi returned to Sudan and served as dean and a Law lecturer at the Khartoum Law Department. At the same time he became politically active and steadily reinforced his status as a senior figure in the Muslim Brotherhood movement in Sudan. During the years 1969-1977, under al Numeiri's government, al Turabi was incarcerated for prolonged periods of time due to his activity in the Islamic opposition. However, in the framework of al Numeiri's "national reconciliation" policy, in 1977, al Turabi was released from prison and his activity was allowed in the Islamic movement.

In 1980, al Turabi founded the NIF (National Islamic Front) party, which constituted a coalition and roof organization of several Islamic parties and organizations, headed by the Muslim Brotherhood. When al Numeiri declared the enforcement of the Sharia as state law in September 1983, the Islamic movement became his main ally in the Sudanese political system. During the years 1983-1985, al Turabi

27

served as attorney general, Minister of Justice, and chairman of the committee for the implementation of the Sharia, and in this framework acted to adapt the Sudanese legal system to Islamic Law.

In 1985-1989, the National Islamic Front, with al Turabi as its secretary-general, constituted the main opposition to the administration of al Mahdi. Following Omar al-Beshir's coup d'état in 1989, political activity was banned and Hassan al Turabi was arrested, but he was released within a short period of time and became al Beshir's main political ally. He quickly became the "strongman" and the true ruler of Sudan. Over the years, al Turabi acquired a reputation inside and outside of Sudan as a renowned Islamic philosopher. He published clerical rulings and books related to various Islamic laws pertaining to daily life and Islamic society.

The Development of the Islamic Movement in Sudan during the Modern Era

In his book *The Islamic Movement in Sudan*[2] al Turabi describes the development stages of the movement in Sudan as part of a current engulfing the entire Muslim world and as a natural, irreversible, and determinist process. He claims that Islam is not to be regarded as "a past glory, but rather as an exact prescription for how humanity must approach current and future challenges."[3]

The roots of the modern Islamic movement in Sudan are embedded in cells of the Muslim Brotherhood, which began organization during 1949 at the University of Khartoum under the influence of the mother association in Egypt. The first framework that was established was called "the Islamic Liberation Movement" (Kharkhat al Takhrir al-Islami) by its founders, and it maintained an organizational and ideological link with the Egyptian movement of the Muslim Brotherhood.[4] In the beginning, the movement had an elitist character and it was accordingly based on a group of students and academics who adopted the movement's principles during their studies at the Universities of Cairo and Khartoum.

In the years 1949-1954 the Islamic movement in Sudan maintained close cooperation with the mother organization in Egypt; the latter granted the Sudanese not only ideological and religious support but financial aid as well. The persecution of the Muslim Brotherhood in Egypt by Nasser's regime, which led to the organization's going underground and to diminished activities, forced the Islamic movement in Sudan to lessen its dependence on the mother-move-ment and establish independent organizational patterns in order to continue activities.

The attempts of al Hadibi (head of the Moslem Brotherhood in Egypt) during the 1960s and 1970s to impose his sponsorship and authority on the organization in Sudan[5] met with substantial opposi-tion on the part of the organization's leaders in Sudan, led by al Turabi, and a rift developed gradually between the two organiza-tions. Al Turabi believed that cooperation and coordination should be maintained between the Islamic movements in the various coun-tries, but in light of the differences stemming from the social-eco-nomic aspects and the countries' regimes it would be best to refrain from establishing one central leadership, and each movement must contend with the problems in its own country. However, all of the Islamic movements should be united around the joint aim of estab-lishing an Islamic faithful society (the Umma).

Hassan al Turabi's movement, much like other Islamic organiza-tions and movements, aspires to establish an economic, political, and social order on the basis of the Sharia and Islamic values, and the Islamic state in Sudan constitutes a stage in the foundation of an Islamic faithful society (the Umma). As stated above, Islam's rise is a determinist and unavoidable process—a natural process that is part of historical development.[6] The failure of the secular ideologies—socialism on the one hand, and liberalism and capitalism on the other—was only to be expected due to their moral bankruptcy; Islam will re-place them and will become the central power in the world. Islam has become a powerful social organization involved in cultural renewal and in the foundation of a new identity. It is gradually taking on a political character, and in the future it is destined to become a global phenomenon that will assume various forms and characteristics.

The achievement of the objectives of the Islamic movement will occur gradually and in several stages:[7] Today, the believers are in the stage of "Innovativeness and Transition" (*Tajdid* and *Antakal*), which constitutes a transition period between the historical stagna-tion of the believers' society when facing the challenges of the West (powerful, materialistic, and technological in nature), and the next stage in which the faithful society will burgeon and prosper on the basis of the adoption of Islamic law. According to al Turabi, the Koran and the Sunna constitute the eternal and undisputed response to the current and future challenges, but the transitional stage in which the Islamic society currently finds itself necessitates *new interpretation* adapted to the spirit of these times, circumstances, and place. Thus, the current Islamic awakening "is not a phenomenon stemming from existing circumstances and is not an event reserved for a certain place, but rather will become a comprehensive factor both in location and time."[8]

Al Turabi believes that the Islamic renewal movement will put down roots and spread to every location where a community of believers resides, and as the movement expands so the community of believers will approach its goal to establish the nation on the basis of the values of the Sharia. The rise of Islam will take place in a gradual, evolutionary process and will be achieved whenever possible in peaceful ways, by educating the individual to lead a religious way of life, which will then lead to the Islamization of society and the state. However, if secular regimes attempt to stand in the way of Islam, then there will be no other choice than for Islam to rise to power through revolution.[9]

The issue of religious legislation served as a yardstick for the Islamic movement's approach to the Sudanese regime. Al Turabi claimed that in the matter of legislation and law, gradual action should be taken in stages:[10] In the initial stage, the existing compilation of laws must be examined by committees composed of religious clerics who will check if the current laws comply with Islamic law and its values, and they will act to amend them as required; in the ensuing stage, action should be taken to fully implement the Sharia as state law. In both stages, state laws must be adapted to local needs and to the spirit of the times, but at the same time it must be ascertained that the latter do not contradict Islamic law.

The National Islamic Front (NIF)—the Sudan Charter[11]

In 1987, the NIF formulated a document called "The Sudan Charter" that summarizes the worldview of the Front in matters pertaining to religion, society, and state, and which constitutes the ideological and political platform of the movement. The charter is composed of four central chapters: national unity, ethnicity and nationality, state and religion, and the constitution. The charter is worded moderately and ensures individual rights and religious freedom for all faiths, but a close inspection of the charter's clauses clearly indicates the preference granted to Islam and the Sharia as the state law.

The Sudan Charter states that the Sudanese are a nation united on the basis of religion, common values, solidarity, and patriotism. Nevertheless, Sudan recognizes and permits diversity in its population on religious and cultural bases, and therefore Sudan is a country whose inhabitants identify with defined nationality and area, but are ethnically and culturally different. Sudan's population is divided into two main groups, a population of Arab descent and a population of African descent. The charter respects ethnic and tribal identities and ensures political and legal equality for the entire population. Moreover, in the area of foreign policy, the country is committed to the development of ties with both the Arab world and the African sector.

Be that as it may, the Sudan Charter emphasizes that the Muslims, who constitute the majority of Sudan's population, are united in their faith and outlook regarding the state's lifestyle, and therefore it is legitimate, in keeping with democratic standards and natural justice, to apply their values and religious rules to all areas of life. In the chapter dealing with state law, the charter notes that the state will establish a legal system that will be suitable for the needs of the Muslim majority but will also meet the needs of the minorities and members of other religions; however, if contradictions arise in the legal area between the needs and desires of the majority and those of the minority, the law will be established according to the majority (i.e., preference will be granted to the Muslim law).

According to the charter, the Islamic laws (Sharia) will constitute the source of the legal authority because:

- The Islamic laws reflect the will of the democratic majority in the country.
- Islamic laws match the values and popular customs of the majority of the population.
- Islamic laws meet all needs related to national laws and principles.

State law recognizes the unique needs in the area of matrimony, family (marriage and divorce), and religious rites. Thus, it is permissible for members of other faiths to stand trial in these connections according to the laws prevalent in their own religions, but it will also be possible for them to be tried according to the Sharia.

The Sudan Charter negates secularism as a political and social pattern because it contradicts the principles of Islam. Nevertheless, the charter makes use of assertions that stem from the Western worldview and terminology, such as democracy. According to the charter's wording, Islamic religious law already contains all of the positive foundations inherent to the secular and Western worldview, but it is free of Western maladies and suits the lifestyle of the country's Islamic population.

The Relationship between The National Islamic Front (NIF) and Islamic Organizations and the NIF's Relationship with the West

Cooperation and coordination with the various Islamic movements constitute a central principle of al Turabi's concept.[12] Al Turabi claims that Sudan is a microcosm of Africa: Southern Sudan is part of the African entirety, Eastern Sudan is part of the Horn of Africa, Western Sudan is part of Western Africa, and North Sudan is part of (Arab) Northern Africa. Therefore, geographically and culturally, Sudan serves as a bridge between the Arab and African cultures.

In his vision, al Turabi foresees the growth of the Islamic movement in Sudan, which will spread beyond all borders and unite peoples and nationalities, much like al Mahdi's historical attempt in Sudan. The roots of his vision are ingrained in the period of Islam's foundation.[13] He maintains that the Prophet Muhammad used his tidings regarding the belief in one God for the establishment of a new social order in society, which at the time was immersed in chaos (*Jahilliya*). Muhammad presented society with the Koran and created a community that established an Islamic empire, which spread from the Himalayas in the East to the Atlantic Ocean in the West, and which attained cultural and social achievements with which no European society could compete. Al Turabi aspires to reinstate Islam's former glory and reestablish the Islamic empire; the way to achieve this is through the study of the Koran and return to life based on the fundamental Islamic principles that led to unity among peoples and the eradication of boundaries between states.[14]

Al Turabi asserts that Islam contains all of the positive values inherent to ideologies that have flourished in Western culture (free rule, human rights, a free economy, justice and equality), and therefore there is no conflict of interest between the ascendancy of Islam and the West. According to his outlook, a strong Islam is not a threatening factor but rather a stabilizing element, because the world is expansive enough for more than one civilization and enables different lifestyles.[15] Al Turabi ponders whether the West is truly consistent in its view of democracy as a universal value or if perhaps this is a selective approach that is not valid when the issue at stake is the desire of Muslim masses to establish Muslim rule, like in the case of Algeria. In his opinion, the Western approach to the developments in Algeria testify to the double standards practiced by the West. When addressing the Algerian example, al Turabi also stated that the illusions of socialism, capitalism, and nationalism had already burst in Islamic societies, and they are returning to the authentic values of Islam.[16] The elite initiates the beginning of the process, and its continuation lies in the mobilization of the masses on behalf of the new movement and spirit. In his opinion, in any Arab country where democratic elections are held, the Islamic movements will prevail, just as the Islamic movement triumphed in Algeria.

Al Turabi incorporated the "Qutuebian" Sunni radical Islamic worldview (Sayyid Muhammad Qutb—one of the founding fathers of radical Islam), and the Shiite Khomeinism, while mediating between the Sunna and the Shia. He emphasized the common factors shared by the two streams over their differences, while stressing the role of Islam as a leading force in human society during the modern era.

Notes

1. *Le Figaro*, January 25, 1994, "Biography of Hassan al-Turabi," in *Human Rights Watch Annual Report on Sudan, 1990-2001*.
2. Hassan al Turabi, *The Islamic Movement in Sudan*, Cairo: The Arab Reader Publishing, 1991.
3. Ibid., pp. 202-205.
4. Ibid., pp. 22-27.
5. Hassan al Hadibi "Dawa and not Kuda," Cairo: Dar Altab'ah and al-Nesher al-Islamiya, 1977.
6. Tim Niblock, "Numeiri's Fall: The Economic Base," Muddathin, Badal, Hardallo, Woodward (eds.), *Sudan Since Independence*, Ipswich, Suffolk: The Ipswich Book Co. Ltd., 1986, pp. 203-206.
7. Hassan al Turabi, *The Islamic Movement in Sudan*, pp. 121-219.
8. Ibid., p. 178.
9. Ibid., p. 177.
10. Ibid., pp. 203-212.
11. Abed Alier, *Southern Sudan*, Oxford: Oxford University Press, 1990.
12. Hassan al Turabi, *The Islamic Movement in Sudan*, Cairo: The Arab Reader Publication, 1991, pp. 252-263.
13. Ibid., pp. 17-19.
14. Abdel Wahad al Affendi, *Who Needs an Islamic State?* London: Grey Seal, 1991, pp. 52-53.
15. *Newsweek*, June 15, 1992.
16. *Newsweek*, June 15, 1992.

3

Sudan and Terror

The Links between Sudan and Iran, and Sudan's Support for Radical Islam

The alliance between al Beshir and al Turabi led to the formulation of a policy for the export of the Islamic revolution and in effect made Sudan a focus of and center for Fundamentalist Islamic Organizations. Due to the change in Sudanese policy, the country also altered its approach to its former allies, Libya and Iraq, and acted to strengthen its ties and form a strategic alliance with Iran. The following considerations were at the root of the links between Iran and Sudan:

- Sudanese readiness (despite the fact that it was a Sunni state) to regard the Iranian revolution as an inspirational model and adopt the "Iranian Revolutionary Message";[1]
- The vital need of the Sudanese regime to receive economic and military aid due to the prolonged war in the south and the regime's political isolation (particularly after its support for Iraq during the first Gulf War);
- Sudan's geopolitical location (bordering on eight countries, some of which are Muslim), which from the Iranian point of view makes it an important base for the dissemination of the Iranian revolution;
- Sudan's large area, which enables the concealment of infrastructures and training bases affiliated with Islamic terror organizations;
- Sudan can serve as a suitable substitute for the activity bases of the Revolutionary Guards and the Hizballah in Lebanon, in the event that they are forced to cease their activities as a result of Israeli or Syrian pressure;[2]
- Sudan's economic and military distress enables Iran to acquire an important base of influence for a relatively low economic price.

The establishment of the special links between Sudan and Iran began in 1990 after al Beshir's regime stabilized and the status of the NIF as the dominant body in the new regime became evident. In October 1990, the level of diplomatic relations between Sudan and Iran was raised to ambassadors, and the individual to be appointed the Iranian Ambassador to Sudan was Akbar Mohtashami who had played a key role in the invasion of the U.S. Embassy by the Revolutionary Guards in 1979, and was one of the founders of the Hizballah in Lebanon when he served as the Iranian Ambassador to Lebanon in 1982. At the same time, intensive efforts were initiated to strengthen the political, economic, and military links between the two countries. In this framework, the Iranian cultural minister visited Khartoum in May 1991 and laid the cornerstone of the Iranian cultural center in Sudan. Since 1991, Iran has been operating widespread informational-religious activity in Sudan, through a network of religious and cultural institutions financed by the Iranians or those acting for that country. Iran offers students from Sudan and all over Africa study scholarships in Islamic centers in Sudan, Qum, and Teheran, and encourages the exchange of religious delegations between the two countries.[3]

On April 25-28, 1991, al Turabi convened an Islamic conference of the Arab nation (The IAPC—Islamic Arab People's Conference)—a roof organization for all Fundamentalist Islamic movements, which he himself headed. The conference was attended by representatives of radical Islam from fifty-five countries, and it was the first attempt to establish a radical Sunni Islamic front in order to respond to the challenge that the West posed to radical Islam when defeating Saddam Hussein in the first Gulf War. The organization's main decisions were not made in the full forum, but rather in a smaller framework in al Turabi's home in Manshia. During the conference it was decided to establish the Popular Islamic Conference (PIC), whose goal (according to al Turabi) was to plan ways of waging war against the West. In addition, a permanent committee was founded in Khartoum that included participants from the fifty-five countries where the struggle of radical Islam prevails.

Shiite Iran was impressed by al Turabi's determination and by the success of the conference in Khartoum, and promised to assist him in advancing his concepts, despite the Sunni inclinations of the organization and its founder. Iran assisted in the founding of the control headquarters of the PIC, and several days after the end of the Khartoum conference, the head of Sudanese Intelligence, Colonel al Fatah Urwa, set out for Teheran for consultations and further cooperation. Upon his return, Urwa brought back Iran's contribution—advanced and encrypted communication equipment for communications between the PIC headquarters and its activists in various countries.

Iranian specialists and consultants arrived, and together with Afghan "alumni" started to establish an effective terror infrastructure in Sudan. Two main bases were established to train Islamic terrorists in the beginning of the 1990s: the al-Shambat and al-Mazraa training camps. Training included the use of light weapons and explosives, the preparation of improvised explosives, use of night vision equipment, and setting up ambushes.

On October 18, 1991, in Teheran, Iran convened the international conference of the Islamic Revolution in support of the Palestinian people, which was attended by over 400 delegates from sixty countries. Among those invited to attend was al Turabi, upon whom special respect was lavished by his Iranian hosts. Upon his return to Sudan, al Turabi took determined action to improve the operational capabilities of the Islamic movements affiliated with the PIC. Al Turabi believed that these movements lacked the tools and experience to act outside of their native countries; therefore, he welcomed the Iranian assistance in promoting the international operational capabilities of the Islamic terrorists.

In September 1991, Sudan received a senior Iranian military delegation, which apparently laid the groundwork in anticipation of the visit of the Iranian President Hashemi Rafsanjani to Sudan. Rafsanjani arrived in Sudan on December 13, 1991, for a six-day visit, at the head of a delegation of 157 members including the Foreign Minister, the Defense Minister, the Director of Intelligence, the Commander of the Revolutionary Guards, and the Minister of Commerce. Rafsanjani's visit to Sudan constituted the zenith of the cooperation process between the two countries, as this was the first visit by an Iranian president since the Khomeini Revolution, a fact that testified to the considerable closeness between the two countries and the importance that Iran attributed to its links with Sudan.[4] During Rafsanjani's visit an agreement was reached regarding strategic cooperation between Iran and Sudan, and a series of economic and military agreements was signed by both countries. In the military sphere, Iran promised to provide military aid in the area of training and in the provision of weaponry (at a scope of $20 million), aid that was vital to Sudan in light of the war in the south;[5] in the economic sphere, Iran agreed to supply Sudan with oil, food products, and various merchandise.[6] At the same time, the presence of Iranian consultants,[7] and possibly also members of the Iranian Revolutionary Guards, became known—they dealt in military consultancy and training, and in disseminating the message of the Iranian Revolution.[8] The cooperation between Iran and Sudan, which was formalized in both countries through the strategic alliance signed between them, in 1992 turned Sudan into a forward base for the export of the Islamic Revolution.

In the course of 1992, a militia of the NIF was established in Sudan—"The Popular Defense Units." The militia, based on the model of the Iranian Revolutionary Guards, was established with Iranian aid and was designated to ensure the control of the Islamic movement in Sudan, to serve as a counterbalance to the Sudanese army in a state of internal crisis, and to constitute the "advance guard" of the Sudanese government forces in the war in the south. From the moment of its foundation, the militia was granted preference over the army in matters relating to the allocation of human resources, funds, and weaponry. Its officers underwent training in Iran,[9] and its scope of forces increased perpetually and was estimated at about 90,000 fighters and volunteers.[10] The militia constituted the Sudanese regime's main support, much to the chagrin of the Sudanese army commanders who were thrust aside for the first time since Sudan had earned its independence and forced to assume a secondary role in the country's political system.

Along with the foundation and fostering of al Turabi's militia, additional links were developed militarily between Iran and Sudan as Iran also assisted in the training of Sudanese Air Force members,[11] in providing spare parts and weaponry, and in dispatching Iranian consultants who supported government forces in the war being waged in the south.[12]

Due to the strengthening of al Turabi's power and status as an Islamic leader of some importance, and Iran's position in supporting the Sudanese regime, Sudan gradually became a magnet for fundamentalists from Arab countries, North Africa and Black Africa, and others.[13] This process was in keeping with al Turabi's aspiration to turn Sudan into a center for Islamic Fundamentalism—first in relationship to North Africa and the Horn of Africa, and subsequently vis-à-vis the entire Muslim world. As stated earlier, al Turabi believed (much like Khomeini) that Islam knows no boundaries and conveys a universal message regarding the establishment of a just

Islamic state, which will serve as a model to be emulated by all of human society.[14]

The Sudanese aid granted to the Fundamentalist movements was expressed in the following areas:[15]

- Convening Islamic conferences, informational activity, and maintaining offices and study centers for Islamic Fundamentalists;
- Maintaining training camps for Fundamentalists from all over the Muslim world under Iranian or Sudanese instructors (generally from the ranks of the "popular defense units"), or recruiting trainers from among the Fundamentalist movements at various locations;
- Supplying weapons and sabotage materials to Fundamentalist terrorists;
- Providing aid vis-à-vis documentation, financing and transferring Fundamentalist activists from Sudan to other countries.

The Fundamentalist activity in Sudan posed a threat against several Arab regimes (Egypt, Algeria, Tunisia, Saudi Arabia), and placed Sudan in a confrontational front against these regimes (particularly Egypt), which intensified the isolation of the Sudanese regime. In August 1993, the Clinton administration placed Sudan on the list of states that supported terror,[16] and in consequence economic and political steps were taken against it thus increasing its political isolation. Following the assassination attempt against President Mubarak during his visit to Ethiopia in 1995, three of the individuals involved in the assassination attempt fled to Sudan. The latter refused to extradite them to Ethiopia. In consequence, several resolutions were passed by the UN—1044, 1054, and 1070—which imposed international sanctions on Sudan.[17]

Hassan al Turabi, who was aware of the fears in the Arab world and the West regarding Islamic Fundamentalism and Iranian activity on Sudanese territory, attempted to play down the importance and scope of the ties with Iran, and denied the allegations that his country supported terror.[18] Nonetheless, there appeared to be a significant gap between the calming messages broadcast by al Turabi in interviews to the Western media, and his statements in internal Sudanese forums, as well as his writings in Arabic. In his book, *The Islamic Movement in Sudan*, for example, he addressed the need for reciprocal aid among the Islamic movements in order to attain their goals, and clearly emphasized the aid that his movement had provided to the Palestinian Islamic Jihad, the Islamic Jihad in Egypt, the Alnahda Organization in Tunisia and the Islamic Front in Algeria.[19]

The links between Sudan and the Palestinian Hamas Organization serve as an example of Sudan's support for radical Islamic groups. On May 29, 1998, Sheikh Ahmad Yassin, leader of Hamas, arrived in Sudan for a visit on his trip throughout the Muslim world to raise support for his organization and his struggle against Israel. In the meeting between Sheikh Yassin and Omar al Beshir, al Beshir declared his country's support for the Jihad that the Hamas was waging against Israel until the liberation of the lands conquered by the Zionists.[20] At the end of a joint meeting attended by Sheikh Yassin and Hassan al Turabi (who at the time was Speaker of the Parliament and head of the PIC), the two called upon the Arab world to unite around the Palestinian struggle against Israel. On June 2, 1998, the Sudanese government decided to allow the organization to open offices in Sudan, and also gave it several farms and land to build training facilities as its contribution to Hamas' struggle against Israel. The Khartoum governor stated that the aid was given "in appreciation to Sheikh Ahmad Yassin, who had contributed to the renewal of the Jihad in Palestine." In addition, the governor appealed to charitable organizations to donate funds to the Palestinian struggle.

While testifying before the United States House of Representatives on May 15, 1997, Kenneth McKune, acting coordinator for counter-terrorism in the American administration, claimed that Sudan supports about ten terror organizations acting in different countries.[21] Sudan's ongoing involvement in terror ensures its continued presence on the U.S. State Department's list of countries that support terror, under a regime of UN sanctions.

Sudan and Bin Laden

Sudan's role as a "magnet" for Islamic Fundamentalists brought many of the Afghan alumni to Sudan, with Osama Bin Laden in the lead. Preparations for Bin Laden's move to Sudan had already begun in 1991, due to the rising tension between him and the Saudi Arabian authorities against the background of Bin Laden's harsh criticism regarding the Saudi monarchy's approach to the first Gulf War issue. Jamal al Fadel, Bin Laden's aide, traveled to Sudan and acquired several properties which were to serve Bin Laden and his organization in the event that they relocated to Sudan.[22] In April 1991, Bin Laden left Saudi Arabia for Pakistan, and from there went to Afghanistan, finally ending up in Sudan at Hassan al Turabi's invitation.

Bin Laden and al Turabi developed a symbiotic relationship—
Bin Laden enjoyed unrestricted movement in Sudan, and in exchange
invested millions of dollars in the country. He purchased communication equipment and weapons for the NIF, which was headed by al
Turabi, and in exchange Sudan supplied Al Qaida with 200 Sudanese
passports that enabled organization members to move from place to
place with new and fictitious identities.[23]

Osama Bin Laden established an "economic empire" in Sudan
thatincluded a series of companies:[24]

- Wadi al-Aqiq—an international commerce company
- Ladin International Company—an international commerce company
- Al-Hijra Construction—a construction company owned by Bin Laden
  and the Sudan government, which paved roads, built bridges, and
  employed over 600 people
- Al-Themar Agricultural Company—an agricultural company that
  employed a staff of some 4,000 people in the company's farms
- Taba Investment Ltd.—a commercial company that held a monopoly
  over the export of agricultural products from Sudan (rubber, corn, sun-
  flowers, etc.)
- The Blessed Fruit Company—an agricultural company for the growth
  of fruit and vegetables
- Al-Ikhlas—a candy manufacturer
- Al-Qudurat—a shipping company
- A leatherwork company
- A bakery
- A furniture factory
- Bin Laden also invested about 50 million dollars in the al-Shamal
  Islamic Bank.

Bin Laden's economic companies made use of bank accounts in
many countries worldwide including Cyprus, Malaysia, Hong Kong,
Dubai, Austria, and England.

In 1991, 1,000 to 2,000 Al Qaida members resided in Sudan.
During the years 1991-1993, Al Qaida members carried out a research project in the framework of which they wrote the *Encyclopedia of the Jihad in Afghanistan.* The encyclopedia specified the nature of the struggle against the Soviets and the pro-Soviet regime in
Kabul, the capital of Afghanistan, and the conclusions drawn from
this war. The research, which covered thousands of pages, was published in several volumes and was also distributed on CDs in the
mid-1990s in Pakistan.[25]

Al Qaida also attempted to develop non-conventional weapons in Sudan, and in the beginning of the 1990s Jamal al Fadel, Bin Laden's assistant, negotiated the establishment of a plant for the production of chemical weapons in the industrial zone of Khartoum (Hilat Kolo) with Sudanese officers. Among other items, the plant was to manufacture chemical shells for artillery.[26] Fadel also conducted negotiations for the purchase of uranium through a Sudanese officer, who served as an intermediary, but his partners in the deal were apparently con men who were trying to swindle him, and ultimately the deal fell through.

The years 1991-1993, during which time Bin Laden resided in Sudan, were also a decisive period in all matters relating to the characterization and formation of the Islamic state in Sudan. At that time, the Muslim world began to recover from the Gulf War, which was perceived as a traumatic event where secular regimes in Muslim states had cooperated with Western infidels in order to defeat another Arab country (Iraq). In radical Islamic circles, this period was called *al-Atzma* (the crisis), a term that comes second in severity only to the term of *al-Nakba* (the disaster), which refers to the founding of the State of Israel. It had been proven once again to radical Islamic circles that secular governments in the Muslim world, like the regimes in Kuwait or Saudi Arabia, survived only thanks to their reliance on America's power. This led them to the conclusion that the way to establishing "real" Islamic regimes in the Muslim world was via an uncompromising struggle against the United States, patron of the corrupt secular regimes.

The sense of emergency and the understanding that the battle of each Islamic organization against the secular regime in its native country was pitted simultaneously against two strong enemies—the internal secular regime and the United States (and the West) coming from the outside—signaled the need to consolidate all of the Islamic forces in a battle against the stronger forces.

This conceptual development led to the formulation, in the early 1990s, of an Islamic "Internacionale," which developed a military branch—"The Armed Islamic Movement." The latter constituted an umbrella organization of Islamic terror organizations worldwide. The leading entities in these organizations were the Afghan "alumni," who had gained extensive operational experience during the Jihad in Afghanistan. At this time, the Islamic movements began dispatching fighters from the Armed Islamic Movement to confrontation points between Islam and its enemies worldwide. Osama Bin Laden, residing in Sudan at that time, played a decisive role in the formulation of the training program of the Islamic entities, their dispatch worldwide, and the establishment of terror infrastructures for the perpetration of attacks against the enemies of Islam.

To summarize, the early 1990s and particularly 1992 constituted a historical turning point in the consolidation of international Islamic terror due to the following causes:

- The trauma of the first Gulf War
- The Islamic Jihad's triumph over the Soviet Union in Afghanistan (the collapse of the pro-Soviet regime in Kabul)
- The crumbling of the Soviet Union and the consequent ideological vacuum
- The creation of the Islamic Jihad of mujahidin throughout the Muslim World
- The ecumenical approach of Islam (Sunni and Shiite) consolidating in order to restore the former glory of Islam.

Initially, Osama Bin Laden opened his Sudanese offices in the vicinity of the government offices in the center of Khartoum, but quickly transferred them to a Khartoum suburb, and he spent most of his time outside of Khartoum at a ranch he had purchased in Soba. His home in Soba was a one-story, unfurnished mud house that was situated on the western bank of the Nile. Bin Laden lived there modestly with his four wives and children.

Most of his contracts and business were with the Sudanese government, which identified with Bin Laden's concepts and opinions. The Sudanese government, however, frequently had trouble honoring the contracts and paying for the projects that it had commissioned from Bin Laden, and he was forced to absorb the consequent losses.

According to the Sudanese, during the period that Bin Laden spent in their country he did not deal in terror and it was actually his deportation from the country that pushed him towards terrorism. According to the director of Sudanese intelligence, Gutbi al Mahdi, Bin Laden was occupied with his businesses when he resided in Sudan and he was closely watched by Sudanese intelligence. However, Jamal al Fadel, Bin Laden's former assistant who defected in 1994, told his interrogators that Bin Laden's commercial activities served to finance and camouflage Al Qaida's activities. Fadel revealed that at Bin

Laden's bidding, he had personally been involved in smuggling explosives to Islamic groups in Yemen, the transfer of about $100,000 to a collaborator in Jordan, and the smuggling of weaponry into Egypt. He confirmed that Al Qaida had assisted Islamic entities in Saudi Arabia, Algeria, Syria, Chechnya, Turkey, Eritrea, Tajikistan, the Philippines, Lebanon, and more. Fadel claimed that as early as 1991 Bin Laden had stated in Sudan that a Jihad against the United States was necessary, as the latter had contaminated the holy soil of Saudi Arabia. Bin Laden also claimed that the United States had aided the Christian rebels in southern Sudan and at the same time had initiated its involvement in Somalia.

In 1995, Al Qaida established a pact with the Hizballah. Despite religious and ideological disputes between the Shiite Hizballah and the radical Sunni Al Qaida, they cooperated against the common enemy, the United States. Al Qaida members traveled to Lebanon where the organization purchased a guesthouse. Hizballah instructors trained Al Qaida members in the detonation of large structures. The explosions perpetrated by the Hizballah in 1983 at the Marines headquarters and at the U.S. Embassy in Beirut were models that Bin Laden aspired to emulate. Using this method, Bin Laden believed he could bring about the expulsion of the Americans from Saudi Arabia just as the Hizballah had done in Beirut in 1983.[27] According to the testimony of Muhammad Ali (an Al Qaida member who consented to become state witness in the United States against the organization), Bin Laden met with Imad Muraniya, head of Hizballah's security mechanism.

In 1996, due to combined U.S., Egyptian, and Saudi pressure, Bin Laden was forced to leave Sudan and he returned to Afghanistan. According to the Sudanese authorities, Bin Laden's extradition to the United States or Saudi Arabia was considered at the time, but the fear of the possibility of riots by the strong Islamic circles in Sudan forced the regime to be satisfied with his expulsion from Sudan. Regarding his expulsion proceedings, the Sudanese claimed that the United States held talks with Sudan and demanded that access to Somalia be denied to him; but the CIA had no objection to Afghanistan as his destination. According to economic entities in Sudan, as a result of his banishment and the closing of his local enterprises Bin Laden apparently lost about $30 million.

Sudan and the "Carlos" Affair[28]

An example of Sudan's attempts to portray itself as a state opposed to terror was the extradition to France of the terrorist called "Carlos." During the 1970s and the 1980s, Illich Ramirez Sanchez, dubbed Carlos, was the most wanted terrorist in the world. He was involved in eighty attacks in countries all over the world, and was wanted by their intelligence agencies. Among other incidents, he was involved in the following attacks:

- The kidnapping of eleven of OPEC's oil ministers in Vienna in 1975
- The firing of bazookas at an El Al aircraft at the Orly Airport in Paris in 1975
- The hijacking of the Air France airplane to Entebbe in 1976.

Over the years, Carlos found refuge in Arab and East European countries, where he planned and activated his terror attacks. As a result of the collapse of the Soviet bloc at the end of the 1980s, Carlos fled to Syria, where he wed in 1986. From Syria he returned to Yemen, from there he went to Libya, and finally ended up in Khartoum, Sudan. At some point, he converted to Islam and thought he would find safe refuge under the radical Islamic rule of al Beshir and al Turabi in Sudan. He arrived in Sudan in 1883, changed his name to Ali Barkat and took a second wife (Lana Zerar, a Palestinian woman he had met in Jordan). In 1994, French Intelligence discovered his whereabouts (he was wanted in France for a series of attacks that he had perpetrated on French territory), and France exerted heavy pressure on the Khartoum authorities to extradite Carlos. The French pressure bore fruit and the Sudanese government finally consented to extradite him to France.

Carlos, who was hospitalized in a Sudanese hospital for surgery, was to be transferred to another hospital on the pretext of increasing security, but during the transfer process Sudanese and French agents took over the ambulance and transported Carlos to a military airfield, where he was placed aboard a French airplane and flown directly to detention in Paris.

It would seem that the Sudanese authorities preferred to "sacrifice" Carlos, who, in any case, was not identified with Islamic terror circles and in practical terms was a wanted terrorist lacking in any real source of power, in favor of Sudanese interests to remove international pressure from Sudan as a state that supported terror. The extradition of master-terrorist Carlos was to serve as clear proof of the Sudanese government's claim that it did not support terror, and to enable it to continue its practical sponsorship of Islamic terror entities, including Bin Laden and Afghan alumni. Sudan perceived France as a country (in contrast to the United States) that did not identify with Islam's foes, and the authorities believed that Carlos would be well treated and given a fair trial in France, a fact that would mitigate the criticism regarding the Sudanese extradition of the master terrorist among radical organizations inside and outside of Sudan.

There is also a possibility that the extradition of Carlos was part of an Iranian-Sudanese-French deal according to which Carlos would be extradited to France in exchange for the release of two Iranian terrorists incarcerated in France for the assassination of an Iranian opposition member.[29] If this version is, indeed, true, this would serve as further evidence of the profound cooperation between Sudan and Iran. Moreover, in an interview, even Carlos himself admitted to relief upon learning that he was being flown to France, because he had feared extradition to Saudi Arabia or Israel. In any case, the Sudanese action was duly praised by France, other European countries, the United States, and even some Arab states that had been victims of attacks initiated by Carlos.

However, at the same time, Sudan continued to serve as patron for Islamic terror organizations and to develop its ties with Iran and with Bin Laden and the Afghan alumni. The most acute expression of Sudan's involvement in Islamic terror is reflected in the aid that it provided to Egyptian terror organizations.

Sudanese Aid to Egyptian Terror Organizations[30]

In the wake of a wave of terror attacks perpetrated by radical Islamic organizations (the Islamic Jihad and the Egyptian Jama'a al-Islamiya) from mid-1992, senior Egyptians accused Sudan and its patron Iran of aiding Egyptian terror organizations. President Mubarak and his special adviser Osama al Baz, spoke of the "Arab Afghans" returning from the Peshawar camps in Pakistan to Iran and Sudan for training, from whence they penetrated Egyptian soil in order to perpetrate terror attacks. Iran's involvement in aiding Islamic terror in Egypt had begun already during the Iraq-Iran war. At that time, Iran established special camps for Egyptian prisoners of war who fought in the Iraqi army. Among the Egyptians there were also activists and leaders of the al-Jama'a al-Islamiya and of al-Jihad, who fled from Egypt to Iraq and joined the latter's army. Iran established the first nucleus of terror groups from among these Egyptian prisoners. They were trained in Peshawar, like volunteers from other Arab countries. Hundreds of Egyptian Islamic extremists arrived at these camps and later joined the mujahidin in Afghanistan. When the Soviets were defeated in Afghanistan, the extremists returned to Peshawar for refresher training and continued on to Egypt via Sudan, in order to take part in terror activity.

The alliance between Iran and the front of Hassan al Turabi, leader of the Sudanese Islamic movement, facilitated this activity. In Sudan, the men returning from Afghanistan were received in camps established by the Iranian Revolutionary Guards. These camps also absorbed the fundamentalists who fled from Egypt, Algeria, and Tunisia. Over time, scores of training camps were established in Sudan, on the shore of the Red Sea, at Khadolfi, al-Grif, Shambat, Benda, Karda, Bahra and other sites.

Sudan absorbed leaders of terror groups, particularly members of Jama'a al-Islamiya, and offered them places to live and Sudanese papers. A prominent example in this context is Mustafa Hamza, a senior member of Jama'a al-Islamiya who was sentenced to death in Egypt. Hamza organized the transfer of his organization's men from Peshawar to Sudan, and from there to Egypt.

The Egyptian authorities believed that the Iranian and Sudanese governments knew about all of the activities of the various terror organizations in their countries, and offered them assistance to the best of their ability. This is why Egypt has made major efforts to achieve cooperation with Arab and other states against Sudan and Iran's terrorist activities.

The "crowning glory" of Sudan's involvement in terror against Egypt expressed itself in the assassination attempt against President Mubarak during his visit to Ethiopia in 1995.

Sudanese Involvement in the Assassination Attempt against the Egyptian President

On June 26, 1995, a six-member terrorist cell attacked a convoy of vehicles that was escorting Egyptian President Mubarak en route from the Addis Ababa airport to his hotel in the city, where he was scheduled to attend a conference of African countries. The attackers attempted to block the convoy's passage and isolate the president. Their intention was to shoot at the bodyguards' vehicles and storm the president's car, launch an RPG rocket at it, and finally place a suitcase bomb on its roof. The plan ultimately failed due to an error committed during the blocking of the Egyptian bodyguards' vehicles by the forerunner cell, and the Egyptian president emerged unscathed (see further elaboration of this incident in Part IV).[31]

Two Egyptian organizations claimed responsibility for the attack: Jama'a al-Islamiya" and Tla'a al Fatah (pioneers of the victory). The Egyptian president accused Omar al Beshir and Hassan al Turabi, Sudanese leaders, of involvement in the assassination attempt and of supporting Islamic terror against the Egyptian administration and other Arab-Muslim countries.[32] An investigation of the incident did indeed confirm that the assassins apparently had arrived in Ethiopia from Sudan, and some had fled back there after the assassination attempt.[33] According to senior Egyptian figures, the leader of the Jama'a al-Islamiya, Mustafa Hamzah, and other leaders of that organization resided in Sudan and enjoyed the support and patronage of Hassan al Turabi.[34]

In response to the assassination attempt, Egypt began placing pressure on the Sudanese administration in the form of:

- Widespread informational activity to condemn and isolate the Sudanese government in the Arab and international communities as a regime that supported and was even involved in terror.
- Exerting military pressure in the controversial area between the two countries at Halaib-Shalatin, including the invasion of several Sudanese guard posts, during which fire was exchanged and some Sudanese policemen were wounded or taken prisoner, in addition to reinforcement of relatively large Egyptian forces in the sector as well as increased air and sea activity near the border as a show of force.[35]
- Conveying stern messages that Egypt would use force against the Sudanese regime if the latter did not cease its hostile activity towards Egypt.[36]
- Egyptian entities repeatedly stressed that Egypt had nothing against the Sudanese people, but only against its leadership, which they believed was causing severe damage to the Sudanese people and the Arab nation in general.[37]

The leaders of the Sudanese regime hastened to deny Egypt's allegations, and claimed that Egypt was trying to cast the blame on

Sudan in order to conceal the Egyptian regime's failure to solve its own internal problems vis-à-vis the Egyptian opposition.[38] Sudan condemned Egypt for its aggressive actions in the Halaib-Shalatin sector, which it claimed had caused unnecessary casualties, and announced that the Halaib-Shalatin area was sovereign Sudanese territory and that the Sudanese army would defend all Sudanese land.[39]

At the same time, the Sudanese authorities took a series of steps in response to Egypt's diplomatic and military actions, including:

- President Omar al Beshir called on the country's citizens to volunteer for the defense of the homeland: "We will provide weapons to anyone who can carry them, we will train all of our youth to protect our homeland and honor." [40]
- The Popular Defense Forces (al Turabi's militia) declared general mobilization and the readiness of its members to sacrifice themselves in the framework of the Jihad.[41]
- In various cities throughout Sudan mass demonstrations were orchestrated to increase support for the regime and in protest against the Egyptian aggression.
- An information drive was launched among Arab states with the aim of blocking the Egyptian steps against Sudan and convincing the Arab countries that the Sudanese position was just.[42]
- Sudanese forces took over the vacation home of Egypt's military attaché in Khartoum and expelled its staff. In addition, expulsions and arrests were made against Egyptian citizens in Sudan.[43]
- Sudanese forces were reinforced in the area of Port Sudan and at the focus of conflict, Halaib-Shalatin.[44]
- President Omar al Beshir appealed to Iranian President Rafsanjani in a personal letter to support his country's stance.[45]
- Hassan al Turabi warned Egypt that military action against Sudan might induce it to tamper with the Nile's sources and block Egypt's water supply.[46]

Hassan al Turabi, who was the focus of the Egyptian accusations as a supporter of Islamic terror and who the Egyptian's believed was involved in the assassination attempt, responded to these allegations in several interviews that he granted to the media. His responses to the events present an excellent opportunity to perceive his worldview and the tactics that he uses against his adversaries, with clear differentiation between the messages addressed to his supporters in Sudan and radical Islamic circles on the one hand, and the "reassuring" messages transmitted to Egypt and the West, on the other. Here follow several central issues that he addressed, as quoted in the various media:

1.   In an interview granted to the CNN,[47] al Turabi denied his country's and his own personal involvement in the assassination attempt and claimed that "Mubarak attacked the Sudan government and me personally because he wanted to divert attention from problems that were plaguing his regime in Egypt. Assassination attempts have occurred in Egypt several times in the past, and this is a problem between the government and the opposition."

2.   Al Turabi denied accusations that his country was training and aiding terrorists and claimed that "most of the terrorists had been trained by the United States in Pakistan and Afghanistan in the framework of their battle against the Russians, and Sudan itself lacks the means to train anyone."

Regarding the possibility that Egypt might take military action against Sudan, al Turabi claimed that his country "will not take the course of war...but Sudan can respond in other ways, as the Nile flows into Egypt from Sudan...and Sudan can always respond in its own way." When asked directly if it was possible that Sudan might cut off Egypt's water supply, al Turabi responded that he did not think that his country had the means to block the water supply.

3.   Completely different positions were expressed by al Turabi in a speech delivered in Medani (in Sudan) before an audience of National Islamic Front activists. In his speech he viciously attacked President Mubarak's regime and claimed "Egypt is totally lacking in Islamic faith, which was a disaster for Egypt. But Allah wishes the revival of Islam to emerge from Sudan and burst forth along the length of the Nile in order to purify Egypt of its impurity."

Al Turabi expressed his admiration for those who had carried out the assassination attempt against Mubarak, called them "mujahidin" (holy warriors) and added "when Mubarak dared to visit Addis Ababa in order to participate in meetings of the organization for African unity, the mujahidin rose up against him, ruined his plans and made him rush home anxious and frightened, to the extent that he was forced to hurl accusations against Sudan." In an unprecedented personal attack, al Turabi noted that in the past he had discussed topics such as philosophy as well as state and religion with Mubarak, and "I came away knowing that this man is on a lower level than myself and too stupid to understand what I said."

4.   When relating to Islam and the West, al Turabi stated that in his opinion Sudan had a leading role to play in the revival of Islam, and his assessment was that the West was fearful of the wave of Islamic renewal because the unity of Muslims posed a threat to Western interests.[48]

As a result of the assassination attempt, tension also erupted at Sudan's borders with Ethiopia and Eritrea.[49] Sudan accused Eritrea of committing acts of provocation at the border between the two countries, supporting the rebels in southern Sudan, and aiding opposition factors in attempts to topple the regime in Khartoum. Sudan reinforced its forces along the Eritrean border, and the Sudanese Foreign Minister, as well as senior security figures, toured the border and Eritrean refugee camps on Sudanese territory.

Reinforcements were also dispatched to the Ethiopian-Sudanese border, and an alert was declared against the background of Egyptian and Ethiopian accusations that the assassins had arrived in Addis Ababa from Sudan.

In light of the tension at three of Sudan's borders (Egypt, Eritrea, and Ethiopia) and its increasing political isolation, Sudan President Omar al Beshir sent a letter to the Iranian president in which he described the repercussions of the events and denied Egyptian accusations that Sudan had been involved in the assassination attempt. President Rafsanjani replied that restraint should be practiced and action should be taken to ease the tension between Khartoum and Cairo.[50]

Al Turabi and al Beshir's responses after the assassination attempt against the Egyptian president faithfully reflect Sudan's political double standards. On the international level, for the ears of the West and its neighbors, Sudan disassociates itself from terror and strives to present itself as a moderate and peace loving country, in order to prevent damage to its economic and security interests, and its relations with Egypt and the United States. The other dimension of Sudanese policy, which was fed by its alliance with Iran,[51] was its support for Fundamentalist terror organizations and its aspiration to export the revolution via terror to its neighbors.

The American Attack against a Factory in Sudan in 1998

In August 1998, suicide attacks were perpetrated against the U.S. Embassies in Kenya and Tanzania. The United States accused Al Qaida of carrying out the attacks, and retaliated by firing cruise missiles at Bin Laden's camps and facilities in Afghanistan as well as at a factory in al-Shifa, near Khartoum, which, according to the United States, had served Bin Laden for the development and production of chemical warfare. The U.S. cruise missiles demolished the factory in al-Shifa. The Sudanese claimed that it was a civilian pharmaceutical factory that produced medication, but the United States remained adamant that the factory had been involved in the production of chemical combat materials for Bin Laden.

As stated earlier, at the beginning of the 1990s, when Bin Laden was reinforcing the infrastructure of Al Qaida in Sudan, the organization launched negotiations to acquire the ability to develop or purchase non-conventional weapons. Bin Laden's assistant, Jamal al Fadel, negotiated with Sudanese officers in order to found a factory for the production of chemical combat materials. The factory was to be established in Khartoum's industrial zone and serve, among other aspects, to produce chemical shells for Sudanese army artillery.[52]

The United States justified the destruction of the factory based on the following arguments:[53]

- Bin Laden maintained an infrastructure of manpower and companies in Sudan, and served as an intermediary between Iraq and the Sudanese authorities in an attempt to develop military cooperation between the countries.
- The Sudanese army closely guarded the factory, which would not be the case if it were indeed an innocent pharmaceutical company.
- The al-Shifa factory manager lived in Bin Laden's former residence.
- The CIA dispatched an agent who collected soil samples in the factory's vicinity. In the laboratory tests traces of a substance called Empta were found. The sole use of this substance is for the production of the VX nerve gas.
- This information came in addition to tips that Bin Laden had been making repeated attempts to obtain chemical weapons.

There exists a whole set of counter-arguments that supposedly refutes the U.S. allegations one by one and proves that the demolished factory was indeed a pharmaceutical company. However, to date, no testimony has been found to enable an unequivocal resolution as to which of the two sides is correct.

In an interview for the *Christian Science Monitor*,[54] after the U.S. assault of the "pharmaceutical " factory near Khartoum with cruise missiles, al Turabi stated that the American action had been a terrorist attack aimed at toppling the Sudanese regime. He declared that Islamic Sudan was strong and capable of protecting itself. He claimed to know the American people well, and noted that they were not imperialist or hostile towards Islam; his accusations were directed at the American leadership. Al Turabi argued that the U.S. attempt to harm Bin Laden through the missile attack would, in fact, achieve the opposite effect and lead to the creation of 10,000 new "Bin Ladens." He claimed that Bin Laden is a fighter and a businessman. "And who trained him to be a fighter?" asks al Turabi and then replies that Bin Laden started out as an Islamic freedom fighter who was trained by and cooperated with the CIA against the Soviets in Afghanistan during the 1980s. After the war ended he lived quietly in an area far removed from Sudan, but the Americans turned him into a symbol of the anti-West power and since then all the youth from all over the Muslim world regard him as a symbol and a model for emulation.

The opinions regarding the attack at the pharmaceutical plant remain divided in the United States as well. Critics claimed that "the retaliation attacks may have signaled U.S. determination, but in fact they did not inflict any serious damage vis-à-vis Al Qaida capabilities. But on the other hand, they might have caused damage to America's moral status. Instead of emphasizing that the majority of those hurt by Arab terror are Africans, it appeared as though the United States was bombing Muslim countries."[55]

Power Struggles between Omar al Beshir and Hassan al Turabi (1999-2002)

The power struggles between Hassan al Turabi and Omar al Beshir, which began at the end of 1999, had a significant impact upon Sudan's policy regarding the export of the revolution and the assistance granted to Islamic terror. Al Beshir began to suspect that al Turabi was attempting to undermine him and initiated a series of steps meant to restrict al Turabi's actions and influence.[56] On December 27, 1999, al Beshir convened an emergency meeting of the Advisory Council of the National Congress Party at which it was decided to reorganize the government and the Parliament.[57] At the end of December, al Beshir dissolved the Parliament and initiated contacts to establish a new government, while simultaneously declaring a state of emergency in the country.[58] On May 6, 2000, al Turabi's appointment as the Secretary General of the National Congress was rescinded, and in an address to the nation that al Beshir delivered that month, he announced that he was freezing the activity of the party's Secretariat including that of its Secretary General, and reiterated his accusation that al Turabi and his men were attempting to undermine the legitimate state government.[59]

In an interview from his home in Khartoum, al Turabi accused al Beshir of taking undemocratic steps that were leading Sudan into a dangerous state, which could deteriorate into revolution.[60] Due to the continuing tension, and in consequence of al Turabi's bitter criticism of al Beshir, al Turabi and four of his aides were arrested on February 21, 2001. They were thrown into prison on a charge of conspiring to dispose President al Beshir. Due to al Turabi's senior status and age (al Turabi was about 70), he was released from prison in May 2001 and placed under house arrest.

On April 4, 2001, thirteen senior Sudanese officers were killed in a plane crash, including the Deputy Defense Minister Colonel Ibrahim Shams a-Din, who was a member of the Revolutionary Council and al Beshir's accomplice in the 1989 coup. Shams a-Din played a central operational role in the war against the south, and along with him twelve other officers with ranks of colonel and general perished. The SPLA (The Sudanese People's Liberation Army—the rebel organization in Southern Sudan) denied any connection with the plane crash, and some commentators believe that the crash was connected to power struggles within the Sudanese regime.[61]

Following contacts between close associates of both of the individuals[62] the dispute between the two was temporarily resolved, and in a speech delivered by al Beshir in the Parliament on January 4, 2002, he withdrew the allegations against al Turabi and his associates. This declaration paved the way for al Turabi's release from house arrest and his return to politics. Al Beshir did not explain why he had withdrawn his charges against al Turabi, but when relating to the release of detainees from the opposition circles, he explained that his intention was to strive for national reconciliation and to incorporate these entities in the Sudanese political system.

In March 2004, police arrested Turabi and about seventy party members, including some military and police officers, accused of being involved in an alleged plot to overthrow al Bashir, and Turabi's party was suspended.[63] Turabi was accused of inciting sedition, sabotage, hatred against the state and undermining the regime. Turabi and his party members have denied the accusations.[64]

The internal power struggles and the weakening of al Turabi's status caused a revolutionary change in Sudan's policies. Seeking to reinforce his government, Al Beshir initiated contacts with the rebels in the south (using the United States as his intermediary), and aligned himself alongside the "Coalition against Terror" after September 11, 2001, in the fear that his country would become a target in this battle.

The Shift in Sudan's Policy following September 11, 2001

As stated above, following the September 11 attacks, President Omar al Beshir decided to change Sudan's policy and align itself with the United States in its war against terror. One of the main reasons for this shift, in addition to the country's aspiration to achieve stability and the abolition of the UN sanctions, was the discovery of large quantities of oil in the state's southern area, the site of constant skirmishes between the government and rebel forces.[65]

On August 30, 1999, Sudan celebrated the opening of the oil port Port-Bashir, from which the first shipment of oil export (600,000 barrels) was launched on a ship to Singapore. President al Beshir, who attended the ceremony, presented awards and medals to companies and countries that supported the project, such as Canadian, German, and Italian enterprises, but also included companies from Iraq, Iran, Yemen, Saudi Arabia, and more. The equipment for building the port and the refineries was transferred to Sudan despite the economic sanctions imposed due to a UN resolution in 1997. Against this background there is no doubt that the end of the war in the south with international intervention will enable Sudan to take advantage of the economic resources in the region for the restoration and development of the whole country's economy.[66]

Parallel to al Beshir's turnabout in the matter of his policy vis-à-vis the United States, he also initiated reconciliatory advances towards al Turabi. As stated earlier, it was al Turabi who had invited Bin Laden to settle in Sudan in the early 1980s and assisted him in setting up a business and terror infrastructure in Sudan and worldwide. In consequence the United States had accused Sudan of supporting terror, as a result of which international sanctions had been imposed. Following Bin Laden's attacks at the U.S. Embassies in Kenya and Tanzania in 1988, the United States launched a cruise missile attack against a factory in al-Shifa near Khartoum, which it claimed had served for the production of chemical warfare substances for Bin Laden.

After the September 11 attacks, al Beshir feared a second U.S. reprisal in Sudan, and therefore rushed to close one of the largest industrial centers in the country, some thirty kilometers away from Khartoum (the Glad Center), which produced combat means for the Sudanese army. Al Beshir's fears focused on this center because the owner of the center, Idris Salah, was one of Bin Laden's associates (Salah was also the owner of the factory in al-Shifa which had been attacked by the Americans). However, the change in Sudan's policy led to a reconciliation with the United States, and Secretary of State Powell lauded Sudan for contributing intelligence to the United States in its war against terror and even arresting terrorists. According to American sources, some thirty Afghan alumni living in Sudan were arrested after September 11. In exchange, the United States agreed to the rescinding of the UN sanctions against Sudan.

On January 10, 2002, Sudan hosted a conference of the heads of seven East African countries, which discussed the resolution of regional conflicts and the struggle against terror.[67] The conference was attended by Sudan, Somalia, Uganda, Kenya, Ethiopia, Eritrea, and Djibouti. This was an additional step aimed at revising the earlier image of the Sudanese regime in the West as an administration that aided Islamic terror.

In May 2002, the Sunday *Times* of London reported that Sudan had arrested one of the most senior terrorists wanted by the United States. President Bush had referred to the prisoner—Abu-Anas al-Libai—as "one of the twenty-two most dangerous people in the world." The newspaper, which quoted U.S. intelligence sources, described Abu-Anas as a senior military entity in the Al Qaida network, who, among other campaigns, had planned the attacks at the U.S. Embassies in Kenya and Tanzania in 1998. A source associated with the CIA told the newspaper, "He is one of the nine fighters apprehended in Khartoum and he is now being handed over to the U.S. authorities."[68] Abu-Anas had resided in Manchester (in northern England), but had fled after the United States issued a warrant for his arrest. In May 2000 (according to the *Times*), the British police arrived at his front doorstep only a short time after he had fled.

The al Beshir administration also revised its policy vis-à-vis the issue of the war against the south, and expressed its willingness to come to an agreement. In 2002, three central factors led to the achievement of a ceasefire and the initiation of peace talks between the warring sides:

- The internal political struggle within the Khartoum administration weakened the status and influence of Hassan al Turabi, who had held an extremist position regarding the struggle in the south.
- The attacks on September 11, 2001, the U.S. declaration regarding a war against terror, and al Beshir's fear that Sudan would become a target in this war caused a shift in Sudan's policies and motivated it to cooperate with the United States, and also with the American intermediary who acted to achieve a ceasefire in the civil war.
- The oil produced in the south could significantly change Sudan's economic status, but that depends on the achievement of peace and internal stability.

The Sudanese government and the rebel organizations led by John Grange launched negotiations through a U.S. Intermediary, which were held first in Switzerland and then moved to Kenya. In the meantime, the parties achieved a ceasefire agreement, and it was agreed that the talks would continue, with the aim of putting an end to the war, which to date has claimed almost two million victims. The rebels' spokesman, Samson Kuwaja, told the BBC that the two parties had agreed to hold a referendum after a period of six years regarding Southern Sudan's right to self-definition and also concerning the enforcement of Islamic law in Northern Sudan only. The government's representative to the talks, Gazi Salah a-Din, noted that the agreement included a plan that would resolve all of the substantial problems related to religion and state, as well as the question of autonomy in the southern region. "These are the two most serious problems that we had," added Salah a-Din.

The agreement was signed after five weeks of negotiations in the city of Machakos, Kenya, and its implementation was contingent on the cessation of hostilities. The agreement was signed between the government and the SPLA along with several additional factions, but it does not cover all of the rebel organizations active in the south. At the present time it seems that all of the parties committed to the agreement are acting to implement it, but the fundamental problems between the north and south are far from resolved. In effect, the willingness of the north to join the peace process stems mainly from the American pressure placed on al Beshir's regime based on the "carrot and the stick" method, the "stick" being the American threat to use force against Sudan, while the "carrot" lies in the rescinding of the sanctions against Sudan and the anticipated economic boost for the country upon the cessation of the civil war, which costs the state millions of dollars a year (see elaboration in Appendix A). Alongside the information testifying to the changed attitude of the Khartoum government, there are also contradictory reports regarding continued links between the Sudanese and Al Qaida. According to the *Washington Post*, which bases itself on U.S., European, and Pakistani intelligence sources,[69] in mid-2002, Al Qaida transferred its gold reserves from Pakistan to Sudan. The reference is to an unknown number of cases of gold bars, which were disguised as other merchandise and transferred in small boats from the port of Karachi in Pakistan to Iran and Dubai, and from there they were flown on cargo planes to Khartoum. The value of the transferred gold is unknown, but the newspaper's quoted sources stated that it was a considerable amount.

Al Qaida has always maintained most of its assets in the form of gold. After the September 11 attacks and the U.S. declaration of war against Afghanistan, Al Qaida members, with the help of the Taliban regime, moved most of the gold reserves outside of the region. The gold's initial destinations were Dubai and Iran, but from there it was dispersed to various hiding places worldwide. The information regarding the route of Al Qaida's gold substantiates the American claim that Iran is becoming an active partner of terror organization, and that that country supports it in various ways. This refers mainly to Iranian intelligence units, which are associated with senior entities in the Teheran government who take a radical stand and offer patronage and aid to Al Qaida members seeking refuge and requesting assistance for reorganization outside of the boundaries of Afghanistan and Pakistan.

The exposure of the gold transfer also stresses Sudan's role as a financial center for Al Qaida, after countries like Saudi Arabia and the United Arab Emirates clamped down on money transfers and assets from their territories, as a result of the global war against terror. This new information proves that despite the blow that the organization sustained, it is succeeding in its reorganization and controlling its economic assets.

Sudanese sources in Washington denied the report that the Al Qaida gold was transferred via their country, and emphasized that they are cooperating with the United States in the war against terror; however, although in the past the United States lauded the Sudanese government's counter-terror actions, the situation has changed. Intelligence sources, both in the United States and Europe, claim that Sudan continues to serve as a base for Al Qaida, and that the organization still has many supporters in that country, mainly due to Bin Laden's ties that were created during the years that he lived there.

Indeed, among researchers there is controversy regarding Sudan's policies. There are those who believe that the alleged change in Sudanese policy is not a substantial strategic shift but rather only a tactical move meant to temporarily serve Sudan's interests, that is, rescinding of the sanctions and removing the American threat to attack the country due to its links with Islamic terror in general and Bin Laden, in particular. Others point to Sudan's cooperation with the United States in connection to the war against terror, the peace accord with the rebels in the south, and the agreement for cooperation against terror that it recently signed with Yemen and Ethiopia,[70] as steps that attest to a substantial change in Sudan's policy.

Notes

1. *Ha'amshari*, Iran, January 24, 1993—an interview with Hassan al Turabi.
2. *Conflict International*, September 1994.
3. *Al-Watan alArabi*, Lebanon, December 18, 1992.
4. *Teheran Times*, December 14, 1991; *Teheran Times*, December 15, 1991; *Teheran Times*, December 14, 1992; *Al-Watan alArabi*. Lebanon, December 18, 1992.
5. *Conflict International*, September 1994.
6. *IRNA Agency*, Teheran, December 8 1992; *Al-Watan alArabi*. Lebanon, December 18, 1992.
7. *Al-Watan alArabi*. Lebanon, December 12, 1992.
8. *Al-Muswar*, Egypt, December 2 1992; *al-Ahram*, Egypt, December 8, 1992; *Al-Sharq al-Awsat*, London, December 6, 1992; *Conflict International*, September 1994.
9. *Alkhalma Almamnoa*, Britain, February 1993.
10. *Alahad*, Jordan, December 21, 1993.
11. *Al-Watan alArabi*, Lebanon, March 12, 1993.
12. Report from Reuters dated January 27 1993. Reuters quoted the German TV network MDR, which reported that some 3,000 Iranians were fighting alongside al Beshir's forces in the war in southern Sudan.
13. *Al-Hayat*, Lebanon, November 27 1992; *Conflict International*, September 1994.
14. Hassan al Turabi, *The Islamic Movement in Sudan*, Cairo: The Arab Reader Publications, 1991, pp. 252-256.
15. *Al-Hayat*, London, February 10, 1993.
16. *Guardian*, December 10, 1992; *Conflict International*, September 1994.
17. George F. Moose, Assistant Secretary for African Affairs, Statement before the Subcommittee of Africa, Senate Foreign Relations Committee, Washington, D.C., May 15, 1997, U.S Department of State.
18. *Al-Muharar*, Lebanon January 13, 1993—an interview with the Sudanese Information Minister.
19. Hassan al Turabi, *The Islamic Movement in Sudan*, pp. 252-256.
20. *Al-Gumhuriya*, Egypt, May 30, 2001.
21. Kenneth R. McKune, acting coordinator for counter-terrorism, statement before the Subcommittee on Africa, Senate Foreign Relations Committee, Washington, D.C., May 15, 1996, U.S. Department of State.
22. Yosef Bodansky, *Bin Laden—The Man Who Declared War on America*, New York: Forum, 2001, p. 33.
23. Ann M. Lescht, "Osama Bin Laden's 'Business' in Sudan," *Current History*, January 2002.
24. Alan Fever, "Bin Laden Group had Extensive Network of Companies, Witness Says," *New York Times*, February 13, 2001.
25. Yosef Bodansky, *Bin Laden—The Man Who Declared War on America*, p. 91.
26. Ibid., p. 92.
27. Ibid., p. 93.
28. Based on an article in *Yediot Aharonot*, Tel Aviv, April 6, 2001.
29. Survey of Sudan's involvement in terrorism, http://www.ict.org.il/articles

30. This section is based on Nahman Tal, A *Confrontation at Home—Egypt and Jordanian Handling of Radical Islam*, Tel Aviv University: Papyrus Publications, 1999, pp. 152-153.
31. *Time*, July 10, 1995, pp. 20-22.
32. *Al-Ahram*, July 1, 1995; *Al-Waffad*, June 30, 1995.
33. *Al-Mazwar,* Egypt, June 30, 1995.
34. *Al-Gomhoria*, Egypt, July 9, 1995.
35. *Al-Waffad*, June 30, 1995
36. *Al-Watan alArabi*, Lebanon, July 6, 1995.
37. *Al-Watan alArabi*, Lebanon, July 6, 1995; *al-Ahram*, July 1, 1995; *al-Ahram*, July 8, 1995.
38. The Arab News Agency, Khartoum, July 4, 1995; *Alasuak*, Jordan, July 3, 1995; Reuters, Khartoum, June 30, 1995.
39. *Alahbar*, June 27, 1995; Reuters, Khartoum, July 1, 1995.
40. The French News Agency, Khartoum, July 13, 1995; *Alrai Alahar*, Sudan, July 4, 1995.
41. The French News Agency, Khartoum, July 13, 1995.
42. *Al Sharq*, June 30, 1995; *Alasuak*, Jordan, July 2, 1995.
43. *Al-Waffad*, June 30, 1995.
44. *Al-Hayat*, London, July 10, 1995
45. Teheran Radio, July 12, 1995.
46. An interview with Hassan al Turabi (CNN), June 30, 1995.
47. CNN, June 30, 995.
48. The French News Agency, Khartoum, July 5, 1995;The Sudanese News Agency, July 5, 1995.
49. *Al-Hayat*, London, July 1995.
50. Al-Shark Radio, July 13, 1995.
51. *Al-Ahram*, July 13, 1995.
52. Yosef Bodansky, *Bin Laden—The Man Who Declared War on America*, p. 91.
53. Ibid.
54. Hassan Turabi, "Islam Now Entrenched," *Christian Science Monitor*, September 9, 1998.
55. Martha Crenshaw, "Why America? The Globalization of a Civil War," *State and Society*, 2, issue 2, August 2002.
56. *Dawn* (Internet edition), January 2, 2000.
57. Ibid.
58. Ibid.
59. *Dawn* (Internet edition), May 7, 2000.
60. "Turabi Party: Sudan is a Police State in Need of Change," Khilafah.com, January 5, 2002.
61. "Sudan: Case Against Islamic Ideologue Dropped," Khilafah.com. January 5, 2002.
62. The talks were held with former Senator John Danforth serving as intermediary.
63. *Sudan Tribune*, Khartoum, July 1, 2004.
64. Ibid.
65. Randolph Martin, "Sudan's Perfect War," *Foreign Affairs*, March/April 2002.
66. Ibid.
67. CNN.com. world, "East Africa Leaders Meet on Terror," January 10, 2002.
68. *Sunday Times*, May 23, 2002.
69. *Washington Post*, May 22, 2002.
70. Sudan.Net, December 28, 2003.

Part II

Somalia and Islamic Terror

4

Somalia—Background and Historical Review

Following the September 11, 2001 attacks, Somalia made headlines as a country that might become a target in the U.S. war against global terror, due to its ties with Osama Bin Laden and with additional Islamic terror organizations.

Somalia, situated in the African Horn—an important strategic location overlooking the passageway between the Red Sea and the Indian Ocean—became an early target for Western colonialism from the sixteenth century up until the twentieth century, and alternated between Portuguese, Italian, French, and British control. The independent Republic of Somalia was founded in 1960 on the basis of the consolidation of two colonies—one British and the other Italian—into one state. Since its establishment, Somalia has suffered from political instability and inter-tribal conflict. The Somali state attempted to establish "greater Somalia" and consolidate a central government and a Somali national identity in a society clearly characterized by schisms on a tribal basis. Somalia's demand to control settled regions in Somalia caused a war with Ethiopia (1977-1978) and border clashes with Kenya.

Somali Society

Most of the Somali population is Sunni Muslim, but despite religious homogeny the Somali society is characterized by tribal division and infinite rivalries against a background of personal and sectorial power struggles.

The majority of the Somali population (about 80 percent) is nomadic and composed of four main tribes:[1] Dir, Isaaq, Daarood, Hawiye. These four tribes are divided into sub-tribes, extended families and clans, which either cooperate or compete with each other. The strongest basis for loyalty is the family and extended family,

63

while on the tribal and national plane the level of solidarity and loyalty becomes steadily weaker. This phenomenon explains why the two prominent Somali leaders—General Muhammad Farah Aidid and Ali Mahdi Muhammad—are both from the Hawiye tribe; they could not rely on broad support on the tribal level and have mainly the support of sub-tribal and familial solidarity groups. Confrontations between the various social components have been a frequent phenomenon throughout Somali history, however, at the same time there were various institutions charged with resolving these conflict, such as councils of the tribal leaders and elders, and various Islamic institutions.[2]

Most of Somalia's population is split between nomadic tribes and non-nomadic tribes with permanent residences. The Digil and Rahanwein tribes, for example, were permanent residents who dealt in agriculture in northern Somalia. These fertile and cultivated lands served as Somalia's wheat granary and provided a solution in the years of drought when the roaming residents relied on the produce of the farmers, either via commerce or by invading the area and forcibly confiscating the food.[3] Another component of Somali society is the urban class, consisting mainly of merchants and clerks that were closer to the secular culture and had moved a relatively long way from the religious and tribal systems.[4]

Thus, most of the internal conflicts in Somalia during the modern era have erupted due to the uprising of one of the tribal groups against an attempt to impose a collective Somali identity, and the group's desire to protect its self-definition and freedom as a group.

The Period of Ziad Barre's Administration

In the first nine years of its existence, the Republic of Somalia, which had been established in 1960, was a parliamentary democracy that allowed unrestricted political activity; the political and social systems incorporated traditional tribal norms and values together with Western lifestyles and values.[5] An expression of the conservative aspect was the marginal role of women in the political system, so that only in May 1963 was the right to vote granted to all Somali women. In March 1969, however, Somali democracy came to an end: a coup d'état, headed by General Ziad Barre, took place and the elected president Amdi Rashid Ali Shermarke was deposed.

Muhammad Ziad Barre was orphaned at the age of ten, and until adulthood he struggled to support himself as a goatherd in Somaliland, which at that time was an Italian colony. He joined the Italian colonial police and quickly rose in the ranks. In 1960, when Somalia was granted independence, Barre was appointed deputy commander of the Somali army, which was being founded at the time, and five years later he was appointed commander of the Somali army. In March 1969, Barre initiated a military coup and seized control.

Barre did not only introduce governmental changes, but also aspired to instigate a Marxist revolution that would introduce fundamental changes in Somalia's political, social, and economic system. The Revolutionary Council with Barre at its head served as Somalia's government, changed the political and organizational structure of the government, and formulated a new ideology that incorporated Islam and Communism. In 1971, Barre declared his intention to convert the revolutionary, military regime into a civilian government, thus leading to the establishment of the governmental party—the SRSP (Somali Revolutionary Socialist Party); members of this party's central committee were also members of the Revolutionary Council.[6]

In this framework, Barre became a close ally of the Soviet Union in East Africa. The Soviets supplied Barre with weapons, military equipment, and advisers, and with their help Barre proceeded to build up a strong army with which he attempted to resolve conflicts with his neighbors and his adversaries from within.

In 1977-1978, a brutal war raged between Somalia and Ethiopia due to Somalia's demand to control the Somali population in the Ogaden Desert. The Somali forces were defeated, and more than a million Somali refugees fled from Ogaden to Somalia, placing an onerous burden on Somalia's already collapsing economy. Somalia's defeat in the Ogaden War, which culminated in a peace agreement with Ethiopia (1978), the problem of the refugees (as the result of the war about one million refugees arrived in Somalia from the Ogaden Desert), and the severe economic crisis that struck the country from the mid-1970s, forced Barre to appeal to the international community in order to solicit humanitarian aid.[7]

The economic and social crisis also led the establishment of pockets of opposition to Barre's regime within his own tribe and party, in addition to the adversaries from rival political and tribal circles. Facing the threat to his regime, Barre began a campaign to suppress his adversaries—many were arrested, tortured, and even executed, and tribes that were hostile to the regime were severely punished. The economic and political distress from within and Barre's disappointment with the Soviet stance during the Ogaden War triggered a significant shift in his policies; he abandoned his alliance with the Soviets and appealed to the United States and the West for aid.[8] The United States hastened to assist Barre, thus ousting the Soviet Union from this important strategic stronghold at the shores of the Red Sea. The United States granted Barre generous aid, directly and via the international bank, to enable his regime to survive.[9] In exchange, Somalia allowed the United States to utilize docking services at the strategic port of Berbera, which had previously served the Soviet Navy.

Parallel to the stream of economic and military aid pouring in from the West, it was requested of Barre that he implement a more liberal policy, preserve human rights in his country, and act to establish a democratic political system. Due to these pressures, in December 1979, Barre declared elections for the parliament in which the "People's Parliament" was elected, but in effect all of the elected parliament members were affiliated with the SRSP, the governing party. Following the elections, Barre also introduced changes in the composition of the executive branch. In this framework he rescinded the roles of the three vice presidents and consequently reinstated the Revolutionary Council (in October 1980). As a result of these changes, in practical terms three congruent bureaucratic mechanisms functioned in one governmental system:[10]

1. The Party's politburo, which held executive authority through the Central Council (which was an executive entity);
2. The Council of Ministers or the Government;
3. The Senior Revolutionary Council (SRC).

The multiplicity of mechanisms and the competition between them enabled Barre to fortify his own status and left him with the decision-making process through the strategy of "divide and conquer." However, the failing bureaucracy and the political power struggles prevented the restoration of the Somali economy despite the economic aid received from the West. Against this background, in February 1982, Barre set out for the United States. On the eve of this visit, in order to minimize the criticism against his regime, he made the gesture of liberating two political prisoners who had been incarcerated since 1969. But at the end of his visit, when he saw that political criticism in his country was rising, he initiated a new wave of suppression of opposition members in addition to those entities whom he perceived as a threat to his status. On June 7, 1982, Barre demanded the arrest of seventeen leading politicians and public figures, including the chief of staff, the former vice president, a former foreign minister as well as some politburo members. The arrests triggered an atmosphere of terror and crisis, and as a result opposition elements consolidated into a united front, mainly on a tribal basis, with the aim of toppling the government.

In July 1982, Somalia faced not only internal problems but also an external threat in the form of an invasion by Somali exiles, with the aid of Ethiopian army units and combat planes, into the state's northwestern regions and its center, thus threatening to cut the country in two. Barre declared a state of emergency and requested Western aid in repelling the invaders. The U.S. administration agreed, rushed weapon shipments and doubled its economic aid. After several weeks of fighting, the invasion was deflected and Barre was again free to deal with his adversaries at home.

In December 1984, due to his desire to intensify his government's legitimacy, Barre introduced several amendments to the constitution, including the extension of the president's term of office from six to seven years, as well as an amendment according to which the president would be elected in a referendum, and not by the National Council (the executive body). It is to be noted that in referendums that Barre held during his term of office he always won 99 percent of the votes, and therefore the amendment of the constitution in this matter was geared at fortifying his control and granting his regime a broad, popular basis of support.[11]

A short time after his ascendancy to power in 1969, Barre had declared that he would act against the tribal and sectorial characteristics of Somali politics and society. He claimed that the tribal mentality constituted a threat against Somalia's unity, and in the name of the struggle against this danger he banned all political and party activity. But in practical terms, in the twenty-one years of his regime, Barre also based his political power on tribal and sectorial loyalty. Most of the influential and powerful positions were allocated by Barre among the three main clans of the Daarood tribe:

1.   The clan to which he himself belonged—Mareehaan;
2.   The clan of his son-in-law—Dulbahante;
3.   The clan of his mother—Ogaden.

The remaining tribes and clans were permitted to claim the "left-over" crumbs from the Somali government's "cake." The ban on political and party activities made the tribal association the only legal possibility for group organization, and therefore a clear link was created between the tribal and political interests.

The establishment of the SRSP government party did not constitute a proper and real response to the Somali society's political needs, and therefore protest activity was channeled into illegal directions related to political subversion and terror. Regardless of the fact that Ziad Barre's regime relied solely on force and lacked broad political support, it succeeded in surviving twenty-one years, but ultimately the domestic opposition forces finally overcame him and put an end to his regime at the end of 1990.

The Rival Factions in Somalia

As noted earlier, Somali society was characterized by a large range of powerbrokers arrayed on a tribal, clan, and extended family basis. Some of these power centers established political movements and militias aimed at protecting the group's interests in the Somali political system. It is possible to count five main movements, all on a tribal and regional basis, that were prominent in the power struggles in Somalia during the early 1990s:

1.   The USC (the United Somali Congress)—of the Hawiye tribe in central Somalia, the dominant movement in the state;
2.   The SNM (Somalia National Movement)—of the Isaaq tribe in the Somaliland area;
3.   The SPM (the Somali Patriotic Movement—in the Ogaden area;
4.   The SSLF (the Somali Salvation and Liberation Front)—of the Mayerteen tribe;
5.   The SDM—(the Somali Democratic Movement)—of the Rahanwein tribe in north Somlia.

The movements were generally divided into two main groups:

1.   North Somali movements, headed by the SNM, which represented tribes and populations from the former British colony;
2.   Central Somali movements, headed by the USC, which represented tribes and populations from the former Italian colony.

Although the regional and tribal division provides a relatively convenient way to distinguish between powerbrokers, the political reality was actually far more complex, and splits and rifts within the ranks of the political movements, in addition to a shifting of loyalties, were prevalent in Somali society.

The End of Ziad Barre's Government and the Civil War

At the end of 1990 and the beginning on 1991, there was widespread insurrection initiated by the tribes and powerbrokers in Somalia against the government of General Barre, who had governed Somalia for twenty-one years. Due to the insurrection, Barre was forced to flee Somalia (he was given political sanctuary in Nigeria, where he died in 1995). Most of his associates and supporters, who fulfilled central roles in the administrative and governmental mechanisms, also fled Mogadishu, and the capital was left in governmental chaos.

Due to the collapse of Barre's government, political struggles erupted over control in Mogadishu in particular and over the entire country, in general. The two main contenders for control came from the ranks of the United Somali Congress (USC)—the dominant political movement in Somalia at that time. The two were:[12]

1. *Ali Mahdi Muhammad*, one of the USC leaders and a member of the Hawiye tribe and the Abgal extended family, which resided mainly in the Mogadishu area.

Muhammad had been a teacher and a government clerk prior to his election to the House of Representatives (the Republic's National Congress) in March 1969. Following Ziad Barre's coup in Ocrober 1996, Muhammad was arrested along with many other politicians. He was released from prison several years later and launched a career in business. In the 1980s he served as manager of the UN offices in Mogadishu. At the same time, Muhammad used his financial resources in order to assist guerrilla fighters affiliated with the USC in their struggle against Ziad Barre.

In May 1990, Muhammad was among those who signed a petition demanding that Ziad Barre introduce democratic reforms. Barre responded with a rash of arrests; Muhammad fled to Rome where he continued to act against Barre's government from the USC offices there. In the framework of the internal

struggle in the ranks of the USC, Ali Mahdi Muhammad relied
on the support of circles within the USC, members of his own
tribe, and a loose coalition with other tribes.

2. *General Muhammad Farah Aidid*, also one of the senior leaders of the USC, and a member of the Hawiye tribe, but he belonged to the Habar Gidir extended family, which resided in
central Somalia.

Although his father was a simple camel raiser, Aidid studied in Italian schools and subsequently in the Soviet Union.
Aidid spoke several Western languages and was considered an
intelligent, though somewhat erratic, individual.

During the administration of President Ziad Barre, Aidid
fulfilled senior roles; he served as a senior officer in the army
with the rank of general, a cabinet member, ambassador to India, and director of Somalia's intelligence. However, subsequently Barre suspected that Aidid was subverting him and incarcerated him for a period of six years.

In the framework of the internal struggle in the ranks of the
USC between Aidid and Ali Mahdi Muhammad, Aidid was supported by his tribe and a relatively broad coalition of tribes, as
well as political and military powerbrokers, called the Somali
National Alliance (SNA).

Following the collapse of Barre's regime, the USC declared the
establishment of a temporary government, but its actual rule was
limited. The USC elected Ali Mahdi Muhammad as its temporary
president. According to the 1979 constitution, the president serves
as the head of state and he is authorized to appoint a government;
accordingly, Ali Mahdi Muhammad appointed Omar Arta Galib, of
the Isaaq tribe, as temporary prime minister. The latter established a
government with twenty-seven ministers and eight deputy ministers. This step accentuated the importance that Muhammad attributed to the establishment of a coalition on a tribal basis and to the
broadening of the legitimacy basis for his government.

In June 1991, elections were held for the leadership of the USC,
and Aidid was elected chairman of the movement, however, despite
the defeat within his movement, Ali Mahdi Muhammad refused to
relinquish the presidency, which he had taken at the end of 1990.
Due to Muhammad's actions, Aidid strengthened his links with his
allies from the SNA and initiated forceful steps to depose Ali Mahdi

Muhammad and his associates.[13] Ali Mahdi Muhammad declared that it was his true intention to hold general elections the moment that security circumstances enabled it, but the internal power struggles in the USC and the resistance of opposition elements to Muhammad's government prevented any possibility of holding elections, and the country rapidly deteriorated into a civil war.

Thus, in the beginning of 1992, a civil war erupted in Somalia, which quickly spread from Mogadishu to the other parts of the land. In the fighting in Mogadishu, Aidid had the upper hand and his forces overtook most parts of the city, but they were unable to uproot Ali Mahdi's forces in several quarters, leaving the capital divided. After their relative success in the capital, Aidid and his men set out to dominate the central and southern part of the country.

The ruthless battle between the rival tribes and factions, the collapse of all governmental systems, including the supply of basic products, in addition to the severe drought that prevailed in the area (which reportedly caused the deaths of some 300,000 people in 1992)—all of these factors contributed to major disaster for Somali residents. Due to the growing anguish, the UN decided to offer aid to Somalia and in December 1992 operation "Restore Hope" was launched in an attempt to restore order in the state and enable the distribution of food to its inhabitants. The UN offices in Mogadishu were opened shortly after the victory of Aidid's forces over Ali Mahdi Muhammad, and in this situation it was clear to the UN representatives that they were too late to achieve any kind of compromise between the warring parties. Therefore, the UN activity focused on humanitarian aid in order to ease the starvation and suffering of the inhabitants.[14] The UN Secretary-General defined the situation in Somalia as anarchy, and viewed the achievement of a ceasefire and the confiscation of weapons from the rival sides as a pivotal step towards resolving Somalia's problems.

Therefore, the UN decided (with U.S. support) to dispatch an international force under UN auspices with the following roles: providing humanitarian relief for Somali's starving population, disarming the fighting sides, and forming a stable central government based on the Western model.[15] The UN's steps met with dogged resistance on the part of traditional powerbrokers and entities with political interests in Somalia, and the UN's humanitarian mission rapidly deteriorated into a violent confrontation with local militias, particularly with the forces of General Aidid, which inflicted heavy casualties on the UN forces.

The rival parties in Somalia understood that the humanitarian aid arriving via the UN constituted the key to control of the state and its population, and therefore did everything in their power to achieve control over the distribution of humanitarian relief.[16]Ali Mahdi Muhammad, who continued to claim that the role of state president was his even after his defeat at the hands of Aidid, argued that he should be the only person with the authority to supervise the allocation of humanitarian aid and set standards for eligibility and prioritization for its distribution. When the UN refused to accept this demand, his forces bombed Mogadishu port and attacked distribution sites of humanitarian aid. Ali Mahdi Muhammad claimed that the attacks were carried out by desperate and uncontrolled elements among his forces, but it was evident that he was the person who decided to deprive the general population of humanitarian aid if its distribution was not conducted under his control. General Aidid argued that the distribution of the relief should be handled by his own people, who controlled most of the country's territory, and accused the UN and the Arab countries with which they were taking sides in the conflict of being accomplices to Ali Mahdi Muhammad's actions.

In November 1992, in view of the increasing difficulties surrounding the distribution of the humanitarian aid in Somalia, the United States decided to dispatch a large military force whose role would be to enable the UN delegation to assist the suffering Somali citizens. The U.S. decision came up against the strong opposition of various powerbrokers in Somalia, who were afraid of losing their power if they relinquished their control over the supply of food and international humanitarian aid.[17]

On November 2, 1992, Aidid threatened that any deployment of foreign forces in Somalia would end in bloodshed, and the USC spokesperson stated that the reference was to the American armed forces that were impairing Somali sovereignty. Due to U.S. and UN refusals to take his side in the confrontation, Aidid launched a series of steps aimed at reinforcing his status in anticipation of a possible confrontation with the Americans. Aidid convened a conference of leaders of various sectors in Somali society to gain their support for the SNA and their loyalty to its leadership. At the same time (on November 10, 1992), Aidid's forces took over fifteen central intersections from gangs and local powerbrokers, thus achieving control over the country's main roadblocks and axes.[18] At the end of November, Aidid visited Kismayo—a city in the southern part of the

country with an important port, an airport, and a central junction—
and he signed an agreement with several important powerbrokers,
including:

- Ahmad Omar Jays, chairman of the SPM, whose people controlled the
  area (Aidid appointed him deputy chairman of the SNA);
- Muhammad Nur Iliau, leader of the SDM in the north;
- Leaders of the "Army for the Liberation of Somalia"—a relatively
  large underground movement whose main bases were in nearby Kenya.

In a meeting with these leaders Aidid described the dangers threatening their control and demanded cooperation in order to protect
joint interests. At the same time, Ali Mahdi Muhammad acted to build
up a counter-coalition, and held meetings with powerbrokers from
Eritrea and Ethiopia in order to recruit aid in his struggle against
Aidid.

However, despite the threats, on December 1, 1992, the two warring sides welcomed the arrival of the American forces. Nevertheless, each of the sides demanded that the UN and the United States
recognize his as Somalia's legitimate leadership, and that the U.S.
forces take action against his adversary if he should disrupt the distribution of humanitarian aid.

Islamic Involvement in Somalia[19]

The involvement of Islamic relief organizations in Somalia began
as early as the late 1970s, when Ziad Barre severed his ties with the
Soviet Union and the Communist Bloc. Islamic charity and aid organizations, with the encouragement of Saudi Arabia and the Persian Gulf States, poured financial and humanitarian aid into Somalia, most of which was transferred to the government via a Somali
liaison named Muhammad Sheikh Othman.

In the summer of 1991, following the collapse of Barre's regime,
Othman transferred his camp's loyalties to General Aidid. This step
was apparently taken with the blessings of the Islamic entities that
made use of Othman's services, as the ideological and financial support of these entities was also transferred to Aidid's camp.

During the civil war in Somalia, Islamic factors from Saudi Arabia
and the Gulf states were active in the country; they incorporated
humanitarian aid with Islamic preaching aimed at bringing the Somali population closer to their religious worldview. These organizations were diverse and represented various interested parties and

several religious sects from the Arabian Peninsula, that sought exclusivity in aiding Somalia. They regarded UN and U.S. involvement as counterproductive to their interests and as an attempt by Western superpowers to take over Somalia under a pretext of humanitarian aid. Thus, for example Islamic charities like the Islamic World Association and the Muslim World Relief Organization declared that "only Muslim organizations act to provide true humanitarian aid to Somalia, and the humanitarian relief from the West is meant to serve Western control of Somalia."[20]

Among those entities active in Somalia under the guise of charitable organizations was Osama Bin Laden, who acted in coordination with the radical Islamic leader of Sudan—Hassan al Turabi. Bin Laden viewed the deterioration of the central government in Somalia and the intensification of radical Islamic influences in this country as a window of opportunity to develop and boost an Islamic terror infrastructure. The Islamic terror infrastructure that Bin Laden deployed all over the world relied on a network of companies and financial institutions that served as camouflage for the terror networks and ensured the flow of required resources for their operation. Thus, with the aid of Muhammad Sheikh Othman's financial infrastructure, Somalia quickly became an important component in the financial, worldwide network established by Bin Laden.

Bin Laden's activities in Somalia were largely coordinated with Sudan, whose leader—Hassan al Turabi—regarded Somalia as an important destination for the export of the Islamic Revolution; the Sudanese involvement was supported by Iran, Sudan's patron at that time, and became a part of an Iranian strategic plan to export the Islamic revolution to Africa and to attain important strategic footholds in the Horn of Africa and on the shores of the Red Sea.

It is thus accurate to state that since the beginning of the civil war in Somalia four radical Islamic entities have acted there simultaneously and sometimes even in coordination:

1. Iran—Directly and indirectly through its ally Sudan;
2. Sudan—Directly and through Somali powerbrokers that it supported;
3. Bin Laden and Al Qaida—Independently, but in coordination with Sudan;
4. Radical Islamic entities from Saudi Arabia and the Emirates in the Persian Gulf.

Somalia rapidly turned into an arena of confrontation between the United States, which aspired to restore stability and peace and to strengthen its own status and influence in the area of the strategic Horn of Africa on the one hand, and the Islamic powerbrokers, who aspired to perpetuate the anarchy in Somalia with the aim of strengthening the influence of Islam and achieving a free hand for Islamic terror entities in this country, on the other.

Iranian Involvement in Somalia[21]

Iran regarded the Horn of Africa, Somalia included, as an important target for the export of the Islamic Revolution and as a key to achieving control over the coasts overlooking the vital waterway between the Red Sea and the Indian Ocean. The creation of a chain of Fundamentalist Islamic regimes associated with Iran would have generated a new geopolitical reality which would enable Iran to "surround" the Arabian Peninsula—from Iran in the east, on to the Horn of Africa states in the west, and finally Yemen in the south—in addition to intensifying the Islamic threat against Egypt and the North African countries.

Under the government of Hassan al Turabi and Omar al Beshir, Sudan had already become Iran's close ally in 1990, and served as an active partner and a springboard for the realization of strategic Iranian interests in the region. Iran and Sudan regarded the United States and the West as the main enemy impeding the realization of the Islamic vision in the Horn of Africa, and therefore took joint action to block and remove this threat.

On November 28 1992, following the U.S. declaration of its intention to dispatch forces to Somalia, an Iranian delegation headed by Ayatollah Mohammad Yazdi arrived in Khartoum for consultations. During the visit, a new security cooperation agreement was signed between Iran and Sudan, according to which Iran undertook to boost Sudan's military and security capabilities and to help with the building of the necessary infrastructures for the export of the Revolution to African countries. Iran and Sudan decided to establish a joint committee headed by the Iranian General Rahim Safawi and Ali Othman Taha, al Turabi's aide, who had planned the action in the Somali arena against the American forces with the help of local powerbrokers (the SIUP—the Somali Islamic Union Party). In addition, Iran decided to establish the SRG (the Somali Revolutionary

Guard), to be funded by Iran. Its members were to be trained in Sudanese camps by Iranian and Hizballah experts. The establishment of the SRG was placed in the hands of an Iranian intelligence officer named Ali Manshawi.

The strategy formulated by Ali Othman Taha's team postulated that the Islamic activity should focus on inciting the Somali public against the American presence and encouraging guerrilla and terror activity by local powerbrokers; however, a frontal confrontation between the organizations supported by Sudan and the United States was to be avoided as long as the conditions were not yet ripe, and providing that there was no direct threat against Sudanese and Iranian interests.

Nonetheless, the Iranians believed that there was an urgent need to perpetrate terror acts against the United States, which would give expression to radical Islam's opposition to the American presence and activity in Somalia. The target for attack was Aden, which served as a base for American activity in Somalia but was located outside of the boundaries of the African continent. The mission in Aden was assigned to Osama Bin Laden, who undertook the task with alacrity and efficiency (see subsequent section in this chapter on this issue).

In the framework of preparations for activity in the Horn of Africa, Iran incorporated the "Al-Quds forces," whose role was to facilitate the export of the Revolution via subversive activity in the target countries. Several hundred Afghan alumni were active in these activities, some of whom were sent by Iran to Sudan prior to their operations in the Horn of Africa. In addition, Iran presented Sudan with Stinger anti-aircraft missiles for their possible use in Somalia. At the end of 1992 and in the beginning on 1993, groups of Al-Quds fighters were dispatched from Sudan to Somalia and Ogaden in order to organize infrastructures and prepare for their operation.

In February 1993, a conference was held in Khartoum under the patronage of Hassan al Turabi, and with the participation of senior Iranian representatives, the SIUP representatives and delegates sent by Aidid, with the aim of establishing a combat strategy against the United States. After the conference, in the following six to eight weeks, Aidid and several of his senior aides visited Iran, Yemen, and Sudan numerous times in order to coordinate the aid to be offered his forces in Somalia. The Iranians poured combat means, instructors and consultants into Sudan and through that country into Somalia; according to various reports the latter helped the Islamic forces and Aidid's people in the fighting in Mogadishu.

The U.S. decision to withdraw its forces from Sudan following the losses that it had sustained there (particularly in the fighting on October 3-4 1993; see subsequent elaboration) was perceived by the Iranians and the Sudanese as a major victory of radical Islam over the American superpower. Iran, which had succeeded via the Hizballah in causing the withdrawal of U.S. forces from Lebanon in 1983, again forced a humiliating retreat on the United States, this time in Somalia. On March 1, 1994, most of the U.S. forces withdrew from Somalia, and the country was plunged into total anarchy, which enabled Iran and its allies—Sudan and Bin Laden—to tighten their grip on strategic territory that in practical terms had ceased to function as a state.

The Sudanese Involvement in Somalia[22]

The escalation and deterioration vis-à-vis the situation in Somalia occurred at the same time as (and perhaps as part of) an Iranian-Sudanese campaign aimed at exporting the Islamic Revolution to East Africa. During the years 1990-1991 an infrastructure of training camps was established in Sudan, which was sponsored by the NIF (the National Islamic Front). Islamic volunteers from Ethiopia, Eritrea, Kenya, Uganda, and Somalia arrived at these camps. Dr. Ali Alhaj, one of al Turabi's cronies, was responsible for the operation of these training camps and for the training of the foreign terrorists.

In the fall of 1992, al Turabi ordered an escalation of the campaign to undermine the stability of regimes in East Africa, and the terrorists who had completed their training were sent back to their native countries in order to facilitate and lead the subversive Islamic activity. This step by al Turabi was initiated around the time that the United States decided to send a humanitarian task-force to Somalia.

The civil war and the anarchy that prevailed in Somalia presented a convenient opportunity for Iran and Sudan, its ally, to attain influence and a grasp in a strategically located Muslim country on the shores of the Red Sea. The American involvement in Somalia was perceived by Iran and Sudan as a threat against the interests and actions that they aspired to facilitate in this country and as renewed American Imperialism under the guise of humanitarian aid. Thus, in the eyes of Iran and Sudan, the U.S. forces became a central target, which should be expelled from Somalia through a terror and guerrilla campaign that would be based on local powerbrokers hostile to the Americans and the UN.

Sudan aided Islamic terrorists trained in its camps to reenter Somalia via various routes (the sea, Ethiopia, and Kenya) and supplied them with weaponry. Al Turabi's three main allies in the Somali arena were:

1. Abdel al Rahman Ahmed Ali Tur, an Islamic leader in the Somaliland area who enforced a rigid Islamic regime in the area under his control and enjoyed Sudanese and Iranian aid;
2. General Muhammad Abshir, former chief of the Mogadishu police and a central figure in the leadership of the SSDF (the Somali Salvation Democratic Front); because of his close ties with al Turabi, the militia was joined by many volunteers from Sudan, Egypt, Pakistan, and Afghanistan;
3. General Aidid was al Turabi's most important ally, but the extent of Sudanese or Iranian influence on his actions was relatively limited.

Sudan granted Aidid financial and military aid with the aim of broadening and boosting its influence in Somalia, and al Turabi even sent volunteers trained in Sudan to fight alongside Aidid against the forces of Ali Mahdi Muhammad, but Aidid succeeded in maintaining a large degree of political independence, and his dependency on his friends in Khartoum and Teheran was limited. As noted earlier, through Osama Bin Laden al Turabi established a covert financial and logistic infrastructure in Somalia for the funneling of financial aid to al Turabi's allies. In 1992, Al Turabi established the SIUP (Somali Islamic Union Party) in Somalia, an umbrella organization that consolidated several radical Islamic entities sharing a common denominator of tribal loyalties. The SIUP became the main and direct platform for infiltrating the Sudanese influence into the Somali arena, under al Turabi's express guidance.

The formal leader of the SIUP was Mohammad Othman, who was based in London and dealt mainly in informational and propaganda-related activities, but the subversive activities and the fighting were run by local commanders in Somalia, who received instructions directly from Sudan and Iran. The SIUP initiated military activity in June 1992 via an offensive launched in the area of Bosaso, North Somalia, but the attempt failed. Following the military debacle, a delegation of experts headed by Rahim Safawi, the deputy commander of the Iranian Revolutionary Guard, and Ali Othman Taha from Sudan arrived in Matka, Somalia, in August 1992 to investigate military and other needs of the SIUP, together with the latter's commanders, and prepared a plan for the improvement of its operational skills. Starting from the fall of 1992, weaponry was supplied and training camps were set up for the organization in Somaliland and in Ogaden inside Ethiopian territory (Bin Laden played a major role in arranging the establishment of the camps on Ethiopian soil).

Following the landing of the U.S. Marines in Somalia, a joint Sudanese-Iranian decision was made to initiate a struggle against the American presence, on the basis of Sudan's allies in the Somali arena and the terror infrastructure established in the country prior to the arrival of the American forces.

Osama Bin Laden and the Campaign in Somalia[23]

From the beginning of the 1990s, Osama Bin Laden resided in Sudan, and under the patronage of the regime of Hassan al Turabi and Omar al Beshir, built up an economic empire and a terror infrastructure on the basis of which he planned to launch a Jihad against the West. Bin Laden, who was a close associate of Hassan al Turabi, became an active partner in the granting of aid to various Islamic terror organizations who gained al Turabi's support.

Bin Laden and his organization, Al Qaida, were partners to the formulation of the Iranian-Sudanese strategy for the dissemination of the Islamic Revolution in the Horn of Africa (Bin Laden's main partner in the Somali activity was his right-hand man Aiman A-Zawahiri). Admittedly, most of the tasks assigned to Bin Laden were logistic and organizational, but they enabled him to accumulate valuable experience in organizing a structural framework to support the complex system against the United States in East Africa, and to fit in as a significant player in the decision-making processes and their realization in the workings of the Iranian-Sudanese coalition.

The establishment of an effective front for the Islamic terror organizations in the Somali arena necessitated building a logistic and financial operation to provide fighters, weaponry, and funds. As noted, the task of establishing and operating this infrastructure was assigned to Bin Laden, who employed his economic and organizational experience, as well as his worldwide connections to accomplish this, and within a short period succeeded in placing an efficient logistic and financial infrastructure at the disposal of Iran and

Sudan. Bin Laden founded several international companies that dealt in agricultural development in Ethiopia, Somalia's neighbor. In the Ogaden Desert, near the Somali border, these "companies" established farms that served as cover for training facilities for Somali terrorists, storage for combat equipment and the supply of money for funding activities.

Towards the middle of 1993, in the framework of preparations for the escalation of the struggle against the American forces in Somalia, Bin Laden managed a complex campaign involving the transfer of Afghan alumni from Pakistan and Yemen to Somalia. Some of the fighters were transported in a fleet of fishing boats and dropped off at desolate beaches in Somalia, from whence they were taken by local networks to the Mogadishu combat area; others were flown in on light aircraft, which landed during the night at landing areas situated in Somalia; the rest infiltrated Somalia via its borders with Ethiopia and Kenya.[24]

Bin Laden apparently visited Somalia several times but did not take part in the fighting. Nonetheless, his right-hand man and assistant Aiman A-Zawahiri, and Ali al Rashidi (an activist of the Egyptian Islamic Jihad), who was an Afghan alumnus and Aiman A-Zawahiri's closest aide, reportedly were in direct command of the fighting forces in Mogadishu. Bin Laden's main involvement with the Somali campaign was his connection in organizing the attack against U.S. targets in Aden (see subsequent elaboration).

The heavy losses that the United States sustained in the fighting in Somalia and the decision to withdraw its forces from this country by March 1, 1994, was perceived by Islamic entities and the Somalis, as well as by Bin Laden, as proof of their ability to defeat and crush the United States. In an interview with Robert Fisk of the *Independent*, Osama Bin Laden declared:[25]

> We believe that God used our holy war in Afghanistan to destroy the Russian army and the Soviet Union...and now we ask God to use us one more time to do the same to America to make it a shadow of itself.
>
> We also believe that our battle against America is much simpler than the war against the Soviet Union, because some of our mujahidin who fought here in Afghanistan also participated in operations against the Americans in Somalia, and they were surprised at the collapse of American morale. This convinced us that the Americans are a paper tiger.

In another interview that Bin Laden granted to the Al-Jazeera television network, he stated:[26]

Based on the reports we received from our brothers, who participated in the Jihad in Somalia, we learned that they saw weakness, frailty and cowardice of US troops. Only eighteen US troops were killed. Nonetheless, they fled in the heart of darkness, frustrated after they had caused great commotion about a New World Order.

The Campaign in Somalia—Summer 1993

In the beginning of the summer of 1993, Iranian and Sudanese preparations for the campaign in Somalia were completed, and Islamic terror cells started to act against the UN forces in the neighborhoods that were under Aidid's control. The attacks included ambushes and the planting of explosive devices.[27] These activities peaked on June 5, 1993, in an ambush laid by the terrorists for a Pakistani UN force, in which twenty-six Pakistani soldiers perished. Following this brutal attack against the Pakistani force, the UN declared the SNA an illegal organization. Aidid was officially estranged from the contacts for the economic and political restoration of Somalia, and the commander of the UN forces declared a prize of $25,000 for anyone who could bring about the capture of Aidid. The attack, which was attributed to Aidid, boosted his stature among the Somali public, and many tribes as well as powerbrokers joined the SNA coalition under Aidid's leadership. The counter-response of Aidid's radio station to the UN's declaration was to offer a prize of $1 million to anyone who would bring in the commander of the UN forces in Somalia, Admiral Howey, dead or alive. Following the heavy losses suffered by the UN forces, they began to respond with heavy fire against the terrorists, and in the exchange of fire Somali citizens were often hit.

On June 11 1993, Aidid and several of his aides set out for Khartoum in order to coordinate the coming steps with Sudan. The Sudanese propaganda machine blamed the United States and the UN for the deterioration of the situation in Somalia, and alleged that the US aim was to take over the entire Horn of Africa, with Somalia only the first target in the overall American plan. The Sudanese Foreign Minister warned the United States that if it attacked Sudan the former would encounter harsh opposition and the declaration of a Jihad against the United States.

Following Aidid's visit to Khartoum and according to Sudanese instructions, Bin Laden poured weaponry and additional fighters into Mogadishu, with the aim of fortifying the combat ability of the Islamic entities. In June 1993 the Islamic forces in Somalia included the following:[28]

- Aidid's forces under the SNA umbrella (whose headquarters were located in Mogadishu and Galacio);
- The SIUP forces (whose headquarters were in Maraka);
- The forces of the SRG accompanied by Iranian advisers (whose main base was in Bosaso);
- Forces and volunteers from Iraq.

The forces were equipped and prepared to operate a prolonged terror campaign and guerrilla warfare against U.S. and UN forces, according to the policy and instructions issued by Iran and Sudan.

During June 13-15 1993, the United States conducted a series of land and air offensives against Aidid's positions and forces. On June 17, Aidid's house was raided—the house was surrounded and searched but Aidid was not found.[29] In response to these actions, the SNA announced that it would fight until the last UN soldier departed from Somalia, and Aidid's people called on the residents of Mogadishu to go out and fight the Americans and give their lives for the freedom of Somalia. Aidid's troops intensified the attacks against the UN forces in Mogadishu and throughout Somalia, and his followers incited demonstrations and riots of unarmed citizens against the presence of the UN forces in the country. The violent activity of Aidid's troops was accompanied by an intensive war of propaganda in which the UN forces were accused of neo-colonialism under the guise of humanitarian aid, and the American forces were charged with the genocide of the Somali people and the destruction of mosques and holy sites.

In August, Islamic volunteers acting under the organizational name of "The Vanguard of the Islamic Salvation" arrived in Somalia. The organization founded its own radio station, which broadcasted propaganda, including a call to the Somali nation to join a Jihad against America's diabolical forces.[30] Aidid and the Islamic forces continued with their preparations in anticipation of an American offensive against Aidid. On August 11, Aidid's men activated an explosive device by remote control and caused the death of four American soldiers. The attack was perpetrated by a new organization that was established on the basis of fighters from Aidid's extended family—Habar Gadir. The organization was called the SISM (Somali Islamic Salvation Movement).[31]

In September 1993, the Sudanese instructed the SIUP to join in the fighting against the Americans. Although the SIUP was established and prepared for combat even prior to the Americans' arrival in Somalia, it was not active before September 1993, and up to that time only Aidid's forces were involved in the fighting in this arena.[32] Already on September 3 1993, the organization's spokesman announced from Iran that his organization had perpetrated a series of attacks against UN forces in Somalia. The situation in Somalia continued to deteriorate and on September 5, Aidid's men attacked a Nigerian UN force and killed seven of its members. Only massive U.S. intervention enabled the rescue of the Nigerian force.[33]

On September 10 1993, with Sudanese encouragement, a new phase was initiated in the combat against the UN forces. Islamic forces from Aidid's extended family of Habar Gidir began attacking Somali individuals identified as UN supporters throughout Somalia. In consequence, widespread riots and fighting erupted throughout the country. The UN and U.S. forces were summoned to restore order, but soon found themselves trapped in ambushes laid in advance by the Islamic forces.

The fighting spread from the periphery to the capital Mogadishu, and on September 13, heavy fighting broke out between the U.S. troops and Aidid's forces. The Americans sent in Cobra helicopters to fight Aidid's forces and among other sites hit a hospital that also served as Aidid's headquarters and logistical warehouse. Many Somali civilians were hurt in this attack, and Aidid's supporters called for revenge. On September 15, Aidid's troops attacked the UN headquarters in Mogadishu with mortar fire, and in retaliation, U.S. forces bombed Aidid's headquarters. Aidid's supporters, including women and children, stoned UN patrols on the streets of Mogadishu, and UN soldiers opened fire and injured Somali citizens. This incident exacerbated the situation in the city even further and Ali Mahdi Muhammad, Aidid's opponent, took advantage of the window of opportunity and accused Aidid of bringing disaster and destruction on the country.

The United States, which up to that time had carefully refrained from taking a formal stand in the internal Somali conflict, decided to come out publicly against Aidid in September and to attempt to break his strength. At the end of September a task force of Rangers raided Aidid's headquarters and captured his right-hand man, Othman Hassan Ali Ato. Aidid retaliated with ambushes aimed at knocking down U.S. helicopters, and on September 26, his men did indeed succeed in shooting down an American "Blackhawk" helicopter over Mogadishu. An enraged crowd mutilated the bodies of the American pilots and dragged them along the streets of Mogadishu. The incident, which was documented on television, shocked the American public and forced the American forces to respond ruthlessly. The confrontation between Aidid, the Islamic forces, and the U.S. task force culminated in a battle on October 3-4, which constituted the watershed line in the American involvement in Somalia.

The Battle of October 3-4, 1993—The "Snatch and Grab" Mission[34]

The aim of the "Snatch and Grab" mission was to apprehend two of Aidid's senior aide—Osama Salah and Muhammad Hassan Awali. The aim was to apprehend them at the Olympic Hotel in an area called the "Black Sea," General Aidid's stronghold, located near the busy marketplace in Mogadishu, the Somali capital. The mission was based on intelligence information that necessitated rapid organization on the part of U.S. forces in order to execute the mission while its targets were at the said location. The Ranger task force, under the command of General William P. Grison, had drilled similar missions many times and had also acquired combat experience prior to the "Snatch and Grab" campaign. But what had originally appeared to be a simple mission, based on precise intelligence, rapidly evolved into a bitter battle that generated far-reaching consequences.

The American task force blundered into a well-planned ambush laid by hundreds of Somali and Islamic fighters, and during the fighting two Black Hawk helicopters were downed and an additional helicopter was forced to make an emergency landing in the Mogadishu airport. The American force took over its target and apprehended Aidid's aides, but were swiftly surrounded and forced to fight for their lives. An end was finally put to the ensuing bitter combat only after a rescue mission was launched by land forces using attack helicopters. Eighteen American fighters were left dead and seventy-eight wounded. American pilot Michael Diorent was taken captive by the Somalis.

The mission of the U.S. task force had been accomplished despite the delay and the heavy toll in casualties and injuries. General Grison's men did indeed win the battle but it was a "Pyrrhic victory," which led to U.S. defeat in the overall war.

Information gleaned from various sources indicates that forces of Islamic volunteers made up of Afghani alumni participated in the

October 3, 1993 battle, and not only the forces of the warlord Aidid.[35] According to this version, the entire operation was under the command of A-Rashidi (an Egyptian Jihad activist and Afghani alumnus, personal aide to Aiman A-Zawahiri, head of the Jihad organization and Osama Bin Laden's partner).

The main assault force was made up of SIUP fighters and Afghani alumni, who used anti-aircraft 23-mm. artillery and RPG7 launchers to shoot down the helicopters. Aidid's people, who played a secondary role in the fighting, isolated the battle arena and instigated mass riots of unarmed civilians, which made the American rescue mission even more cumbersome. These claims were confirmed in the charge sheet brought against twenty-one Al Qaida members who were accused of assaulting U.S. and UN forces in 1993 and with directing terror conspiracies together with Sudan, Iraq, and Iran.[36]

The consequences of the action were disastrous for the United States. The heavy losses and the traumatic film footage aired on television channels worldwide of masses mutilating the bodies of American soldiers aroused strong opposition in American public opinion and in the Congress to U.S. involvement in Somalia. Following the military fiasco in Mogadishu and due to the combined pressure of public opinion and the Congress, President Clinton decided to discontinue the activities of the U.S. task force in Somalia. As a lesson drawn from the activities of the American forces in Somalia, the Clinton administration established the principle of "involvement without intervention," according to which the United States would refrain from sending soldiers to fight in foreign countries in order to realize goals that do not directly serve American interests. An inquiry committee was set up in the U.S. Senate, which heard testimony about the action in Somalia. At the end of the hearings, the committee published a paper placing the blame for the debacle on the president and Defense Secretary Les Aspin. Aspin submitted his resignation two months later, and General Grison ended his career earlier than planned.[37]

The American experience in Somalia in general and in the October 3 battle in particular, became a warning sign for the United States in all matters related to the sending of troops to resolve conflicts overseas. This was apparently the reason for the lack of UN and U.S. intervention in the civil wars in Zaire and Rwanda. The American policy was revised in connection to Bosnia and Kosovo when there was a fear that the conflict would spread outside of the Balkan.

It also underwent change as a result of the attacks of September 11 2001, which led to the U.S. declaration of war against terror, the offensive in Afghanistan, the resultant collapse of the Taliban regime (Bin Laden's sponsor), and the destruction of the Al Qaida organization's infrastructure in this country.

Somalia Today—For and Against Terror

Somalia after the Withdrawal of UN troops (1995-2002)

Following the withdrawal of the UN forces from Somalia in 1994, the civil war continued and UN efforts to achieve a ceasefire and reconstruct the country's political system were temporarily put on hold.

General Muhammad Farah Aidid died on August 1, 1996, at the age of sixty and there are various versions regarding the circumstances surrounding his death; according to "South Mogadishu Radio" he died of a heart attack; other sources claim that he was injured on July 24, 1996 in fighting against a rival faction, and subsequently died due to infection.

Aidid had fourteen children, most of whom grew up in the United States and live there to date. Muhamad Farah Aidid's heir was his son Hussein Aidid who also was raised and studied in the United States, served in the Marines, and even arrived in Somalia with the Marines forces in 1992. After completing his military service Hussein Aidid remained in the United States several more years and returned to Somalia in 1995. After his father's death he became the leader of the factions that had supported his father and continued (to this very day) in the rigid policy of struggle to gain control of Somalia.

Beginning 1995 various political entities renewed their attempts to intermediate in the matter in an effort to stop the war in Somalia. Among those intermediaries are:

- Neighboring countries—Kenya, Ethiopia, Djibouti;
- International organizations—Islamic organizations, African Unity Organization and more;
- European and Islamic countries;
- Various UN committees.

Over the years several conferences were held, leading to the establishment of two central political and tribal blocs:

1. Transitional National Government—TRG, which controls most neighborhoods in Mogadishu and several districts in the state;
2. Somali Reconciliation and Restoration Council—SRRC, an umbrella organization of some 120 militias structured on a tribal basis and headed by Hussein Aidid, whose only common interest is to oust the Transitional National Government (see subsequent elaboration on this matter).

The declaration regarding the establishment of the TRG in August 2000 came after two months of discussions conducted in the framework of the Somali National Peace Conference held in the city of Arta in neighboring Djibouti. Previous attempts to achieve national agreement had failed and had put in question the ability to achieve national reconciliation in this country. The conference in Arta instilled cautious hope regarding the chances to implement its resolutions.

The transitional government was the result of a sensitive agreement regarding the manner of distributing power in the country; each tribe was assigned representation in the Parliament, which contains 245 seats, in addition to several key roles in the national transition government. Ali Caliph Galiar was appointed prime minister, and Abed al-Kassem Salad Hassan was appointed president. Hassan is the son of the leader of the extended Habar Gidir family, one of the most important families in Somalia. He served as a minister in Barre's cabinet and when Barre's government was ousted in 1991, he fled to Egypt. Several years later, Hassan returned to Somalia and began to boost his political power with the ultimate goal of restoring Somali national unity and putting an end to the civil war. The establishment of a temporary government headed by Hassan received an enthusiastic welcome in large sections of Somalia. The residents of Mogadishu were the government's most prominent supporters because its foundation assured the return of public order and the provision of services and work places.

The leadership of the transition government dealt extensively in the restoration of Somalia's diplomatic status, and accomplished several significant achievements when it reinstated Somalia's representation at the UN, the Arab League and the Organization for African Unity. These accomplishments notwithstanding, few countries in the world recognized the transitional government in Somalia, while the United States and most Arab states decided to adopt a policy of "wait and see" prior to recognizing the government. The transitional government appealed to various countries worldwide to introduce a "Marshall Plan" for the restoration of Somalia, but the response was minor (the funds allocated as aid for Somalia are estimated at only $20 million, most of which came from Saudi Arabia). Other countries and organizations stipulated that the provision of funds would be contingent upon proof that the interim government was indeed in control of the country.

The unwillingness of the Arab world and the West to come to the aid of the transitional government caused considerable frustration among its members and increasing difficulties due to the lack of economic resources to enforce its authority over the country. In September 2001, the transitional government was immersed in a serious governmental crisis. It did not succeed in establishing an efficient administrative system even in Mogadishu, and half of the city was under the control of opposition factors. Moreover, the government did not succeed in reopening Mogadishu's airport or seaport, and the enforcement systems vis-à-vis law and order functioned on a very limited basis.

The transitional government gradually lost the support and legitimacy that it had enjoyed in the beginning, and opposition entities—including the rulers of the northern districts (Somaliland and Pontland), the SRRC organization and some of the heads of the stronger militias—posed an acute challenge vis-à-vis its very existence and control. Hyper-inflation, resulting from financial manipulations and accusations regarding corruption and the theft of donation funds, also contributed to the weakening of the transitional government.

Aside from the internal problems in Somalia, the transitional government also needed to contend with an external adversary—Ethiopia—which had originally supported the establishment of a temporary government but quickly revised its policy and regarded it as a threat due to its close relationships with Arab and Muslim states. Ethiopia suffered from the activities of a radical Islamic movement within its own boundaries, and due to the long border that it shared with Somalia was sensitive to any internal shift in Somalia that might turn that country into a base for radical Islamic activity against it. Ethiopia claimed hegemony in the region of the Horn of Africa and regarded itself as party to a drawn-out competition vis-à-vis Egypt and Arab states in relationship to its status and influence in the region.

The transitional government in Somalia made no effort to improve its ties with Ethiopia and alleviate its fears. On the contrary, it invested serious efforts in reinforcing its ties with the Arab world, thus increasing the tension with its neighbor. In consequence, several months after its establishment the Somali transitional government was forced to contend with opposition groups that enjoyed Ethiopian support. The tension between the sides developed into the form of "a war of emissaries," with the opposition forces supported by Ethiopia acting against the Somali government, which had the support of the Arab countries. In the meantime, autonomous regions cropped up in Somalia that declared their independence and enjoyed the aid of the SRRC and countries such as Ethiopia and Kenya.

Despite the perpetuation of the political and tribal adversity, during the years the fighting died down (although it never stopped completely) and a status quo of parallel governments by rival factions prevailed in different areas.

However, the terror infrastructures established during the 1990s by Iran, Sudan, and Bin Laden continued to exist in the country without disruption, under the patronage of local allies, but the focuses of activity and the issue of Islamic terror gradually shifted to new destinations. U.S. and Saudi pressure finally induced neighboring Sudan to expel Bin Laden from its territory, to "lower its profile" and to some extent reduce its support of terror; nevertheless, East Africa remained an important focal point for Islamic terror, and several prominent attacks were executed there:

- The assassination attempt against Egyptian President Hussni Mubarak in Addis Ababa, Ethiopia (1995);
- Attacks against the U.S. Embassies in Kenya and Tanzania (1998);
- The attack at the Paradise Hotel in Mombassa, Kenya (2002).

Nonetheless, quite surprisingly the terrorists did not avail themselves of the Islamic terror infrastructure in Somalia, but acted on the basis of terror networks prepared in advance in the target countries. After the September 11 attacks and the war that the United States declared against terror, Somalia's name resurfaced as a possible target for an American offensive against Islamic terror points. Towards the end of the campaign against the Taliban and Al Qaida in Afghanistan, the United States suspected that Bin Laden and his people might try to flee to Somalia and reconstruct the organization's infrastructure from there.[38] Thus, in October 2001, the United States and its allies began air and sea patrols opposite the Somali shores in order to locate Al Qaida activity in this arena. The United States noted two entities in Somalia that it believed were involved in Bin Laden's terror activity: One was the al-Itihad al-Islamiya, which the U.S. included in its list of terror organizations; and another—an economic concern called "al-Barkat," that deals in a wide range of economic activities such as banking, international commercial companies, cellular companies, and more. The United States suspects that this organization has commercial ties with Bin Laden's businesses and serves for the transfer and "laundering" of funds for him.[39]

Opposition factors in Somalia opposed to the TNG point out the links and ties between the government and the al-Itihad and Al Qaida organizations, and call upon the United States to topple the government and expel the Islamic terrorists from Somalia.[40] The president of the transitional government of Somalia, Abed al Kassem Salad Hassan, denies any presence of Islamic terror entities in his country as well as any ties with them, and charges the opposition with casting false accusations against his government.[41] In the meantime, it is not clear whether the accusations against the Somali government are based on actual fact or if opposition entities are simply trying to enlist the United States to their side in an internal-Somali conflict.

In any case, the United States is operating intelligence surveillance vis-à-vis the Islamic activity in Somalia and maintains connections with Somali powerbrokers—including Hussein Aidid, head of the SRRC, who has declared his desire to mend fences with the United States and with members of the RRA (see subsequent elaboration)—in the event that it might need to act against Islamic terror entities in Somalia.[42] At the same time, meetings have been held between U.S. political and military entities and the heads of neighboring states—Ethiopia, Kenya, and Djibouti—in the event that an U.S. offensive becomes necessary in the Somali arena.[43] If the United States decides to act in Somalia, al-Itihad al-Islamiya and the Al Qaida infrastructures will be the main targets for any operation, and it is reasonable to surmise that the SRRC, and particularly the RRA, will facilitate the U.S. steps.

Al-Itihad al-Islamiya (The Islamic Union)

One of the Somali movements that cooperated with Bin Laden and Al Qaida was al-Itihad al-Islamiya (the Islamic Union). This group first emerged in the late 1980s in Mogadishu, and most of its members were young academics who had studied in Middle Eastern schools. They believed that the only way to liberate Somalia from the corruption, oppression, and tribalism that characterized Ziad Barre's regime was to adopt political Islam. In this, al-Itihad was similar to many Islamic movements in the Middle East and the Muslim world.

After the collapse of the governmental system in Somalia, in 1991, this movement made an attempt to take over strategic assets such as seaports. It was not able to hold on to the northern port of Bosaso, but it maintained temporary control of the Kismayu and Marka ports as well as the economically vital intersection near Luuq in south Somalia, near the Ethiopian border. At the same time, the movement established cells in various locations in Somalia, which attempted to expand the movement's influence. Al-Itihad controlled Luuq during the years 1991-1996 and imposed the Sharia (Islamic rule). Ironically, the security situation in Luuq was better than other places in Somalia, so the international relief organizations preferred the regime of the al-Itihad to the control of the other powerbrokers in Somalia.

In 1996, the Ethiopian arm of the al-Itihad movement was involved in several terrorist attacks in that country, including the planting of two bombs in hotels and an assassination attempt, in the framework of a campaign to impose the Sharia on the Somali population in Ethiopia. These activities were the reason why the al-Itihad movement was included in the U.S. State Department's list of terror organizations, and spurred the Ethiopian government to take firm action to thwart the activities of this movement in Ethiopia. In this framework, Ethiopia launched military action against the movement's strongholds in the area of Luuq, in consequence of which al-Itihad was forced to withdraw from this vicinity.

From the year 1996 onwards, al-Itihad adopted a new strategy:

- The movement decided not to hold on to territories on a permanent basis, as this turned them into an easy target for Ethiopia and other enemies.
- The movement decided to assimilate and act within various Somali communities, a fact that made it difficult for its adversaries to thwart its activities. Based on the understanding that the Somali tribalism found it hard to accept an integrative Islamic perception, the movement decided to act on a tribal basis and leave the goal of a united

Somalia under the wings of an Islamic regime for the subsequent stages. The movement achieved varying levels of influence in different tribes, but no tribe agreed to subjugate its leadership to the movement's policies.

- The movement became decentralized, much like the social structure of Somalia, causing the movement to take on a different character in the various areas of Somalia. In some areas the organization cooperates with Western relief organizations and refrains from maintaining ties with radical Islamic organizations, while in other locations the movement acts independently, and in still other areas it is involved in violent activity against Somali adversaries and Westerners.

- Al-Itihad has decided to attain its long-term goals—the establishment of the Islamic regime in Somalia— through "*dawa*" activities (education, indoctrination), and it pursues the development of long-term political and social infrastructures by investing in education, in the development of a local judicial system based on Islamic law, in communications and information. The organization operates relief and charitable organizations and deals in the development of the movement's economic infrastructure and in the recruitment and infiltration of its members into influential focal points in Somali society.

There is some controversy regarding the movement's power— there are those who believe that the organization is powerless and insignificant, while others argue that it is gathering strength and is becoming a major source of power in the Somali arena. Following the September 11 attacks, suspicions were raised regarding cooperation between al-Itihad and Al Qaida. According to the United States, al-Itihad enabled Al Qaida to use its bases and other infrastructures prior to Al Qaida's terror attacks in 1998 against the U.S. Embassy in Nairobi (Kenya) and in Dar al-Salaam (Tanzania). The Al Qaida liaison vis-à-vis the al-Itihad organization was Osama Bin Laden's aide Muhammad Attaf, who was killed in the U.S. offensive in Afghanistan.[44]

The al-Itihad Organization apparently continues to operate several training camps for Islamic terrorists, including the Ras Kamboni Camp located near the Kenyan border. According to U.S. sources, this camp served as a base for Al Qaida terror activity in Africa (mainly in nearby Kenya). The Americans claim that the al-Itihad organization is also linked with the "al-Barkat" company, which allegedly served Al Qaida for money laundering services.[45] In view of the links between al-Itihad and Al Qaida, it was feared that al-Itihad might offer Al Qaida members fleeing Afghanistan a safe haven in Somalia, and that the latter would serve as the organization's main base to replace the lost one in Afghanistan.

Al-Itihad has a strong infrastructure in Mogadishu, and it operated a legal system based on the Sharia in that city before the temporary government was founded. The movement supported the Arta process and the establishment of the temporary government, and in exchange demanded government portfolios, particularly the Ministry of Justice (due to its critical importance to the application of the Sharia as the state law), but this request was turned down and instead it had to be satisfied with several seats in the Parliament. This support served as the basis for charges that the temporary government was merely a Trojan Horse planted by al-Itihad, as Al Qaida's tool. From this point of view, the temporary government in Somalia is perceived as similar to the Taliban government in Afghanistan, which championed the Al Qaida organization.

Ethiopia and its allies in Somalia (that portray themselves as parallel entities to the "Northern Alliance" in Afghanistan) aspire to present this theory to the United States in order to elicit its aid in banishing the temporary government from Somalia. The temporary government adamantly repudiates these charges and argues that Al Qaida has no bases or influence in areas under its control. It even issued an invitation to the United States to investigate the matter,[46] and announced that it was arresting individuals suspected of being involved in terror activity—all with the aim of preventing U.S. action against Somalia. Somalia's Foreign Minister Zakaria Mahmoud Abdi claimed that[47] "The TNG... is the light for the Somali people at the end of the tunnel. Ethiopia wants to destroy that small candle, claiming that the government has links with terrorism."

Although it is difficult to refute these fears, it is possible to point out several "reassuring signs" in this regard:

- Somalis were not directly involved in Al Qaida terror campaigns and attacks.
- No Somalis were found among the higher echelons of Al Qaida.
- Somalia would be a problematic haven for Al Qaida activists, as rival factions would be willing to turn in Al Qaida activists in exchange for money and bribes. Moreover, it would be difficult to conceal the presence of Al Qaida members due to the country's social and political reality. Therefore, it is highly doubtful whether Al Qaida members will try to turn Somalia into a substitute for Afghanistan.

It appears that the temporary government in Somalia is not a Trojan Horse, and if it could it would expel the al-Itihad members from its ranks. However, it is currently weak and cannot risk a face-to-face collision with that organization's members at a time when it is facing numerous threats from its various other adversaries. In any case, it is currently impossible to describe the TNG as a government that explicitly supports radical Islamic positions.[48]

Islamic Charitable Organizations in Somalia

Islamic charities in Somalia do not maintain ties with Western and other philanthropic organizations, and do not adopt the behavioral norms and transparency customary in organizations of this sort. The "closed" policy of these Islamic organizations enables them to cooperate closely with radical Islamic organizations that exploit these charities to promote their goals in the country. It is also possible that some of the Islamic charities actually constitute "front organizations" for al-Itihad as well as other radical Islamic organizations.

An example of the involvement of a Somali charitable organization in terror can be found in the Al-Haramain organization. Al-Haramain is a Saudi, privately owned organization, whose aim is to disseminate Islamic studies worldwide. Funding for the organization's activities came from donations of Muslim countries, prosperous Muslim donors, and from fundraising campaigns that the organization initiated worldwide. The organization established an infrastructure of offices worldwide, including one in Somalia.

The office in Somalia had strong contacts with Al Qaida and with the al-Itihad al-Islamiya organization. At its offices, Al-Haramain employed al-Itihad al-Islamiya activists and paid them salaries through Bank Al Barakaat, which was also connected to Al Qaida's financial infrastructure.

Over the years, a substantial amount of money was channeled through Al-Haramain, which was originally raised for the foundation of mosques and orphanages for the al-Itihad al-Islamiya organization. Following the September 11 attacks, the Al-Haramain organization and Bank Al Barakaat were declared organizations that supported terror in the United States. Their activities were banned and their assets in the United States frozen.

The Somali Reconciliation and Restoration Council (SRRC)

The SRRC is an umbrella organization that incorporates the entities opposed to the national transitional government in Somalia. The organization was established in 2001 with the aid and support of

Ethiopia, which regards the transitional government as a threat to Ethiopian interests. The SRRC is headed by Hussein Aidid (son of Muhammad Farah Aidid), one of the leaders of the USC and the extended Habar Gidir clan. Additional powerbrokers in the SRRC are: the RRA, the factions led by Othman Hassan Ali Ito (who was the ally and right-hand man of the senior Aidid), leaders of the autonomous northern region, and others.

The SRRC is conducting a political propaganda blitz in an attempt to persuade the UN and international countries to recognize the SRRC as a legitimate governmental factor in Somalia, and at the same time is waging a violent campaign against the TNG forces. In its attempt to win over Western support, the SRRC emphasizes its aspiration to establish a Western-style democratic state in Somalia and insists that radical Islam is the main common enemy of the West and Somalia.

The Rahanwian Resistance Army (RRA)

On September 17, 1995, militias of General Muhammad Farah Aidid invaded Baidoa, most of whose inhabitants are members of the Rahanwein tribe, and established a tyrannical regime based on terror. On August 1, 1996, upon the demise of Muhammad Aidid, his son Hussein took the reins of power and continued his father's policy, inflicting punitive actions and massacres in order to sustain his control in that region. Despite the efforts to establish a reconciliatory government in Somalia, Hussein Aidid remained in the opposition and continued to control certain areas including the Riverine region and Baidoa in its center.

The Rahanwein Resistance Army (RRA) was founded in October 1995, in order to combat the invasion and liberate the region of Aidid's men. For some four years the RRA underground waged its battle until finally on June 7, 1999, it succeeded in defeating Aidid's men and liberating Baidoa. In the following months, the RRA succeeded in liberating most of the Riverine region, and on December 9, declared the establishment of an autonomous government in the area. On May 18, 2000, convoys carrying food and UN humanitarian aid (via the World Food Program) succeeded in reaching Baidoa and provided assistance to the population, which was in severe distress. During the year 2000, once security and stability had been restored in the region, economic rehabilitation began with the assistance of the UN and humanitarian aid organizations such as Care International.

The RRA is headed by Colonel Hassan Muhammad Nur Shargodod, who advocates the idea of establishing autonomous governments in various regions of Somalia, which will eventually be incorporated into an integrated federal administration. Shargodod opposes attempts to establish a central government that will control all of Somalia, and refrained from attending talks held in Djibouti with the aim of introducing a peace agreement in Somalia, claiming that this was a conspiracy designed to promote foreign interests.

RRA leaders expressed their support for the American decision to dispatch forces to Somalia in order to arrest or eliminate Al Qaida members active in this state.[49] One of the more senior RRA members claimed that Somalia is a paradise for terrorists, due to the lack of an effective central government, and noted that Afghanistan and Somalia are very similar. Thus, he stated, only the United States can help to banish the terrorists from this country.[50]

According to the Governor of Baidoa, Aduwan Muhammad, his organization aspires to liberate all of Somalia, and talks have been ongoing between his organization and U.S. entities regarding the possibility of aiding the RRA in the event of a U.S. decision to act in Somalia.

The Relationship between Somalia and Ethiopia

Somalia shares a long and problematic border with Ethiopia in the Ogaden Desert. Territorial and ethnic controversies, which have yet to be resolved, led to the eruption of the "Ogaden War" in the 1970s, which claimed many victims in both countries and created pressing refugee problems in Somalia.

The loss of a central government in Somalia, which occurred in the early 1990s, had a crucial impact on the relationship between Somalia and Ethiopia, which became particularly complex and problematic. Ethiopia fears the spreading of radical Islam from Somalia into its own territory, and therefore takes resolute action against these entities inside and outside of Ethiopia. In the framework of the internal Somali conflict, Ethiopia supports the powerbrokers who are willing to serve Ethiopian interests. This support is reflected in the provision of economic and military support, and when necessary also in the form of direct military intervention in Somali events.

In the long-term view, Ethiopia is interested in the establishment of a stable government in Somalia that will maintain good neighborly relations and prevent the penetration of subversive Islamic influences into its territory. Therefore, it supports the various intermediary processes aimed at restoring government and stability to Somalia. However, as long as the reality in Somalia does not change, Ethiopia acts concurrently against internal Somali powerbrokers in order to ensure its interests in this arena, thereby contributing to the continued internal power struggles and instability. The relationship between the two countries has experienced ups and downs during recent years. On June 9, 2001, the provisional government in Somalia accused Ethiopia of invading its territory. Diplomatic dialogue was launched between the two countries in order to defuse the tension, but it ended without any positive results, and the temporary government in Somalia continued to accuse Ethiopia of meddling in its internal affairs.

In November 2001, the relations between the two governments deteriorated further. On November 15, Ethiopia shut down the offices of the largest commercial Somali company—Al-Barkat. This step was initiated after the United States had frozen this company's assets due to the suspicion that it was linked with Al Qaida. The company's management and the Somali government adamantly denied any connection with Al Qaida, and were even willing to expose the company's documents and accounts to an external auditor in order to prove the justice of their claims, but to no avail. Moreover, the Somali government claimed that during November 2001 Ethiopian forces invaded Galkayo in northeast Somalia. This area, which had declared itself autonomous and does not accept the authority of the temporary government, is under the control of Colonel Abdallah Yusuf Ahmad, who declared the entire Galkayo region an autonomy. The Somali government claims that the invasion of the Ethiopian forces was in response to a request made by Abdallah Yusuf Ahmad, with the aim of reinforcing his forces in the internal Somali conflict. The Ethiopian government refuted the Somali claims regarding any request to dispatch its forces and denied their presence in Somalia.[51]

On May 20, 2002, the Somali government lodged a complaint with the Security Council, in which it accused Ethiopia of invading its territory and supplying combat means to various powerbrokers in the country. In response, the Ethiopian Ambassador to the UN accused the Somali government of trying to impede the discussions to achieve a peaceful agreement between the rival factions in Somalia, and denied any military involvement of his country in the internal Somali conflict. He reiterated that his country has a vested interest in a stable Somalia ("It is in our interest to have a stable Somalia.")

Notes

1. James Cameron, *The African Revolution*, London: Thames and Hudson, 1981, pp. 176–80.
2. Ibid.
3. Ibid.
4. *CIA Fact Book*, Somalia, 2000.
5. Ibid.
6. Robert F. Goreman, "The Anatomy of Somali Civil War and Famine," *Washington Report on Middle East Affairs*, March 1993, pp. 9-18.
7. Ibid.
8. *CIA Fact Book*, Somalia, 2000.
9. AbcNews.com, "Somalia's Hopes," October 26, 2001.
10. *CIA Fact Book*, Somalia, 2000.
11. Ibid.
12. "The Civil War in Somalia," in *CIA Fact Book*, Somalia, 2000.
13. Ibid.
14. NomadNet.com, "Mission in Somalia," December 5, 1993.
15. Ibid.
16. Robert F. Gorman, "The Anatomy of the Somali Civil War and Famine," pp. 9-18.
17. NomadNet.com, "Mission in Somalia," December 5, 1993.
18. Ibid.
19. This chapter is based on Yosef Bodansky's *Bin Laden—The Man Who Declared War on America*," New York: Forum, 2001.
20. Ibid.
21. Ibid.
22. Ibid.
23. Ibid.
24. Peter L. Bergen, *Holy War Inc.—Inside the Secret World of Osama Bin Laden*, London: Weidenfield & Nicolson, 2001.
25. *Independent*, March 1, 1994.
26. Interview with Al-Jazeera television network, June 10 1999.
27. Yosef Bodansky, *Bin Laden—The Man Who Declared War on America*, pp. 62-64.
28. Ibid., pp. 65-70.
29. Mark Bowden, *Black Hawk Down, A Story of Modern War*, New York: Atlantic Monthly Press, 1999, p. 89.
30. Yosef Bodansky, *Bin Laden—The Man Who Declared War on America*, p. 69.
31. Ibid., pp. 69-70.
32. Ibid., pp. 69-70.
33. Keith B. Richburg, "UN Officials Misjudged Size of Aidid Militia Armaments," *Washington Post*, October 8, 1993.
34. This section is based on the book, Mark Bowden, *Black Hawk Down, A Story of Modern War*.
35. The source for this information is the book by Yosef Bodansky, *Bin Laden—The Man Who Declared War on America*.

36.   Martha Crenshaw, "Why America? The Globalization of the Civil War," *State and Society*, 2, Issue 2, August 2002.

37.   Patrick J. Sloyan, "Somalia Mission: Clinton Called the Shots in Failed Policy Targeting Aidid," *Newsday, Inc.* December 5, 1993.

38.   Charles Cobb, Jr., "Hints of Military Action Cause Puzzlement and Worry," allAfrica.com, December 23, 2001.

39.   Jeff Koinange, "US Seeks Allies against Terror in Somalia," CNN.com.world, January 13, 2002.

40.   Ibid.

41.   BBCnews.com, Decmber 21, 2001.

42.   Jeff Koinange, "US Seeks Allies against Terror in Somalia."

43.   An interview with Hussein Aidid—allAfrica.com, February 1, 2002.

44.   Charles Cobb, Jr. "Hints of Military Action Cause Puzzlement and Worry."

45.   *Dawn*, November 26, 2001.

46.   An interview with Hussein Aidid—allAfrica.com, February 1, 2002.

47.   CNN.co.world, "East Africa Leaders Meet on Terror," January 10, 2002

48.   Ken Menkhaus, "Somalia: In the Crosshairs of the War on Terrorism," *Current History*, May 2002, pp. 210-218.

49.   BBCnews.com, "Somalia's Role in Terror," December 21, 2001.

50.   Jeff Koinage, "US Seeks Allies Against Terror in Somalia."

51.   ArabicNews.com, November 24, 2001.

Part III

Yemen and Islamic Terror

5

Yemen—Historical Background

Yemen's geographical location along the coast of the Red Sea and its proximity to the Indian Ocean, as well as its control of the Bab el-Mandeb Straits, grants this desert-like country geo-strategic importance.

In the seventh century, most of the Yemenite population converted to Islam, and Yemen became part of the Muslim caliphate that grew in the Arabian Peninsula. In the ninth century, the Zaidite Dynasty took over Yemen, and its descendents continued to govern Yemen until 1962, when the last ruler from this dynasty was deposed in a military coup d'état. Ninety-five percent of Yemen's population is Arab, the majority of which is Sunni (55 percent). However, a large Shiite minority constitutes some 42 percent of the general population, which totals about 17.5 million people.

From the sixteenth century up to the twentieth century most of Yemen's territories were part of the Ottoman Empire, but already in 1839 the British were occupying Aden, and consequently, after the opening of the Suez Canal, Aden became a port of economic and strategic importance to the British Empire. Following the collapse of the Ottoman Empire (1918) Britain and the League of Nations granted independence to Yemen's northern area, while South Yemen and particularly the region of the Aden port remained under British control (the Aden Protectorate). Upon the death of North Yemen leader Imam Ahmad in 1962, his successor was ousted in a military coup d'état initiated by Colonel Abdallah Salal and North Yemen became a republic. The uprising caused the outbreak of a civil war between the republicans and the monarchists, which lasted until 1970.

In 1963, in the framework of its preparations to grant South Yemen independence, Britain united the relatively developed colony of Aden with other districts of the South Saudi Arabian Federation. National-

ist circles in Aden were opposed to the British action, and in light of
the dissension and terror, Britain established of an emergency government in South Yemen. In June 1965, Britain declared the main
opposition organization—the NLF (National Liberation Front)—illegal and responded to the escalating violence by freezing the constitution in September 1965.

In February 1966, Britain announced that it would withdraw from
South Yemen in 1968. Against this background of the anticipated
British withdrawal, terror increased and the confrontations between
various local powerbrokers escalated. The NLF refused to cooperate with the British in an orderly transfer of the government; thus,
upon the withdrawal of the British forces, the loose Federation created by the British collapsed, and the NLF took over most of South
Yemen, with the exception of Aden, which remained under British
control. In 1967, an agreement was finally signed between the British and the NLF that enabled the completion of the British withdrawal, and on November 30, 1967, South Yemen was granted its
independence. The new country was called the Popular Republic of
South Yemen, and in 1969 its name was changed to the Democratic
Popular Republic of Yemen.

The War in North Yemen 1962-1970[1]

On September 26, 1962, with the cooperation of republican
Yemenite leaders based in Aden, a military junta instigated a coup
d'état against the regime of the Imam al Bader, who had inherited
his position from his father Ahmed only eight days earlier. Several
days after the coup the monarchist camp geared up its organization,
with Prince al-Hassan, who had rushed back from the United States,
at its head. However, in contrast to rumors, in mid-October it became clear that Imam al Bader had not perished in the bombing of
his palace. The two reached a general agreement according to which
al Bader would serve as the Imam and al Hassan would be prime
minister. They succeeded in gathering tribes loyal to the monarchy
around them, and with external aid—mainly Saudi and Jordanian—
threatened the existence of the fledgling republic.

Egypt's Incursion into Yemen

In the beginning of October, it became clear to the republicans
that they would not be able to withstand the monarchists on their

own and they appealed to Egypt for assistance. Already on October 7, Egypt announced its willingness to comply and dispatch Egyptian forces to Yemen. Egypt's response to the Yemenite appeal stemmed from a combination of several factors:

- From the political and economic aspect Egypt regarded this as a golden opportunity to obtain a foothold and base of influence in the southern part of the Arabian Peninsula, in close proximity to the wealthy oil-countries.
- Egypt maintained traditional ties with some of the revolutionary leaders.
- The Egyptian regime felt an ideological "obligation" to promote a "progressive" revolution in an Arab country (similarly, at the end of 1963, when they were already deeply sunk in the "Yemenite bog," the Egyptians dispatched army units to aid the "progressive" Algeria, in its battle against "reactionary" Morocco.

When it intervened in Yemen, Egypt failed to consider the country's topographical character as well as the tribal and ethnic structure of the population. Therefore, it made the erroneous assessment that several elite regiments could rapidly wipe out the monarchist pockets of resistance. Within a short period of time it became clear to the Egyptians that they had become mired down in severe military and political problems that necessitated an ever-increasing allocation of means and personnel.

Military Entanglement

The military campaign in Yemen can be divided into two main stages. In the first stage, until March 1963, the Egyptian army was engaged in campaigns aimed at occupying and holding as much area as possible. These campaigns were based on the concept that it was possible to achieve control only in areas where there was the physical presence of military forces. Another consideration was that by occupying the border areas between Yemen and Saudi Arabia, Egypt would be able to block the monarchists' supply routes. This stage ended with the failure of a large-scale offensive in the area of Ahl-Juf, which, although initially successful, subsequently collapsed. From this point on there developed a standoff: The Egyptians and the republicans controlled Southern Yemen, while the Egyptian army controlled only the small towns and isolated strongholds in the north; all the rest was continuous monarchist territory.

The Egyptians' basic strategy was to spread their forces in small concentrated groups over a huge area. This network of isolated strongholds, each in the hands of a small force and linked by long supply routes, enabled the monarchist fighters to take full advantage of the mountainous and transverse terrain. The monarchists adopted a tactic of attacking these isolated strongholds and cutting off their supply routes. When Egyptian reinforcements were dispatched, which proved too strong to succumb to an ambush, the monarchist forces would then withdraw to their mountainous strongholds. Due to these monarchists' guerrilla tactics, the Egyptians could not tap their army's power and technical strength, and translate it into an advantage in the battlefield.

The monarchists' guerrilla combat created a standstill that necessitated a constant influx of Egyptian forces, the numbers of which grew incessantly and in 1963 came to over 30,000 soldiers (according to British sources their numbers reached 50,000). The hopes of the Egyptian leadership to release part of this force by training the regular Yemenite army were also dashed, and the dispatch of three regular Yemenite army divisions to Egypt with the aim of completing their training failed to create a military power capable of accepting the task of defending the Yemenite Republic.

The Egyptian-Saudi Arabian Confrontation

The Egyptian intervention in Yemen initially aroused considerable fears in Saudi Arabia and in other conservative Arab countries, as well as among Western countries with interests in the region. The situation subsequently reversed itself, however, when it became clear to Egypt that it was militarily and politically "sunk in the mire." Egypt itself became interested in pulling most of its forces out of Yemen as quickly as possible. Nevertheless, despite the shifting trends, the basic conflicts of interests continued to prevail, and Egypt still viewed Saudi Arabia and Britain as her main adversaries.

While Egypt encountered ever increasing difficulties—that stemmed from the occupation of its forces in Yemen as well as the related expenses, and the severe domestic criticism leveled against the unsuccessful escapade—Saudi Arabia offered the monarchists aid at a relatively cheap price, and its leaders were able to claim a better bargaining position. In addition to their greater economic means, the Saudi rulers also enjoyed the advantage—in contrast to

King Hussein of Jordan, for example—of not having to deal with hostile public opinion at home, as the monarchy was fully aware of the anticipated threat to which they themselves were exposed as a result of the Egyptian influence in Yemen. Attempts to intermediate, as well as Egyptian pressure on Saudi Arabia during 1963 did not yield results. Even the pressure imposed on the Saudis at the first Arab Summit in Cairo in January 1964 did not induce them to change their positions, and at the end of the Summit close to 40,000 Egyptian soldiers were still stationed in Yemen.

The War in Yemen 1964-1967

The monarchists' accumulated successes in guerrilla warfare heightened their self-confidence, and in April 1964 they tested their mettle in a frontal attack against the town of Haja in central Yemen. Up to that time the monarchists had limited themselves to guerrilla warfare and had refrained from undertaking wide-scale offensives against the republican and Egyptian forces. In the attack on Haja, the Egyptians had all the advantages; they were deployed in fortified defense strongholds and they effectively operated their new and heavier weapons, while the monarchists used out-of-date methods of attack and old equipment. The resounding defeat that the monarchist units sustained partially paralyzed their activity in this sector and in other sectors as well, and the Egyptians took advantage of the fact to expand upon their achievements and the area under republican control through a combination of bombings, bribery, and persuasion vis-à-vis tribal leaders and the population, in order to acquire their cooperation.

This period of relative calm for Egypt came to an end in the months of June-July, with the renewed military activities of the monarchist elements. Renewal of the monarchists' guerrilla warfare, combined with an inflexible Saudi policy, forced the Egyptians to make another effort to find a resolution that would enable them to withdraw their forces from Yemen. Thus, prior to the second Arab Summit that was scheduled to convene in September in Alexandria, the Egyptians aspired to obtain a military breakthrough in Yemen that would have political significance.

In August 1964, the Egyptians (who in this offensive relied mainly on regular Yemenite and tribal forces) launched a broad attack in Northwest Yemen. Its objective was to close off the Yemenite-Saudi border, cut off the monarchists' supply routes, and if possible, to apprehend the Imam el-Bader. As had occurred several times in the past in Egyptian attacks in Yemen, they experienced initial successes, but these were arrested subsequently. The initial success brought Marshal Amar to Yemen; he arrived to personally supervise the campaign, apparently in order to ensure that this time the vital achievement they anticipated would indeed be obtained. The "pep talks" that he delivered to the soldiers were full of optimism, but the campaign, which was launched with "a bang," ended with scarcely "a whimper," and bore witness to the Egyptians-republicans' dismal failure. Moreover, the revolution's collapse and the monarchists' renewed occupation of the northwestern part of Yemen, alongside the Saudi Arabian border, caused even greater damage to Egypt's prestige and facilitated the crumbling of the republican camp.

The success of the monarchists triggered Egypt, according to both breakaway monarchists and republicans, to use poison gas again in order to extricate itself from a bad situation, as had happened a year earlier in Yemen. As the result of the deterioration in the military and political situation, Marshal Amar arrived in Yemen in January 1965 for yet another visit.

This fresh failure to achieve a military resolution in Yemen once again made clear to Egypt that in order to end the Yemenite escapade they must reach some sort of an arrangement with Feisal, the Saudi leader. The deterioration of the economic situation in Egypt and the growing criticism against the regime in various circles (in July 1964 there were persistent rumors regarding a thwarted attempt to assassinate Abd al-Nasser), intensified Egypt's desire to extricate the Egyptian army from Yemen. The pressure that the Egyptians placed on Feisal grew and climaxed at the second Arab Summit in September 1964, one month after King Hussein of Jordan was forced to pay the price for his improved relations with Egypt and recognize the republican regime in Yemen.

In the meantime, the Saudi ruler Feisal was having trouble resisting the constant pressure. The argument that Egypt was unable to meet its full commitments vis-à-vis "Palestine" due to the fact that its forces were bogged down in Yemen placed Saudi Arabia in an untenable situation vis-à-vis Arab public opinion. Abd al Nasser took advantage of the atmosphere at the summit—which to a large extent was fostered by him due to his entanglement in Yemen—in order to try and resolve this fiasco. It was clear to Feisal that a resolution for the Yemenite problem must be found, and there was no reason not to agree to a solution if it met his threshold requirements. Therefore, in the following months several attempts were made to resolve the differences of opinion; nonetheless, the parties were ultimately unable to reach an agreement.

The question of the evacuation of Egyptian forces was important to both Yemenite camps, but to Egypt and Saudi Arabia it was a crucial issue. The desire to remove the Egyptian army from Yemen constituted a central common denominator for Egypt and Saudi Arabia, but each side sought to perform the evacuation in a way that would protect its own interests. The Saudis were interested in a complete and rapid evacuation as well as a takeover of the traditional elements in Yemen (which were linked to Saudi Arabia and were hostile to Egypt). The Egyptians, on the other hand, could not allow themselves to lose face and forego their influence due to the collapse of the republic and the reinstatement of the Imamite institution in Yemen, in the event of their army's hasty departure. Therefore, the Egyptians preferred a gradual departure and the maintaining of a certain Egyptian presence in Yemen, in order to keep their prestige and their influence in the Arabian Peninsula intact, and to obtain a certain degree of compensation for the money and human lives that they had invested in Yemen.

In 1965-1967, the war continued in Yemen, though each of the sides had reached an impasse, and the political discussions that were simultaneously underway could not achieve an agreement that would put an end to the bloodshed.

The tension that prevailed in May 1967 at the front facing Israel provided a convenient pretext for Egypt to withdraw most of its forces from Yemen in anticipation of the war with Israel, without "losing face." The Six Day War and the subsequent defeat of the Egyptian army in this war put an end to Egypt's military involvement in Yemen. The Egyptian desire to cease its involvement in the Yemenite war was reflected in peace talks between Saudi Arabia and Egypt in the second half of 1967, producing an agreement according to which Egyptian forces were removed from Yemen and Saudi Arabia ceased to aid the monarchists. However, despite the cessation of Egyptian and Saudi Arabian involvement in this war, it continued until 1970 and eventually ended with the victory of the republicans. Saudi Arabia recognized this government.

The Unification of Yemen

As stated earlier, South Yemen was granted independence in 1967, but in its first years the new state suffered from political instability, which during those years also characterized its more veteran neighbor in the north. In the 1970s, friction arose between North Yemen and South Yemen. At times battles broke out between the two countries (in the beginning of 1971 and in October 1972).

In 1978, General Ali Abdallah Salah ascended to power, declaring that one of his main objectives was to unify Yemen. In the beginning of 1979, the tension increased once again between the two countries, culminating in skirmishes during the months of February and March 1979. Due to the intervention of the Arab League, however, the fighting stopped and the sides sat down at the negotiating table in Kuwait to resolve the controversy between them and promote the issue of unification into one country. Contact between the representatives of both countries continued into the 1980s, during which time joint work committees were established to process the unification proposals and formulate a joint constitution. These efforts bore fruit in 1990 when, against the background of the Soviet collapse (South Yemen's ally) and in light of South Yemen's economic difficulties, Salah succeeded in consolidating the two states. The united state was called the Republic of Yemen.

In 1991, a referendum was conducted regarding the constitution of the consolidation, and Abdallah Salah was elected by both parliaments—in the north and in the south—as the president of unified Yemen.

In 1991-1993, Yemen continued to suffer from economic difficulties and internal instability. In 1993, democratic elections were held for the first time in the unified country. Several parties ran in these elections and Abdallah Salah remained president. Since its establishment, the new state was under the hegemony of the northerners, which aroused friction between the two parts of the country. In the beginning of 1994, dissension was growing dissension between President Salah (who was from the north) and Prime Minister Attas (who was from the south), regarding the distribution of political power and economic resources between the north and the south. The end result was a war between the north and the south, in which the north prevailed, thus forcing the south to reenter the amalgamation.

Despite the northern victory, President Salah endeavored to establish a national reconciliation government, in which he granted powerful positions to the southern representatives, and even declared a general amnesty to facilitate the national reconciliation process. In addition, a plan for economic reforms was formulated with the help of the World Bank and the International Monetary Fund. In 1997, elections were held for the first time since the civil war of 1994, and President Salah's party won by a landslide.

This brief historical review reflects the complexity of the Yemenite society and political system. This reality imposes serious limitations upon the central government's ability to maintain control, particularly as it needs to bridge the gaps between a wide range of opponents:

- North versus South;
- A large number of tribes that enjoy a relatively high level of autonomy, and an infinite number of personal and tribal rivalries among these powerbrokers;
- Socialist ideologies versus monarchist/conservative ideologies, and versus Islamic ideologies.

The two civil wars—in the 1960s and in 1994—also left their mark and forced the main government to be especially cautious when handling sensitive issues from the aspect of populations and the various powerbrokers in the country. The hostility directed at the British Colonialism as a central historical narrative, the influence of the Soviets in the 1960s and 1970s, which also left residues of antagonism towards the West, and the growth of radical Islamic movements in the Wahabist Saudi spirit, in addition to the Khomeini Revolution—all of these elements combined to turn Yemen into an apt arena for the activity and establishment of infrastructures on behalf of radical Islamic organizations, including Bin Laden's Al Qaida organization.

Yemen and the Gulf War

Kuwait's invasion by Iraq and the subsequent crisis posed complex dilemmas before the Yemenite regime. Due to its weak economy, Yemen was largely dependent on its economic ties with Iraq, which granted it generous financial aid on the one hand, as did its wealthy neighbor Saudi Arabia, on the other. When Iraq and Saudi Arabia placed themselves on opposite sides of the fence, Yemen had to maneuver between the two adversaries. In December 1990, Yemen was a temporary member of the Security Council, and due to its interests and its temporary political status it initiated intermediary efforts to resolve the crisis in Kuwait. In the beginning of January 1991, the president of Yemen set out on a peace initiative to resolve the crisis. However, this initiative failed and did not prevent the outbreak of the war.

During the Gulf War, Yemen took Iraq's side and condemned the coalition's military steps. This stand won public support in Yemen, but caused considerable tension between Yemen and Saudi Arabia, as well as the other coalition states.

In response to Yemen's pro-Iraqi stand, Saudi Arabia decided to cancel work permits for Yemenite citizens and deported many of the 850,000 Yemenite citizens working in that country. The Saudi step dealt a hard blow to the Yemenite economy, as it staunched the flow of funds which these workers had transferred to Yemen and caused a significant rise in unemployment in Yemen. The United States also ceased the economic aid it had been giving to Yemen due to that country's policy.

The friction between Yemen and Saudi Arabia was also reflected in controversial areas along the joint border between the two countries. Discussions between the two countries related to these issues were held during the years 1992-1995 without yielding results, and from time to time border skirmishes erupted. Only from the mid-1990s and onwards did Yemen begin to revive its ties with Saudi Arabia and the United States, which remained suspicious due to the stand that the former had taken in the Gulf War and its support of Islamic terror. A significant change in Yemen's ties with these countries took place only after September 11, 2001, which will be discussed subsequently.

The Growth of Radical Islam in Yemen

The demographic-social structure of Yemen, the tribal branches, the prolonged civil wars, and the absence of an effective central government have turned the country into a convenient arena for the development of radical Islam. This reality was aptly described by Abdel Aziz Ulamasudi, an Arab history lecturer at the Sanaa University, during an interview with the *Christian Science Monitor*:[2] "This is a tribal state…it's the Wild West here, and the government doesn't have even close to enough money…to pacify all these tribes."

The Jihad in Afghanistan, in which many mujahidin from Yemen were active, constituted a central milestone in the consolidation of radical Islam in Yemen. One of the key figures in the formation of radical Islam in this country was Sheikh Abdel Majid al Zindani.[3] Al Zindani, a senior Islamic religious leader, was a central activist in recruiting Yemenite volunteers for the Jihad in Afghanistan, and even took part in the combat against the Soviets. During his years in Afghanistan he met and became acquainted with Osama Bin Laden and cooperated with him in the campaign against the Soviet Union. In the beginning of the 1990s, al Zindani returned to Yemen and established the "Islah" Islamic movement, which subsequently became an important political movement in Yemen's political system.

In 1994, with the outbreak of the war between the south and the north, al Zindani sided with the Salah regime that ruled the north, and recruited Afghan alumni for the campaign. The Afghan alumni regarded the campaign between the north, with its Islamic leanings, and the south, with its Marxist inclinations, as the natural continuation of the Jihad that they had waged against the Marxist regime in Afghanistan, and enthusiastically hoisted the banner of the new challenge.[4] After the north's victory over the south, for which the Afhan alumni could claim a good deal of credit, the country was reunited under the rule of General Salah, and the rulers of the united country rewarded the Afghan alumni for their contribution by incorporating their leaders, such as Abdel Majid al Zindani, in senior positions in the Yemenite government.[5]

Over the years, al Zindani and the Islah party became a pivotal political entity in the Yemenite administration, and though Islah adopted a relatively moderate Islamic stance, al Zindani kept in contact with radical Islamic entities among the Afghan "alumni," including Bin Laden. In contrast to the Islah movement, which as noted became a relatively moderate component in the Yemenite political system, more radical Islamic movements sprang up which established terror organizations that adopted the route of Jihad as the means to realize their goals.

Yemen and Islamic Terror

Until its unification with North Yemen, the Marxist Republic of South Yemen served as a safe haven for a wide spectrum of Palestinian and other terror organizations, which founded a terror infrastructure that enjoyed the patronage of the authorities. This tradition of supporting subversive organizations persevered even after the unification of the parts, but the Palestinian organizations and the radical leftist movements were replaced by organizations with Islamic orientations.

Yemen, located in the "shadow" of affluent Saudi Arabia, which is affiliated with the West, has traditionally served as a haven for opposition entities to the Saudi monarchy, and has sought allies in the region to balance the asymmetry between Yemen and its rich and large neighbor. Therefore, Yemen was a prime potential candidate for the forming of alliances with Saudi Arabia's opponents, such as Iran, Iraq, and Egypt in the past. It is therefore no coincidence that Yemen was among the few countries to align itself with Saddam Hussein during the first Gulf War and it criticized the United States harshly, as well as Arab countries that cooperated with the superpower against Iraq.

Since the 1990s, Yemen has gradually become a place of refuge and a stopover for radical Islamic entities, including terrorists, due to the tolerant (if not enthusiastic) approach of the Yemenite authorities. During the years of the war (Jihad) against the Soviets in Afghanistan some 30,000 volunteers left Yemen for Afghanistan (according to the estimate of the *Janes Intelligence Review*), most of which returned to Yemen after the Jihad and became the vanguard of radical Islam in this country. Among the radical Islamic entities active in Yemen was Osama Bin Laden, whose father came to Saudi Arabia from Hadramawt in Yemen, and one of his wives is of Yemenite origin. Bin Laden deposited hundreds of millions of dollars in banks in Sudan and Yemen and offered economic support to the regimes in these countries. He opened accounts in Yemen's central bank and at times kept the amount of some $200 million there, part of which was deposited in the name of Sheikh Abdel al Zindani— one of the leading Islamic clerics in Yemen.[6] Aside from the widespread financial infrastructure that Bin Laden developed in Yemen, he also forged close links with the radical Islamic leaders, some of whom he knew from the period of the Jihad in Afghanistan.

The first terror attack that was perpetrated at Bin Laden's initiative in Yemen, and which availed itself of the local infrastructure, occurred at the end of 1992 (see subsequent elaboration).[7] In the framework of the organizational efforts of Al Qaida in anticipation of the attacks at the U.S. Embassies in East Africa, and as part of the

Global Jihad declared by Bin Laden against the United States, early in 1998 Bin Laden established "front headquarters" for Al Qaida near Sanaa, and he himself was sighted during that period in Sanaa. The infrastructure established by Al Qaida enjoyed the patronage of Abdel Majhid al Zindani, the spiritual ruler of Islamic radicals in Yemen.[8]

In the years 1998-1999, Yemen also served as an important base for other organizations, such as the Islamic Army of Aden and Abyan, which was founded at that time. Subsequently, Yemen itself became an arena for terror attacks, some of which were thwarted but others were carried out, such as the kidnapping of Western hostages and the attack against the American destroyer, the *USS Cole*. Yemenite citizens were and continue to be active participants in Bin Laden's terror network, and the following data should be noted in this connection:

- Ramzi Bin El-Shibh (of Yemenite origin) shared an apartment in Hamburg with Muhammad Atta, commander of the terror attacks on September 11.[9]
- One of the hijackers of the airplane on September 11 was Yemenite (Khaled Al-Midhar).[10]
- At least sixty-nine of the Al Qaida prisoners taken captive in Afghanistan who were transferred to Guantanamo, Cuba ,are Yemenite citizens.[11]
- Several Yemenite citizens were involved in the attacks at the U.S. Embassies in Kenya and Tanzania.
- Yemenite Al Qaida activists were involved in the attack against the *USS Cole*.

The American administration, Britain, and other states have acted during the past decade to persuade the rulers in Sanaa to refrain from aiding terror organizations and instead to cooperate with them in the struggle against Bin Laden. The Clinton administration endeavored to improve its relations with Yemen, and President Ali Abdallah Salah visited Washington in April 2000 with the aim of promoting ties between the two countries, but this did not trigger a significant shift in Yemen's policy. The attack against the *USS Cole* and U.S. pressure on the Yemenite regime to cooperate in the investigation of the incident bore little fruit, and the American investigators that arrived in Yemen did not receive noteworthy cooperation from the authorities.

In an interview that President Salah granted to the CNN[12] he addressed most of the U.S. allegations regarding Yemen's involvement in terror. According to him, there is no evidence that the attacks against the U.S. Embassies in Africa (1998) and against the *USS Cole* (2000) were connected to Bin Laden. He also added that Yemen opposes the military offensive in the framework of the "war against terror" that the United States is conducting, and believes that intelligence efforts alone would suffice.

Salah noted that his country continues to honor its agreement with the United States enabling U.S. ships to anchor and refuel in Aden. He expressed the hope that the United States would again utilize the services at his country's ports and promised to take suitable security measures. Salah pointed out the difficulties that he has encountered while endeavoring to implement the war against terror in his country, but claimed that he is making a great effort to persuade the heads of the tribes not to assist extremist entities and Al Qaida members. If the persuasion attempts are not successful, Salah promised to take military steps against them.

The true turning point in Yemen's approach to terror occurred only following September 11, 2001, and the American declaration of a "global war against terror." Out of a fear that Yemen might turn into a target of the war against terror, like the Taliban regime in Afghanistan, the country decided to take a stand (at least formally) alongside the coalition fighting world terror.[13]

In another interview with the *New York Times*,[14] Salah stated that his security forces were encountering difficulties similar to those encountered by American security forces in Afghanistan, whose efforts failed to catch Bin Laden and the organization's leaders. Salah claimed that tribal members that offer refuge to two wanted Al Qaida members—Qaid Salim Sinan al Hariti and Muhammad Hamdi al Adhal—are far more familiar with the mountainous terrain and hiding places than the security forces. Nevertheless, he promised that the search for the two would continue, and their pictures were published in order to facilitate their capture. President Salah claimed that his country was cooperating with the United States in the investigation of the attack against the *USS Cole* and the war against terror, and also noted that he had asked the United States for military and economic aid.

Due to the pressures applied by the United States, Britain, and Saudi Arabia, the Yemenite government began to take practical steps against elements identified with Bin Laden and the radical terror organizations. In the framework of these steps a special counter-terror unit was established in the Ministry of Interior, and Yemen began to cooperate with international elements in the area of counter-terror activity. However, these actions taken by the Yemenite government have met with limited success to date for several main reasons:

- The tribal structure of the Yemenite society prevents the establishment of an effective central government, thus the government's control of remote areas far away from the capital is only partial.
- The leaders of the stronger tribes have their own policies and they support radical Islamic entities due to financial and ideological considerations.
- There are strong circles affiliated with radical Islam that are very popular.
- Corrupt and ineffective administration and supervisory systems make it hard for the central government to control what is happening in the country.

As stated earlier, due to the September 11 attacks and the ensuing "war against terror" declared by the United States, the government in Sanaa became very careful not to provide the United States and its allies with a reason to attack Yemen due to its situation of being a safe refuge and an asylum for Islamic terrorists.[15] In the beginning of February 2002, Central Command Commander-in-Chief General Tommy Franks visited Yemen. Franks announced at the end of his visit that he was pleased with the cooperation between the countries, and added that his country would provide Yemen with military aid and instructors to train units of the Yemenite army in counter-terror combat. In July 2002, it was reported that the first forty Yemenite soldiers had completed their training under American instruction in the area of combating terror. Aside from Franks, Deputy Secretary of State William Burns and the directors of the FBI and CIA visited Yemen.[16]

Indeed, in September 2002, it was announced that Yemenite authorities had arrested over one hundred individuals suspected of been affiliated with or aiding Al Qaida.[17] Be that as it may, the steps taken by the Yemenite government against radical Islamic entities in that country were mainly designated to placate the United States and prevent damage to Yemenite interests. At this present time they cannot be considered an indication of any real intention of the authorities to contend with the problem. Although the regime in Yemen does not support and is not involved in international Islamic terror, many of its senior members have family and other connections with radical Islamic entities in the country and therefore they have no real interest to act against these parties. Moreover, there are many circles in the country's leadership that are hostile to the United States and the Saudi regime, and they would like to see them gone.

In an interview with *Al-Sharq al-Awsat*, the foreign minister of Yemen stated that the Yemen Parliament had established a committee whose role it is to investigate allegations regarding the infringement of human rights on the part of the Yemenite security entities vis-à-vis their activities against those suspected of affiliation with a terror organization. It would appear that the criticism being leveled by opposition groups and by government circles identified with radical Islam reflects the internal opposition to the Yemen government's policy in this matter.

The Yemenite government is therefore wedged beneath a steamroller: On the one hand, there is the United States demanding resolute action against entities identified with Islamic terror, while, on the other hand, there are the Yemenite factions that support radical Islam and are hostile to the United States. Therefore, it is reasonable to assume that only ongoing U.S. pressure will ensure anti-terror activity by the Yemenite government, and without this threat the Yemenite authorities will probably cease to act against Islamic terror in their country.

Local Islamic Terror Organizations Active in Yemen

The two main Islamic terror organizations active in Yemen are the Yemenite Islamic Jihad, which is the more veteran of the two, and a relatively new organization, which was established by a group that split away from the Islamic Jihad, namely the Islamic Army of Aden-Abyan. Both organizations share the same objectives—the establishment of a religious Islamic state in Yemen and the removal of foreign influences from the holy territory of the Arab Peninsula. Both organizations take violent action (Jihad) to achieve these goals.

The Islamic Jihad in Yemen[18]

This organization was founded due to the influence of the Egyptian Islamic Jihad. Many of the organization's members set out for Afghanistan during the 1980s, participated in the war (Jihad) against the Soviets, and at the end of the war returned to Yemen and became the organization's vanguard. In the early 1990s, the Yemenite authorities made efforts to institutionalize the radical Islamic entities in

the country in order to exercise some control over them. In this framework, the authorities offered their patronage to radical Islamic organizations and organizations like the Islamic Jihad, with the intention of even incorporating them within Yemen's armed forces, but
these attempts failed.

The Islamic Jihad in Yemen maintains close links with Islamic
terror entities worldwide, including Bin Laden's Al Qaida. Activists
of the Islamic Jihad enjoy the patronage of various tribal leaders in
Yemen, and maintain an infrastructure of facilities and training camps
in desolate mountainous areas in Yemen.

The Islamic Army of Aden-Abyan

This organization, established in 1998 by a faction that split away
from the Yemenite Islamic Jihad, was headed by Salah Hidara Atawi
and al Midhar (Zain al Abdeen Abu-Bakar al Midhar), also known
as Abu al Hassan. Abu al Hassan fought in Afghanistan in the framework of the Jihad against the Soviets where he met Osama Bin Laden
and was influenced by his ideas. At the end of the war Abu al Hassan
returned to Yemen, joined the ranks of the Islamic Jihad, and subsequently became one of the founders of the Islamic Army of Aden-
Abyan.

In August 1998, after the American attack of cruiser missiles
against Al Qaida targets in Sudan, and in retaliation for the attacks
against the U.S. embassies in Kenya and Tanzania, the organization
declared its support for the Jihad declared by Bin Laden. In a letter
distributed by the organization, Abu al Hassan stated:[19]

> The Islamic Army declares its support and backing for Osama Bin Laden and the
> brothers in Sudan…and appeals to all sectors of the Yemeni people, the descendants of
> the mujahidin conquerors, to kill the Americans and seize their possessions, for their
> blood is proscribed and their possessions are the Muslims' spoils. The Aden Islamic
> Army pledges to destroy US possessions and bases that are being equipped in Socotra,
> Al-hudaydah and Aden.

Similar warnings against foreign residents were issued by the organization in March and May 1999, and were sent to the Arab newspapers *Al Hayat* and *Al-Sharq al-Awsat* that are published in London.[20]

From December 1998 onwards the Yemenite authorities began to
take action against the Islamic Army of Aden-Abyan and its activists, and on December 18, 1998, they succeeded in nabbing the

organization's leader Salah Hidara Atawi. Atawi's arrest, together with the arrest of other organization members, triggered an escalation in the organization's struggle against the authorities, as now it was also acting to free its incarcerated comrades.[21]

The organization began its involvement in international terror activities in November 1998. During that month, Abu-Hamza al Mitsri, one of Bin Laden's aides who resided in London, contacted Abu-al-Hassan and requested his assistance in carrying out attacks against American and British targets in Aden.[22] Abu-Hamza, an Egyptian born in Alexandria, had emigrated to England in his twenties where he completed his engineering training at Brighton University.[23] In 1987, during a pilgrimage to the sites holy to Islam in Saudi Arabia (the Haj), Abu-Hamza met Abdallah Azzam, who dealt in the recruitment of volunteers for the Jihad in Afghanistan. Abu-Hamza joined the Jihad and during the years 1989-1993 lived in Pakistan and Afghanistan and participated in the war against the Soviets.

In 1993, Abu-Hamaza returned to London and became the Imam of the Finsbury Park mosque in London.[24] In the spirit of the Jihad that he had embraced in Afghanistan, together with other Afghan alumni, Abu-Hamza established an organization called the SOS (Supporters of Sharia), which schemed to continue the Jihad activities against the enemies of Islam. The organization believes that the duty of Jihad applies to every Muslim, aside from the elderly, the sightless, and women.

In the mid-1990s, Abu-Hamza traveled to Bosnia several times in order to organize assistance for the Muslims in their war against the Serbs, and after the end of that war began to focus his efforts in Yemen. Abu-Hamza feared that the United States was about to establish strongholds in Yemen. He therefore contacted Afghan alumni in Yemen and Britain, and jointly formulated a plan of ways to fight the American presence in that country. Among others, Abu-Hamza contacted Abu al Hassan and requested his aid in perpetrating terror attacks. The latter acquiesced and stated that members of Abu-Hamza's terror network would be his guests and would be granted his patronage and assistance as needed.[25] Members of the British terror network arrived in Yemen in early December 1998, and the network was activated in order to perpetrate terror attacks in Yemen.

On December 23, 1998, three terrorists were arrested in Aden for a traffic violation. An inspection of their vehicle revealed that it was loaded with explosives and that the terrorists were on their way to carry out a terror attack against the British Consulate located near Aden port.[26] An interrogation of the three led to additional arrests, and eventually all six members of the terror cell were arrested (see subsequent elaboration).

Due to Abu al Hassan's pledge to take care of Abu-Hamza's terror cell, Abu-al-Hassan decided to kidnap Western hostages in order to liberate the detainees (see subsequent elaboration). The kidnapping attempt organized by Abu al Hassan failed and he was apprehended by the Yemenite security forces, made to stand trial, and was executed by a shooting squad.[27] During his trial, Abu al Hassan refused to express regret for his action, called the Western hostages "the grandchildren of pigs and monkeys," and added that if his firearm had not jammed he would have killed additional hostages.

Despite the heavy blows sustained by the organization, it still continued with its activities and maintained ties with radical Islamic organizations, including Osama Bin Laden's Al Qaida. In October 2002, the organization perpetrated the attack against the French tanker *Limbourg* and claimed responsibility publicly for the attack (see subsequent elaboration).

Prominent Attacks in the Yemenite Arena

The Attacks on December 29, 1992[28]

In the framework of Sudan and Iran's struggle against U.S. intervention in the Horn of Africa in general, and in Somalia in particular, Bin Laden decided to organize a series of attacks against U.S. targets in Yemen. In order to perpetrate the attacks as early as possible, Bin Laden recruited Afghan alumni of Yemenite descent. The original plan included the detonation of explosive devices at hotels in Aden where American military personnel usually stayed, as well as attacks against U.S. targets at the Aden airport and seaport.

To enable perpetration of the attacks within a short time, despite all of the difficulties involved, Bin Laden recruited his aide Sheikh Tarik al Fadli who was residing in London, and asked him to personally take command of the mission. In mid-November, Bin Laden enabled Fadli's secret return to Yemen. Sums of money required for the preparation and execution of the attack were transferred to Yemen via bank accounts of companies and businesses owned by Bin Laden in Yemen. Bin Laden and Fadli, who planned the attacks, decided to avail themselves of the aid of the Yemenite Jihad whose people were active in the vicinity of Aden. Al Fadli believed that action should be taken not only against the American presence but against local politicians also. For the attack mission against local politicians, the Yemenite Jihad members were sent reinforcements in the form of demolition experts from among the Afghan alumni.

In preparation of the attacks, a training base was hastily set up in the area of Saadah in north Yemen, near the joint boundary with Saudi Arabia. An expert sapper of Libyan origin was brought in from Afghanistan, and the weapons required for the attack were smuggled in on boats sailing from Sudan via the Red Sea that landed on a deserted beach in Northern Yemen near Al-Khakhah. The Libyan expert trained several "Yemenite Afghans" in the preparation of explosive charges, and subsequently supervised the preparation of the charges used for the attack. After completing the preparations, the Libyan left Yemen one day prior to the attack.

On December 29, 1992, the terror cell planted explosive charges at the Aden Hotel and at the Golden Moor Hotel in Aden. In the resultant explosions, three were killed and five were wounded. Another terrorist cell armed with a launcher and RPG-7 rockets was apprehended near the fence of the Aden airport, as it was about to launch the RPG rockets at American transport planes parked at the airport. The Yemenite authorities launched an intensive investigation and manhunt to locate the perpetrators. On January 8 1993, Sheikh Tarik al Fadli was apprehended along with some of his men.

Despite the failure of the attack on the Aden airport and the arrest of some of the perpetrators, Bin Laden and al Turabi were satisfied with the results, which they felt had conveyed a message to the United States, as well as a warning against continued American involvement in the Muslim world in general, and in Somalia in particular.

The Arrest of the "British" Terror Network in Yemen
(December 23, 1998)

On December 23, 1998, three terrorists were arrested in a car loaded with explosives. They were on their way to perpetrate a terror attack against the British Consulate in Aden. As the result of their interrogation another three cell members were arrested and a safe house was found that contained mines, rocket launchers, computers, encrypted communication means, and many cassettes belonging to the SOS (Supporters of Sharia). Thus, an organization that had been planning a series of attacks against British and American targets was apprehended in Yemen.[29]

Five of those arrested were carrying (original) British passports, and the sixth was carrying original French documentation. Their questioning revealed that they were members of SOS in London, headed, as mentioned earlier by Abu-Hamza al Mitsri, a radical Islamic leader associated with Bin Laden.[30] Among the cell's members were two relatives of Abu-Hamza; his cousin Muhsein Gailan, who was arrested in Yemen, and his son Muhammad Mustafa who succeeded in eluding capture.

The network's members arrived in Yemen in mid-December, and according to the testimony of at least one of the arrested suspects, they met with Abu al Hassan (one of the leaders of the Islamic Army of Aden-Abyan), who provided them with weaponry and instructions for perpetrating attacks.[31] Their intention was to carry out a series of attacks on Christmas Eve against Western targets in Aden including the British Consulate in Aden, an Anglican church, and a group of Americans dealing in the removal of mines from Yemen who lived in the "Movenpick" Hotel in Aden.

Abu-Hamza denied any connection with terror activity in Yemen and claimed that the detained suspects were not members of the "Sharia Supporters" organization. He also claimed that his organization dealt with religious studies and adhered to the laws of Britain.[32]

The Kidnapping of Tourists on December 28, 1998[33]

One of the most obvious expressions of the ongoing ineffectiveness of Yemen's central government is the phenomenon of tribal entities kidnapping foreign residents and holding them as hostages, usually with the aim of furthering their interests in the struggle against the Sanaa authorities. Since 1991 there have been over one hundred incidents of kidnapping of foreign residents, generally by tribal entities that demanded ransom money for their release. When the ransom was paid, the hostages were usually released unharmed.[34] During the years 1996-2000, the Yemenite kidnappers held 150 hostages, including 122 foreign residents.[35] Following are several examples of kidnappings of foreign residents in Yemen:[36]

- January 26, 1996—Seventeen elderly French tourists were kidnapped by tribal members in the Maareb area. The kidnappers demanded the release of one of their tribal members who had been arrested. The kidnappers released the hostages on January 29, 1996.

- October 20, 1996—A French diplomat was kidnapped in Sanaa and was released on November 1, 1996, after the Yemenite authorities capitulated to the kidnappers' demands.
- March 4, 1997—Seven German tourists were kidnapped, and the kidnappers demanded $12 million for their release. The hostages were released on March 12, 1997.
- March 27, 1997—Four German tourists were kidnapped and the kidnappers demanded $3 million for their release. They were released on April 6, 1997.
- In the first week of December 2001, a German citizen employed at the Mercedes dealer in Sanaa was kidnapped by armed men. The kidnappers, apparently from the Zubian tribe, transferred the victim to a hiding place in a mountainous area some 170 kilometers east of the capital, Sanaa. The Yemenite security forces pursued the kidnappers and conducted a manhunt.[37] On December 6, the security forces surrounded the village of al-Muhgiza and carried out a gunfight against the tribe members, who they believed were involved in the kidnapping. In the exchange of fire three tribe members were killed as well as two policemen and many more were injured.[38]

It is clear that most of the kidnappings did not stem from religious or ideological motives as expressed in the kidnappers' demands and in their choice to not cause the hostages any physical harm. Nevertheless, it seems that this modus operandi was also adopted by terror organizations to further their interests, as witnessed by the events at the end of 1998.

On December 28, 1998, sixteen tourists from various countries were kidnapped (twelve British, two American, and two Australian citizens) while they were touring the Abyan region in Yemen. The convoy of five vehicles in which the tourists were traveling was attacked about 60 kilometers northeast of Aden by an armed group who kidnapped the tourists and held them hostage. The latter were transferred to a hiding place in a remote mountainous region that served as a camp for the terror organization's members. On the night of December 29, 1998, a spokesman for the terror organization the Islamic Army of Aden-Abyan stated that members of his organization had kidnapped the tourists, and he made several stipulations for their release:

- The release of the "British" network's members (sent by Abu-Hamza) and members of the Islamic Army of Aden-Abyan;
- The cessation of U.S. and British aggression against Iraq;
- The banishment of the British and U.S. presence in the Arabian Peninsula.

Yemenite authorities refused to meet the kidnappers' demands, and the Yemenite security forces found their trail and surrounded them and their victims in their place of hiding. In the course of the Yemenite forces' rescue attempt several hostages were killed and others were wounded. At least three of the kidnappers were killed in the incident and three others were caught, including Abu al Hassan. In his interrogation, Abu al Hassan confessed that the kidnapping was to have brought about the release of the organization's members and that of the British terror network members incarcerated in Yemenite jails. According to the testimony of one of the kidnapped victims, during the kidnapping Abu al Hassan held a telephone conversation with General Ali Muhsan al Ahmar, a relative of President Salah, in an attempt to get the latter to agree to the hostages' demands, but the Yemenite authorities had already made the decision to take action to secure the release the hostages. As noted, during the 1990s, there were over 100 kidnapping incidents of foreign residents in Yemen, but this particular incident was the broadest in scale and one of the few that ended in the death of hostages.

The Attack against the American Destroyer (the USS Cole)

In December 1998, an agreement was signed between the Yemenite government and the United States according to which American battleships would refuel in Aden port. The presence of U.S. battleships in Yemenite ports was perceived by radical Islamic entities as an additional expression of the U.S. desire to fortify its presence in the Arab Peninsula, a presence that they believed contaminated Islam's holy sites.

The U.S. warships in Aden thus became a target for an attack by Al Qaida and radical Islamic entities in Yemen. Muhammad Omar al Harazi, a Saudi citizen whose family originated from Yemen (much like Bin Laden) was placed in charge of the organizational aspects related to the attack against a U.S. vessel. Al Harazi was an Afghan alumnus who had also been involved in the attack against the U.S. Embassy in Nairobi, Kenya, in October 1998.

Initially, the group headed by al Harazi had planned to attack a U.S. vessel with RPG missiles, but this idea was abandoned when the planners came to the conclusion that this method would inflict only minor damage.[39] Therefore, preparations focused on the construction of a boat bomb that would be navigated by suicide bombers and detonate adjacent to the U.S. warship, thus inflicting more significant damage. In order to perpetrate the attack, the terrorists rented two apartments in the Aden vicinity, one in "Little Aden," which served as the site for the preparation of the boat bomb, and the other in the port area, in order to observe the port and the American vessels.[40]

The first attempt to attack an American vessel was made on January 3, 2000. The chosen vessel was the *USS Sullivan*, which had moored in Aden port that day for refueling. The boat bomb, which had been loaded with hundreds of kilograms of explosives, sank a short time after it set out on its mission from Little Aden, apparently due to an erroneous estimate regarding its load capacity and the improper packing of the explosives. This miscalculation caused a ten-month postponement of the attack. During the ensuing months preparations for the attack continued, with al Harazi and his team applying the lessons learned from the failure of the initial attempt.

On October 12, 2000, a boat bomb containing over half a ton of explosives, navigated by two suicide attackers from the Al Qaida organization, approached the destroyer *USS Cole*. The boat bomb was disguised as a service boat on its way to handle technical repairs on the American destroyer. The two suicide terrorists were dressed in white coveralls and therefore did not arouse suspicion. They attempted to draw up alongside the vessel's stern in order to wreak as much damage as possible, but were unable to do so, and finally detonated the boat near the destroyer's center. Seventeen American sailors perished in the explosion and thirty-five were wounded.

In April 2001, Yemen's Minister of Interior Hassin Muhammad Arab, announced that local security forces had apprehended six terrorists that would stand trial; three of them had been directly involved in the attack and another three had served as collaborators. Two additional members were killed in the attack (the suicide bombers), and another two are still at large.[41]

One of the chief suspects who was apprehended, Jamal Badawi, confessed that he had traveled to Afghanistan in 1997, undergone training in Bid-Laden's camps, and pledged his oath of loyalty. He met his future accomplices in the attack, including Yemen-born Tawfik al Atrash, known by the code name of "Haled." In June 1999, Haled sent two of his men to meet Badawi. They asked him to travel to Saudi Arabia in order to purchase the boat that later served as the boat bomb. The boat was bought with false documentation, in order to conceal the identity of the buyers, and the vessel was ultimately presented to the two suicide bombers.[42] Another detainee, Fahd al Kuzu, recounted that at the time of the attack he was located at the apartment that served as the observation point for surveillance of the port and U.S. battleships, and he was supposed to film the attack on video, but he fell asleep and in consequence failed to fulfill his role.

The Yemenite authorities' initial response was that the explosion on the *USS Cole* stemmed from a technical malfunction; only four days later did the Yemenite government confirm that it was indeed a terror attack, as the United States had claimed.

Following the attack, several declarations claiming responsibility were announced in the name of unfamiliar organizations, including the "Islamic Deterrent Forces." According to their announcement, the organization called "the Brigades of the Martyrs of the Al-Aksa Intifada" perpetrated the attack in order to "defend the honor of the Islamic nation and avenge the blood of the Muslim people subdued in Palestine due to American aid." The Deterrent Forces stated that the attack was a gift to Al-Aksa and a means to promote the objective of flying the Palestinian flag over their people in Palestine. The attack was meant to defend the honor of the Islamic Arab nation so that America would know the price of its attempt to achieve hegemony over Yemenite land through its warships and military bases. The declaration ended with a warning to the United States not to aid and abet the Zionist entity.[43]

Rifai Teh, one of the most senior members of the Jama'a al-Islamiya, who was first presented by the *Al-Zaman* newspaper as Bin Laden's spokesman,[44] denied that Bin Laden was involved but that he welcomed the attack. Rifai Teh stated:

> this was a great campaign perpetrated against the United States, which is a country that harms our lands, our people, our treasures and our honor in Palestine. The lessons to be drawn from this attack are that even the powerful have weaknesses. The practical conclusion is that the United States was forced to have its destroyer towed in the dead of night and moved secretly, as well as raising the alert level in the U.S. Navy in the Gulf."[45]

In his announcement to *Al-Sharq al-Awsat*, Rifai Teh added that the operation had cost $ 5,000, but the damage caused to the American defense system was valued at hundreds of millions of dollars. He added that the attack had been carried out against a fortified military target, and this type of target cannot trigger criticism because it is a military target belonging to a hostile country that aids and abets the enemy.[46]

While the Yemenite authorities aspired to limit the investigation to the levels that were directly involved in the attack, U.S. investigators sought to broaden the inquiry to senior entities in the country's religious and political system. The United States adamantly demanded that FBI investigators be brought into the investigation that the Yemenite authorities had initiated, but due to different approaches and interests the joint investigation ran aground. As was noted earlier, the turning point in the area of cooperation between the United States and Yemen occurred only after September 11, 2001.

The Yemenite authorities arrested seventeen individuals who were interrogated on suspicion that they had been involved in the attack against the *USS Cole*, and they were detained until standing trial. On April 11, 2003, ten of the detainees broke out of prison in Sanaa.[47] Among the fugitives were Jamal Badawi and Fahed al Kozo, who played central roles in the attack. The authorities arrested two senior police officers suspected of involvement in the escape, and an extensive manhunt was launched in search of the fugitives.[48] It was announced in July 2003 that in the process of extensive arrests of individuals in Yemen with suspected links to Al Qaida, two of the fugitives were apprehended.

The Attack against the French Tanker, the Limbourg[49]

On October 6, 2002, the French oil tanker *Limbourg* moored opposite the Yemen coast, after having been loaded with oil at an Iranian port and with the intention of loading additional oil at the port of Debbah in the Hadramawt region of Yemen. When the tanker was about 5 kilometers off the coast of Yemen, a huge blast occurred, igniting the ship. After the crew's attempts to extinguish the fire proved to be ineffective, it was abandoned. In the explosion and subsequent fire twelve crewmembers were injured, and one crewmember was declared missing. An officer on the tanker's crew said that he had seen a small boat rapidly approaching the tanker's side. He believed that the smaller boat's collision with the tanker's side is what caused the explosion. The ship's captain claimed that the explosion that split the tanker's side was external rather than internal.

Yemenite authorities claimed initially that the fire was caused by accident. Yemen's Transportation and Shipping Minister Sa'ad Yifai stated that the explosion was caused by an oil leak from one of the tanks on board, but managers of the French company that had hired the tanker's services dismissed this explanation. The spokesperson for the French Foreign Ministry announced that the matter was being investigated and it was still too early to determine the cause of the collision.

On October 10, 2002, the Islamic Army of Aden and Abyan dispatched an announcement to the media in which it claimed responsibility for hitting the tanker and noted that the attack was meant to avenge the execution of the organization's leader Zain al Abdeen al Midhar (Abu al Hassan) by Yemenite authorities two years earlier. This announcement stated that the attack also came in protest against the U.S. forces and the American intention to initiate an assault against Iraq; according to the organization, the oil transported by the French tanker was designated for this purpose.[50]

A French research team that visited Yemen discovered wreckage of fiberglass near the tanker, which apparently was part of the boat bomb that collided with it. Once the organization had claimed responsibility, official Yemenite entities acknowledged the possibility that the incident had been a terror attack, although they rushed to qualify the statement with the declaration that it was still too early to determine this unequivocally.

This was the first attack to be carried out in the Yemenite arena against a Western target after September 11, and after Yemen had joined the counter-terror war. The ability of Al Qaida or any other radical Islamic organization to carry out a maritime attack of this sort, at a time when the Yemenite authorities were purportedly taking resolute action against Islamic terror entities, constituted a significant blow to Yemenite credibility, and may have a negative impact on Yemen's future relations with the United States and the West. The attack's target, a French tanker, constituted an innovation vis-à-vis the targets of attacks in this arena, and conveyed the message that Islamic terror organizations did not distinguish between French targets and American or British targets.

Currently, Yemenite authorities hold fifteen detainees in connection with the explosion on the *Limbourg*. Two have confessed to assisting in the preparation of the boat bomb which sank the tanker; their interrogation indicates that a Yemenite citizen named Abdel

Hakim Baziya initiated and planned the attack. The authorities believe that he is still hiding in Yemen.[51] Financing for the attack was provided by a Yemenite citizen living in Saudi Arabia.

On June 2004, the fifteen suspected terrorists were charged in Sanaa's court for several terrorist operations and plots. The prosecution charged them with blowing up the French oil tanker, carrying out several bombings in Sanaa, killing one soldier and plotting to blow up the U.S., U.K., French, German, and Cuban embassies in Sanaa as well as plotting to kill U.S. Ambassador to Yemen Edmund Hill.

The prosecutor said before the court that the suspected terrorists rented a house in Hadaramout to store explosives and another to get the boat prepared; he stated that the boat cost was $20,000. They also bought two tons of explosives, and packed the boat with an amount ranging from 1150-1250 kilos of TNT and 20 kilos of C-4 (explosive), plus a number of flashtubes. The prosecutor noted that they wanted to kill the U.S. ambassador in revenge for Abu Ali al Harit, who was killed by Americans in November.[52]

The Murder of the Three American Doctors

On December 30, 2002, an assassin infiltrated a hospital in South Yemen and opened fire. Three American doctors were slain and a fourth was injured.[53] The assassin was Abd al Rezek Kmal, a student at the al-Iman Islamic University in Sanaa, who was affiliated with an Islamic terror organization that planned to assassinate Yemenite and foreign political figures and to attack Western (particularly American) interests in Yemen.[54]

Yemen security forces arrested the assassin as well as thirty other members of the organization.[55] The organization was headed by Ali Ahmad Jarallah, who three days earlier (on December 27, 2002) had assassinated the deputy secretary general of the Yemenite Socialist Party. This party is considered secular and moderate, and the political assassination shocked the political system in Yemen.[56] During their interrogation, the detainees divulged that they had planned assassinations and attacks based on Jarallah's instructions in order to "defend Islam, demonstrate loyalty to Jihad and fight the infidels, secular entities and Christian missionaries in Yemen, and to kill some of them."[57] Explosives and documents containing hit lists were found in the possession of the organization members.

The interrogation of the network's members indicates that some of them had gone to Afghanistan to undergo military training, and many of the members had been affiliated with the Yemenite opposition party "The Yemen Union for Islamic Reform," but they froze their membership in the party and established the terror organization. Among those suspected of membership in the network was Abd al Salam Kamel, son-in-law of Sheikh Abdel Majid al Zindani,[58] the spiritual leader of radical Islam in Yemen. Yemen security authorities believed that the members of the network were not affiliated with Al Qaida, and maintained that it was a local organization of radical Islamic Fundamentalists. On May 10, 2003, Abd al Razak Kemal was convicted of murder by a Sanaa court and was sentenced to death.[59]

Counter-Terror Steps Taken by the Yemenite Authorities (starting from September 11, 2001)

The activities of the Yemenite authorities in the framework of the counter-terror struggle apply to four levels:

1. On the propaganda-informational level, the authorities make frequent announcements and reports of activities conducted by the government in order to eradicate Al Qaida's terror infrastructure in Yemen.
2. The government carries out arrests among students and citizens from Islamic countries that are suspected of being affiliated with radical Islam.
3. Authorities pursue and arrest Al Qaida activists as well as members of other Islamic terror organizations (to date over 200 individuals have been arrested who are suspected of being members of or aiding Al Qaida).
4. Authorities bring to trial those individuals suspected of membership in Al Qaida or other terror organizations.

The Arrest of Individuals Suspected of Affiliation with Radical Islam

On November 2, 2001, Yemen security forces arrested two academics of Sudanese extraction who were suspected of affiliation with Bin Laden's terror organization. The two—Abd al Salam Nuradin and Ahmed Sayyaf—claimed that they had arrived in Yemen to conduct academic research. Nuradin had spent several years in Yemen and taught philosophy at the Aden and Sanaa Universities, while Ahmed Sayyaf had been sent by a British university to Yemen in order to carry out research about the Red Sea states.[60]

Within their planned activities to identify and arrest Al Qaida activists, Yemenite authorities announced that they had arrested ten students of different nationalities at the religious seminary Dar al-Hathat in the Marrab region.[61] Forty-three students with Indonesian citizenship who had been studying at religious seminaries in Sanaa and Hadramawt were also arrested. The Indonesian Embassy protested the arrests and claimed that the Yemenite authorities had failed to present any evidence regarding the students' guilt.[62] On February 2, 2002, the Yemenite authorities announced that twenty-nine of the Indonesian students would be free to continue their studies in Yemen, while the rest would be released from imprisonment but would be flown back to Indonesia.[63]

Following the arrests among the students at religious seminaries, the authorities decided to deport 115 students whose visas had expired or who had entered the country illegally.[64]

The Pursuit and Arrest of Activists Affiliated with Al Qaida and Radical Islamic Organizations

- On December 19, 2001, it was announced that seventeen people, including thirteen policemen, had been killed in clashes between Yemenite security forces and tribal members during searches conducted by the security forces for individuals suspected of membership in Al Qaida. The security forces surrounded the village of al-Hussin in the area of Marrab and a shoot-out was conducted against local residents. The shooting was backed up by Yemenite helicopter gunboats, which attacked the positions of the tribal members in the village.[65]

- The Yemenite newspaper, *The Twenty-Sixth of September*, which is published by the Ministry of Defense, listed the names of two men wanted for their affiliation with Al Qaida:[66] Qaid Salim Sinan al Hariti, also known as Abu-Ali al Hariti; and Muhammad Hamdi al Azhal, also called Abu-Asem al Adhal. In November, al Azhal was caught near Sanaa. The publication of their names was mentioned in an interview granted by the Yemenite president to the *New York Times*. According to U.S. Ambassador to Yemen Edmund Hall, based on information in the possession of the United States, both were senior commanders in Al Qaida, and al Adhal was also wanted for his involvement in the attack against the *USS Cole*. The Yemenite authorities were also searching for a third person of Egyptian descent named "Iman," who apparently is also a senior member of the organization.[67]

- Yemenite police reported on February 14, 2002 that a Yemenite citizen, Samir Ahmad Muhammad al Hada, suspected of being an Al Qaida activist and wanted by Yemenite authorities, had detonated himself in

Sanaa when surrounded by the police.[68] It was believed that he had undergone training in Afghanistan and returned to Yemen with false papers in order to prepare a terror infrastructure in the country.[69]

- Following an FBI warning regarding the intention of Al Qaida activists, some of them of Yemenite descent, to perpetrate attacks against U.S. targets, Yemenite authorities arrested five Yemenite citizens who appeared on the United States' list of seventeen terrorists suspected of involvement in terror activity.[70] The terror cell was headed by Fawaz Yihya al Rabi, a Yemenite born in Saudi Arabia who used various aliases.[71]

- On September 20, 2002, Yemenite security forces raided an apartment in a Sanaa suburb where several individuals suspected of affiliation with Al Qaida were hiding. Two Al Qaida members were killed in the crossfire and three others were arrested (two Yemenite soldiers and one civilian were also injured in the incident).[72] According to various reports, the United States had put pressure on the Yemenite authorities to take firm action against the Al Qaida activists, and in this framework a U.S. ship carrying special forces had sailed from the Djibouti port for Yemen on September 18, 2002. Yemenite authorities, however, denied U.S. involvement in the activity against Al Qaida, and reiterated that they were cooperating with the "Coalition against Terror" headed by the United States.[73]

The Trial of Individuals Suspected of Membership in Al Qaida

On December 3, 2002, Judge Hamud al Hitar announced that seventeen individuals suspected of membership in Al Qaida were to be charged and tried for sabotage—the maximum penalty for this offense in Yemen is the death sentence. He also announced the release of twenty-four individuals who had been suspected of links with Al Qaida but whose guilt had not been proven, in addition to another twelve suspects who had been released earlier in October. The trial of the suspects took place after an inquiry committee of the Yemen Parliament demanded that the government either try the suspects or release them immediately.

Despite Yemen's policy and the steps that it had taken against Al Qaida activists in its territory the attack perpetrated against the French tanker *Limbourg* occurred on October 6, 2002. It would appear that the continued attacks in Yemen against Western targets were among the factors that influenced the United States to intensify its policy vis-à-vis the handling of Islamic terror in this arena. The acceleration of U.S. activity against Islamic terror in Yemen can be observed in the first American "pinpointed thwarting action" in Yemenite territory carried out against Al Qaida activists on November 6, 2002. Six Al Qaida activists were killed by a "Hellfire" missile launched by an American UAV at the car in which they were traveling.[74] This CIA mission was based on accurate intelligence that pinpointed the Al Qaida activists and brought about their termination.

Qaid Salim Sinan al Hariti, one of the senior Al Qaida leaders involved in the attack against the *USS Cole* in October 2000, was killed in the American strike.[75] According to reports in the newspaper, *The Twenty Sixth of September*, al Hariti had also been among the planners of the attack against the French oil tanker, which occurred in October 2002.[76] In addition to al Hariti four other Al Qaida activists were killed in the American attack: Salah Abu-Hama, al Kaija, Abu-Jarah Munir and Ahmed Hijazi, also called Jallal, who may have been a U.S. citizen. Due to the fear of reprisal by Al Qaida or other Islamic organizations in response to the U.S. action, the U.S. Embassy in Sanaa was closed temporarily.

This was the first operational action initiated by the United States in Yemen, as up to this time the Americans had been satisfied with advising and assisting the Yemenite security forces in their activities against Al Qaida and other Islamic terror organizations. The American action increased the tension and exacerbated political sensitivities in Yemen.

In the course of 2003, the Yemenite authorities persevered in their counter-terror activity against Islamic terror organizations. At the end of June, the Yemenite military conducted a widespread sweep in the Abyan region, during which some eighty members of the Islamic Army of Aden and Abyan were either killed or taken prisoner. The offensive came in retaliation for a series of ambushes set by organization members against the Yemenite army in this region, during which a Yemenite Army medical convoy was attacked and seven of its members were wounded.[77] The offensive was one of the most extensive ever to be carried out by the Yemenite Army, with the participation of infantry, the armored corps, special units and gunships.[78]

On July 18, 2003, Yemen's Minister of the Interior Brigadier General Rashid al Alimi announced that Yemenite authorities had arrested 195 individuals suspected of links with Al Qaida.[79] However, along with the successful steps taken by the Yemenite authorities to arrest terrorists, there were also failures. One of the most prominent of failures was the escape of ten prisoners from jail, who were suspected of being Al Qaida members, including some who had been involved in the attack against the *USS Cole*.

Yemenite authorities also acted to extradite two Yemenite citizens under arrest in Germany who were suspected of collaborating with Al Qaida. U.S. Attorney General John Ashcroft stated that one of the detainees—Muhammad al Hassan al Moid—was suspected of serving as Bin Laden's "spiritual consultant," and of handing over some $20 million worth of donations that he had collected in the mosque that he headed in Brooklyn. The second detainee was Muhammad Mussein Yihya Zaid, who was also suspected of links with Al Qaida. The United States requested their extradition from Germany in order to interrogate them and bring them to trial in the United States.[80]

Yemen and the War in Iraq 2003 (Iraqi Freedom)[81]

As stated earlier, during the Gulf War (1991) Yemen was one of the few Muslim countries to support Saddam Hussein's position, but in the months preceding the current U.S. offensive in Iraq, Yemen sided with the United States in its war against terror, and even arrested Al Qaida members in its territory as well as Islamic terrorists from other organizations. The strengthening of ties between President Salah's administration and the United States, and the pursuit of radical Islamic entities in the country, aroused increasing criticism in Islamic circles, with tribal leaders and political representatives in Yemen.

The American offensive in Iraq, which began on March 20, 2003, increased criticism and animosity towards the United States; tens of thousands of protestors took to the streets and threatened to attack the U.S. Embassy. Police failed to break up the demonstration with tear gas and water hoses, and were forced to open fire upon the protestors, many of which were arrested. One policeman and two demonstrators were killed in these incidents and dozens were hurt. The demonstrations and violence began following inflammatory, inciting remarks by Islamic preachers in the mosques during the Friday prayer services. These were the most violent demonstrations to be held in Yemen in recent years. It would appear that the war in Iraq exacerbated the tension between the Yemenite authorities and opposition factors.

Despite the support expressed by large sections of the population for Saddam Hussein, and regardless of its siding with the struggle of radical Islam against the West, it appears that President Salah succeeded in preserving his government, a fact that was reflected in elections held in Yemen, which strengthened the president's status and that of his party. President Salah currently enjoys economic and military aid from the United States, and Yemen's ties with its neighbor Saudi Arabia have also improved. President Salah's consistent approach regarding the struggle against terror is reflected in the agreement that he signed (December 2003) with Ethiopia and Sudan to increase cooperation with those countries in the war against terror.

Notes

1.   This section is based on Haim Shaked, "Yemen—at a Crossroads," *Ma'archot*, Issue 157, February 1964; Abraham Rabinowitz, "The Journey of Egypt in Yemen—Interim Summaries," *Ma'archot*, Issue 165, February 1965; Major Yonah, "The War in Yemen and the Jeddah Agreement," *Ma'archot*, Issue 170, November 1965.
2.   *Christian Science Monitor*, "Yemen Fights Own Terror War," February 5, 2002.
3.   Peter L. Bergen, *Holy War Inc.—Inside the Secret World of Osama Bin Laden*, London: Weidenfeld & Nicolson, 2001, pp. 190-191.
4.   Ibid.
5.   Ibid.
6.   Yosef Bodansky, *Bin Laden—The Man Who Declared War on America*, New York: Forum, 2001, p. 314.
7.   The International Policy Institute for Counter-Terrorism (ICT), Herzliya, "International Terrorism Attacks Results," http://www.ict.org.il.
8.   Yosef Bodansky, *Bin Laden, the Man Who Declared War on America*, p. 246.
9.   *New York Times*, September 18, 2002.
10.   AP Yemen, September 22, 2002.
11.   *Christian Science Monitor*, "Yemen Fights Own Terror War."
12.   Interview on CNN with the president of Yemen, conducted in Sanaa.
13.   *Christian Science Monitor*, "Yemen Fights Own Terror War."
14.   *Yemen Times*, Issue 7, February 17, 2002.
15.   *Christian Science Monitor*, "Yemen Fights Own Terror War."
16.   AP Yemen, September 22, 2002.
17.   Ibid.
18.   Yosef Bodansky, *Bin Laden—The Man Who Declared War on America*, pp. 373-374.
19.   Ibid.
20.   The International Policy Institute for Counter-Terrorism (ICT) Herzliya, "Militants in Yemen Deny Arrests, Threaten Foreigners," http://www.ict.org.il, May 30, 1999.
21.   *Christian Science Monitor*, "Yemen Fights Own Terror War."
22.   The International Policy Institute for Counter-Terrorism (ICT) Herzliya, "Yemen Executes Leader of Islamic Group," http://www.ict.org.il, October 17, 1999.
23.   Peter L. Bergen, *Holy War Inc.—Inside the Secret World of Osama Bin Laden*, p. 195.
24.   Ibid.
25.   Ibid.
26.   The International Policy Institute for Counter-Terrorism (ICT), Herzliya, "The Kidnapping in Yemen: The British Connection," http://www.ict.org.il., January 14, 1999.
27.   The International Policy Institute for Counter-Terrorism (ICT), Herzliya, "Yemen Executes Leader of Islamic Group," http://www.ict.org.il, October 17, 1999.

28. *Christian Science Monitor*, "Yemen Fights Own Terror War."
29. The International Policy Institute for Counter-Terrorism (ICT), Herzliya, "Yemen Executes Leader of Islamic Group," http://www.ict.org.il, October 17, 1999.
30. The International Policy Institute for Counter-Terrorism (ICT), Herzliya, "The Kidnapping in Yemen: The British Connection," http://www.org.il, January 14, 1999.
31. Ibid.
32. *Christian Science Monitor*, "Yemen Fights Own Terror War."
33. This part is based on the following sources: The International Policy Institute for Counter-Terrorism (ICT), Herzliya, "The Kidnapping in Yemen: The British Connection: http://www.ict.org.il, January 14, 1999; The International Policy Institute for Counter-Terrorism (ICT), Herzliya, "Yemen Executes Leader of Islamic Group," http://www.ict.org.il, October 17, 1999; abcNews.com, "US: Yemen—A Known Terrorist Base," February 24, 2000.
34. abcNews, "Yemen—The New Terrorist Capital," October 8, 2001.
35. Peter L. Bergen, *Holy War Inc.—Inside the Secret World of Osama Bin Laden*, p. 193.
36. The International Policy Institute for Counter-Terrorism (ICT), Herzliya, "Yemen Terror Attacks," http://www.ict.org.il.
37. ArabiNews.com, December 6, 2001.
38. Ibid.
39. Peter L. Bergen, *Holy War Inc.—Inside the Secret World of Osama Bin Laden*, p. 201.
40. Ibid.
41. *Al-Halij*, United Arab Emirates, April 2, 2001
42. *Newsweek*, March 19, 2001.
43. The French News Agency, October 17, 2000.
44. *Al-Zaman*, November 15, 2000.
45. Ibid.
46. *Al-Sharq al-Awsat*, November 15, 2000.
47. AP, Sanaa, April 11, 2003.
48. Reuters, Aden, April 13, 2003.
49. This part is based on articles in the newspapers: *Ha'aretz*, October 7, 2002, *Yediot Aharonot*, October 7, 2002; *Ma'ariv*, October 7, 2002; *Yemen Observer*, October 8, 2002; *Yemen Times*, October 7, 2002; *Ha'aretz*, October 11, 2002.
50. *Ha'aretz*, October 11, 2002.
51. AP Sanaa, February 25, 2003
52. Mohammad al Qadhi, "Suspects Admit Plot to Murder US Ambassador," *Yemen Times,* June 6, 2004.
53. *Ma'ariv*, December 31, 2002.
54. Reuters, Yemen, December 30, 2002.
55. *Al-Hayat*, London, January 20, 2003.
56. Ibid.
57. Ibid.
58. Reuters, Yemen, December 31, 2002.
59. AP Sanaa, Yemen.
60. ArabicNews.com, November 2, 2001.
61. ArabicNews.com, December 28, 2001.
62. ArabicNews.com, February 4, 2002.
63. *Yemen Times*, Issue 7, February 17, 2002.
64. ArabicNews.com, February 16, 2002.
65. ArabicNews.com, December 20, 2001.
66. ArabicNews.com, December, 28, 2001.

67.   *Christian Science Monitor*, "Yemen Fights Own Terror War."
68.   ArabicNews.com, February 15, 2002.
69.   *Washington Post*, February 15, 2002.
70.   ArabicNews.com, February 16, 2002.
71.   Ibid.
72.   Reuters, Sanaa, September 21, 2002.
73.   Ibid.
74.   CNN.com.world, November 7, 2002.
75.   AP Sanaa, Yemen, November 7, 2002.
76.   *The Twenty Sixth of September*, Yemen, November 6, 2002.
77.   *Arab News*, Sanaa, Yemen, June 26, 2003.
78.   *Yemen Times*, Aden, June 25, 2003.
79.   *Arab News*, Sanaa, Yemen, July 18, 2003.
80.   AP Washington, March 4, 2003.
81.   AP Sanaa, March 22, 2003; Reuters, Cairo, March 22, 2003.

Part IV

The Terror Triangle and Its Impact on Neighboring Countries

6

Impact of Terror on Neighboring Countries

Introduction

Islamic terror organizations that based their infrastructures in Sudan, Somalia and Yemen regarded the countries in the region—such as Egypt, Ethiopia, Kenya and Tanzania—as preferred arenas for terror activities. These activities were perpetrated according to the organizations' terror policies, but sometimes also with the help and blessings of regimes that support terror, particularly when the attacks were aimed at serving the interests of the supportive countries, an example of which was the assassination attempt against President Mubarak in Ethiopia.

The issue of Sudan's aid for Islamic terror organizations in Egypt has been discussed extensively in previous chapters, but it is important to note that when compared to Sudan's other neighbors, Egypt was the country to suffer most from the Islamic terror organizations. Therefore, Egypt initiated resolute steps domestically and externally which towards the end of the 1990s to bring about a significant decrease in the scope of Islamic terror in Egypt. The Egyptian authorities initiated agreements with Arab and Muslim states regarding intelligence and operational cooperation against Islamic terror, and acted to politically isolate Sudan because of its involvement in terror, an initiative that the United States welcomed and supported.

One of the most pertinent achievements in the cooperative combating of terror was an agreement signed between Egypt and Yemen in 1993. In the framework of this agreement, Yemen undertook to help solve Egyptian security problems that were connected to it. On the basis of this agreement, Yemenite authorities closed down the al-Jihad office in Sanaa, and the exchange of intelligence between the two countries was extended significantly. In early 1996, Yemen extradited wanted Egyptian fundamentalists that had been living in its territory to Egypt, it appears that the cooperation between the two countries continues to date.

In addition, Egypt also made special efforts to reach an understanding with Saudi Arabia and the Gulf States. On the basis of these understandings, the Gulf States extradited twenty-five fundamentalists, members of the al-Jihad and al-Jama'a al-Islamiya organizations to Egypt in 1993. Intelligence and operational cooperation was also achieved between Egypt and Algeria. In this framework it was decided to act against the Iranian and Sudanese support for terror. Delegations from the two countries held several meetings, the most important of which was in June 1993. In addition, a joint Egyptian-Tunisian committee was established in order to expand security cooperation with an emphasis on the exchange of intelligence information. The committee brought about the signing of a security agreement between the two countries. Other states aspired to emulate the Egyptian-Tunisian cooperation model. These countries included Eritrea and Ethiopia, which requested to join the agreement in order to thwart Sudanese subversive activity against them.[1]

The East African states continue to serve as convenient arenas of activity for Islamic terror organizations. In these countries, these organizations, and particularly Al Qaida, develop infrastructures that serve as places of refuge and transit areas for terrorists, assist in the recruitment of activists, in economic activities, and at times, help to perpetrate attacks. Kenya and Ethiopia share joint borders with Sudan and Somalia, and their coasts are near Yemen's coast. These geographical data undoubtedly make it easier for Islamic terror entities to infiltrate these countries. In addition, each of these countries has relatively large Islamic minorities (in Ethiopia some 43 percent of the population, in Kenya, 6 percent, and in Tanzania, 35 percent) as well as Arab and Iranian emigrants. These groups offer terror organizations refuge and aid as well as potential recruits for terror activities.

The governmental structure, as well as the social and ethnic composition of the countries in the region, significantly restricts the supervisory capabilities of the security entities and law enforcement agencies, and this factor also facilitates the activities of terror organizations in these countries.

Despite everything stated above, relatively few terror attacks were carried out in these countries during and after the 1990s; however, the few attacks that did occur were severe and created serious international repercussions. Four critical attacks can be mentioned in this arena:

1.   The assassination attempt against Egyptian President Hussni Mubarak in Ethiopia (1995);
2.   The bombing of the U.S. Embassy in Nairobi, Kenya (1998);
3.   The bombing of the U.S. Embassy in Dar A-Salam in Tanzania (1998);
4.   The bombing at the Paradise Hotel and the attempt to shoot down an Arkia plane in Mombassa, Kenya (2002).

The Assassination Attempt against President Mubarak in Addis Ababa[2]

On June 26, 1995, an assassination attempt was made against Egyptian President Hussni Mubarak while he was en route from the Addis Ababa airport into the city where he was to attend an African unity conference. Occupants of a car suddenly began shooting at his convoy of vehicles and blocked it. Two terrorists were killed in the crossfire as well as two Ethiopian policemen. Mubarak's armored limousine, which was third in the convoy, was about 70 meters away from the site where the road was blocked by the terrorists' car. Following instructions issued by the security staff, the car turned around and raced towards the airport, from whence the president flew back to Cairo. The assassination attempt failed due to the fact that the bullets did not penetrate the armored car in which the president was traveling, and also because of the relatively large distance between the blocking car and the presidential limousine.

This action was planned by the Jama'a al-Islamiya organization over a two-year period prior to its perpetration. The preparations included the construction of a logistic and operational infrastructure, rental of safe houses, smuggling of weaponry and their installation, the acquisition of cars, the systematic gathering of intelligence regarding access roads, planning the obstruction action, the assault, and escape. The organization sent activists to Addis Ababa so that they would become assimilated there. One of the activists even married a local woman and served as a collaborator for the terror cell. All nine of the cell members were Egyptian citizens, born in Southern Egypt. They all had combat experience and underwent training in Afghan training camps. The organization proved to have a high level of sophistication and daring in preparing this kind of action outside of its home country, along with a high personal performance level, despite their ultimate failure due to a marginal but fatal error in one of the operational stages.

Mubarak accused Sudan of serving as the dispatch base for the assassins. He also claimed that Sudan ran training camps and offered refuge and aid to Islamic terrorists. Following the incident, the Ethiopian authorities revealed caches of combat equipment kept by the assassins. Three terrorists were apprehended by the Ethiopians, and three others were slain when the Ethiopian force stormed the building that had been their safe house in Addis Ababa. The Egyptian organization Jama'a al-Islamiya claimed responsibility for the assassination attempt against Mubarak.[3]

The attempted assassination in Ethiopia occurred after Egyptian security forces had dealt a heavy blow to the terror organizations mainly in the Cairo area and in the Delta region. According to one interpretation, the commanders of the Jama'a al-Islamiya transferred the terror action out of Egypt because they were unable to get to the president within the country.

About two months after the attempt the Egyptian daily *Al-Ahram* published new evidence that confirmed the involvement of the Sudanese regime in the assassination attempt. The newspaper published the pictures and names of eight of the nine Jama'a al-Islamiya members who participated in the attack. Those arrested disclosed that Mustafa Hamza, the commander of the Jama'a al-Islamiya's military branch, had planned the attack, instructed the Addis Ababa cell and provided its members with documents and money. Hamza, who had been sentenced to death twice in the past in Egypt, was given special treatment by the Sudanese authorities, and had infiltrated Egypt for the operational activities. Muhammad Srag, another terrorist, had succeeded in fleeing Ethiopia after the failed assassination attempt by using a Sudanese passport.[4]

Although the assassination attempt ultimately failed, its high level of operational planning is obvious. This type of campaign required precise planning for several months. An operational infrastructure had to be established in Addis Ababa that included safe houses and places of concealment for people, weaponry and vehicles. In addition, escape routes had to be planned and equipment, communication means, documentation and identification papers prepared. In the second stage the participants and their equipment had to be transferred from Sudan to Ethiopia. A thorough gathering of intelligence was essential for these preparations. As for the Egyptians, it is highly likely that the Egyptian intelligence had no advance information about the assassination attempt despite the terrorists' intricate and lengthy preparations. Had Egyptian authorities known about these intentions in advance, it is unlikely that they would have allowed Mubarak to leave for the conference in Ethiopia.

The Attacks in Kenya and Tanzania (August 7, 1998)[5]

Al Qaida itself perpetrated only a small number of attacks out of the many that were perpetrated by terror organizations affiliated with Sunni Islamic terror. Al Qaida, which for many years supported a long chain of terror organizations and Islamic terror cells, entered the direct activity related to attacks only after the official declaration regarding the foundation of the umbrella organization called "the Islamic Front for Jihad Against the Crusaders and Jews" (February 1998). From this point on, Al Qaida adopted a leading role in the perpetration of terror attacks, while previously the organization had been satisfied with the training and provision of operational and logistic aid for terror activities that were conducted independently by Islamic terror organizations and terror cells worldwide.

The African continent was chosen as the site for Al Qaida's first attacks because it was a relatively convenient spot for covert, terror activity due to the limited ability of the local security forces to keep a close eye on the preparations and Al Qaida activists who had arrived on the continent at the end of 1993. In addition, the easy passage to and from Africa and to countries on other continents, in combination with the lax level of security at U.S. Embassies in Africa, turned these embassies into attractive targets for Al Qaida attacks.

The first operations perpetrated by Al Qaida members were the suicide attacks at the U.S. Embassies in Kenya and Tanzania in August 1998. While these attacks were planned over a five-year period prior to their actual execution, the timing was chosen by the Al Qaida command in Afghanistan and was meant to demonstrate the Islamic Front's intention to realize its declarations and to lead the Jihad undertaken by Bin Laden at the time of its establishment and the announcement of the *fatwa* (the religious ruling) of February 1998. Al Qaida struck again in Kenya in November 2002, when it carried out attacks against Israeli targets in Mombassa (see subsequent elaboration).

On August 7, 1998, at 10:00 a.m., a car bomb carrying three-quarters of a ton of explosives was detonated next to the United States Embassy in Nairobi. The car was occupied by two suicide terrorists (one of whom, al Awli, survived because he had gotten out of the vehicle to pursue the embassy's guard who was fleeing). As a result of the explosion, 213 people were killed, the majority of whom were Kenyans, as well as a dozen American citizens who were embassy employees. Over 4,000 people were injured. Simultaneously, an additional suicide attack was perpetrated by the same organization near the U.S. Embassy in Dar A-Salaam in Tanzania, in which eleven people were killed and scores injured. These attacks signaled Al Qaida's intention to commit indiscriminate mass slaughter in attacks against American targets throughout the world, and reflected a characteristic modus operandi that would to be expressed subsequently in September 2001 in the United States.

The apprehension of a number of key activists in the terror network responsible for the planning and execution of the attacks led to a series of arrests and the preparation of a detailed charge sheet, which clearly assigned direct responsibility for the terror campaign in East Africa to the organization headed by Bin Laden. The investigation's findings offered a unique preliminary opportunity to observe closely the Al Qaida organization, thus providing in-depth view of its modus operandi.

The Attack in Kenya

The terror cell that perpetrated the attack in Nairobi was composed of a small nucleus of six to eight activists under the command of Fazul Abdallah Muhammad, an Al Qaida member born in the Comoro Islands.[6] The original plan had been to drive a car bomb into the embassy's underground parking, detonate it with the help of suicide drivers and bring the building down upon its inhabitants.[7] The terror team included three people who drove to their destination in two vehicles. The first car was driven by the mission commander and served as an escort vehicle for the car bomb. The second carried the two suicide bombers—the driver who committed suicide and his escort Rashed Daoud al Awali, who survived the attack, and after being apprehended was extradited by Kenya to the United States, where he was to stand trial. The car bomb driver, an Egyptian by origin, tried to enter the embassy's underground parking facility, but was unable to do so because of the Kenyan guard's refusal to open the embassy's gates. His attempt to circumvent the barrier was prevented by a car driving up from the underground parking area that blocked his way. Awali (the surviving suicide terrorist) threatened the guard and demanded that he open the gate, but when the latter refused, he lobbed a stun grenade at the guard and proceeded to run after him, moving away from the vehicle. The driver detonated the bomb in a compound containing three buildings, about ten meters away from the embassy wall. The explosion resulted in a large number of casualties and the collapse of several buildings near the embassy. The embassy building itself, the attack's main target, did not collapse although it was damaged.

Preliminary preparations for the attack already had begun in 1993.[8] Senior Al Qaida personnel including Bin Laden and his assistant, the military commander Abu-Hafez, participated in the planning. Preparations for the attack were divided into several stages: As noted, the first stage occurred in 1993 when Bin Laden conceived the idea and sent his representatives to Kenya. One of them was Muhammad Ali, a former sergeant in the U.S. military who subsequently served as a state's-witness in the trials of the attack perpetrators in Kenya and Tanzania held in New York, and who confessed that he had met with Bin Laden and given him photographs of the embassy in Nairobi. Bin Laden sent several emissaries to Kenya with the aim of learning the lay of the land. Some even married local women and took work enabling them to gather qualitative information about the potential targets, mainly the U.S. and Israeli embassies.

The second stage of preparations in anticipation of the attack was launched in May-June 1998 (about two months before the attack). The decision was made following Bin Laden's public declaration in an interview with ABC in which he threatened to perpetrate mega attacks against U.S. targets in retribution for the U.S.'s anti-Islamic policy. The practical preparations for the attack were administered from the network headquarters in the target country, the Top-Hill Hotel in Nairobi. Network members also rented a house in Nairobi where they hid the weapons: explosives, stun grenades, and handguns smuggled into Nairobi from the Middle East via the Comoro Islands. A short time prior to the attack, three cell members gathered intelligence about the U.S. Embassy in Nairobi, and when all the logistics were in place, the date for the attack was set.

Several days prior to the attack date most of the network members left Nairobi, with the exception of Harun Fazul, the team's commander, who escorted the car bomb with the suicide terrorists to the target in order to personally supervise the operation. After the explosion, Harun returned to the safe house to cover their tracks and then disappeared.

The Attack in Tanzania

On August 7, 1998, a car bomb exploded near the U.S. Embassy in Tanzania. Eleven people were killed in the explosion and about eight-five were wounded, all local residents. The Tanzanian cell contained six members and additional individuals, who assisted in the preparations for the attack in various stages of the planning.

The members of the team underwent training in Afghanistan in the course of 1994, and the cell was composed of a variety of nationalities including Kenyans, Tanzanians, and Egyptians.[9] With the help of local collaborators, the team members rented a private safe house two months before the attack. The house was located outside of the city and was used for storage of the car bomb (a van) and the purchased weapons. The van had been bought two months earlier and was rigged as a car bomb a short time before the attack.

The cell members collected preliminary information about the routine procedure for cars delivering water to the embassies, and took advantage of the information to attempt to infiltrate a car bomb into the embassy. The suicide bomber arrived separately in Dar-A-Salaam and was kept at a safe house. On the day of the attack, the suicide driver drove the car bomb to the embassy building and followed the water truck that arrived at its entrance. When the water truck was about to enter the premises, the car bomb drew up close and the suicide driver detonated the car, which was loaded with a quarter ton of explosives.[10]

The Terror Campaign in Kenya against Israeli Targets[11]

On November 28, 2002, a terror campaign was set into motion in Kenya against Israeli targets:

- A car bomb driven by terrorists exploded at the Paradise Hotel in Mombassa.
- Two Strella (SA-7) shoulder missiles were fired at an Arkia airplane immediately after takeoff but they missed their target.

Responsibility was claimed by an unknown organization called the Palestine Army.

The organization released an announcement via the Hizballah TV station Al-Manarin in which it stated that the attack had been perpetrated to commemorate the 55th anniversary of the UN partition resolution (the 29th of November). The announcement added that the organization's headquarters had decided that the entire world must hear of the suffering of the Palestinian refugees, and therefore it was decided to send a cell to Kenya with the aim of attacking Israeli targets. The message ended with a statement that the attacks had gone according to plan. The leader of the Islamic Organization "Al-Muhajrun" in London, Omar al Bakhri, stated that during the week preceding the attack the organization had issued a warning in chat sites on the Internet that an attack was about to be launched against Israeli targets in Kenya. In an interview with the Al-Jazeera TV network, Bakhri said "our sources are based on open forums on the Internet." According to Bakhri the message was as follows: "Brothers, you will receive good news during the last twenty days of the month of Ramadan," and it was also stated that the target would be in East Africa.

On December 2, 2002, responsibility was claimed via publication in several Internet sites affiliated with Al Qaida al-Jihad. It would appear that it was Al Qaida that was claiming responsibility although the style differed in its characteristics from earlier claims of responsibility issued by that organization.[12] The announcement, which was particularly long and was worded in the organization's characteristic style, also stated that the attacks in Mombassa were aimed at "eradicating all of the dreams of the Jewish-Crusader alliance, meant to preserve their strategic interests in the region." The mission was meant to deal an additional blow to the Israeli Mossad, like the blows that struck the synagogue in Djerba in the past. The announcement went on to say that both attacks, the attack at the Paradise Hotel and the attempt to shoot down the Arkia plane, "were meant to clarify to Muslims all over the world that the mujahidin stand by their brethren in Palestine and continue in their path." The announcement also referred to the Jewish-American connection, saying that the attack was in retaliation for "the conquest of our holy sites" and Israeli acts in Palestine. "For killing our children, we will kill yours, for our elderly we will kill your elderly, and for our homes your turrets" (see the full version of the claiming of responsibility by Al Qaida for the attacks in Mombassa in Appendix B).

With the aim of justifying the attack, in which many Kenyan citizens were killed, Al Qaida appealed to the citizens of Kenya and all of Africa as follows:

> Ultimately these two actions are meant to declare that the nation, including its Arab and non-Arab sons, the black and white ones, stood as one and faced this enemy and this assault that was declared against the Muslims. We call upon our dark-skinned brothers on this continent, the peoples that have suffered most from Colonialism, which stole their lands, robbed their countries, turned them into slaves and deprived them of their basic human rights, that they follow in the footsteps of the heroes of the two missions in Mombassa and turn the land into hell under the conquering feet of the Jews and Crusaders.

The Attack at the Paradise Hotel

On the morning of November 28, 2002, some 200 Israeli tourists landed at the Mombassa Airport, Kenya. They disembarked from an Arkia charter flight, and passed through the various inspections and border control. They boarded two buses and five minibuses, which took them to the Paradise Mombassa Hotel some 35 kilometers north of the city, where they were to spend the Hanukkah vacation.

It appears that already during the journey to the hotel, a green Mitsubishi Pajero jeep was following the convoy. After disembarking from the buses, the Israeli tourists registered at the hotel and most went to their rooms. At about 7:30 a.m., a Landrover jeep burst through the hotel's security gate. According to eyewitnesses, hotel employees and the Kenyan Police, there were three passengers in the jeep. One passenger jumped out of the jeep at a run, entered the reception area, and detonated the explosive charge that he was carrying on his body. At the same time, the two other passengers detonated the booby-trapped jeep, which was carrying 200 kilograms of explosives and gas balloons.[13] A Kalachnikov was found in the jeep's wreckage.

Thirteen people were killed in the attack: three Israelis, and ten Kenyans, including dancers from a dance troupe that received the Israeli tourists at the entrance to the hotel. According to the various reports, sixty to eighty people were injured in the attack, including some twenty Israelis.

The Firing of Missiles at the Arkia Plane

Several minutes after the attack at the Paradise Hotel (shortly after 7:30 a.m.) two shoulder missiles were launched at Arkia flight 582, which was taking off from Mombassa on its way to Israel. The missiles missed the aircraft thus causing no damage. There were 261 passengers on board in addition to ten crewmembers.

About a minute and a half after takeoff, at a height of 3,000 feet, the passengers felt a thump against the aircraft's hull. Immediately afterwards, the flash of two missiles was identified near the aircraft. Crewmembers rushed to report to the security team on land, and the latter searched the area in an attempt to locate the missile launchers. Two missile launchers and two additional S.A. 7 (Strella) missiles were found hidden among the bushes outside of the airport's perimeter, at a distance of several hundred meters from the fence.

According to U.S. sources, the missiles found in Mombassa were from the same series and production line as the missiles fired by Al Qaida at an American military plane in Saudi Arabia earlier in May 2002.[14] Searches carried out by the police investigators in the area where the missiles were fired indicated that the attack had been perpetrated from a hill with an excellent vantage point of the airport and particularly the takeoff areas, which had made the operation easier for the attackers. It was fortunate that they missed the plane they were aiming for as the attack occurred during what is considered the vulnerable point of a flight—takeoff.

The Strella is a relatively outmoded missile that was developed about 30 years ago. It is used by armies and guerrilla organizations and it is known that various groups in Africa also have some in their possession. The Strella homes in on heat. It is usually adjusted according to the heat waves emanating from the plane's engines or its landing and takeoff lights. The missile's effective range is defined at four to six kilometers; its flight velocity is 580 meters per second, and its warhead's weight ranges between 1 kilogram and 1.2 kilograms. The missile is considered uncomplicated to operate and in regular circumstances its ability to hit a passenger plane during takeoff—which is considered an easy target—is relatively high.

The attempt to down the Arkia plane in Mombassa, Kenya, is not the first time that terrorists have tried to fire shoulder missiles at Israeli aircraft, and it is also not the first attempt to be made in Kenya. In 1969, a Palestinian cell was apprehended in Rome, with shoulder missiles in its possession, whose intention was to shoot down an El Al plane. The cell was caught due to prior information obtained in a joint operation of Italian security forces and the Mossad. In the 1970s, two Germans who had been planning to shoot shoulder missiles at an El Al plane were caught in Nairobi, Kenya's capital. The Germans, who were affiliated with left-wing terror organizations in Germany, were extradited to Israel, tried, and imprisoned, but were released several years later.

An investigation of the attacks in Mombassa indicates that the mastermind behind them was Al Qaida senior activist, Harun al Fazul (Fazul Abdallah Muhammad) who was also behind the 1998 attack against the U.S. Embassy. Kenyan authorities arrested five men suspected of involvement in the attack. The five stood trial in June 2003.[15]

Additional Intentions to Perpetrate Attacks in Kenya

In the course of 2003, the U.S. and British intelligence agencies received warnings regarding Al Qaida's intentions to perpetrate additional attacks in Kenya. Thus, in May 2003, due to these warnings El Al and British Airways flights to Kenya were stopped.[16] In June 2003, the U.S. Embassy in Kenya was closed after warnings were received that Al Qaida was planning to attack the embassy by crashing an airplane into the building.[17] In the wake of this threat, Kenya sealed off its airspace to flights from Somalia and banned the flight of small aircraft from local airports in Kenya (flights from the international airport in Nairobi continued undisrupted). Due to the low level of security in Kenya, the U.S. and Britain considered closing their embassies there in 2003, and recommended that their citizens refrain from visiting that country.

Despite efforts made by the Kenyan authorities to improve security arrangements in their country and enhance the supervision over individuals suspected of involvement in terror, it appears that Kenya continues to constitute a relatively convenient arena for Al Qaida terror for several reasons:

- A large and poor Muslim community from which volunteers can easily be recruited to perpetrate attacks;
- The limited supervision and thwarting capabilities of the Kenyan authorities;
- The long and vulnerable border between Kenya and Somalia, which serves as a safe haven for Islamic terror entities.

Moreover, an investigation of the 1998 attack in Nairobi and the attacks perpetrated in Mombassa, Kenya, in 2002 indicated that a senior Al Qaida activist named Harun al Fazul (as mentioned earlier) had commanded the perpetrators of these attacks. Al Fazul has yet to be apprehended despite the fact that he is one of the most wanted terrorists in the world and continues to plan attacks in the East African arena. His personal story largely reflects the inherent potential ease with which the East African Muslim population can be recruited into the ranks of fundamentalist Islam.

Al Fazul was born in the Comoro Islands in East Africa and studied at a *Madrasa* (an Islamic school) funded by Saudi Arabia. At the age of sixteen, he was granted a study scholarship for the Wahabian Madrasa in Pakistan, and upon completing his studies there he moved to neighboring Afghanistan and joined Al Qaida. After intensive training at the camps in Afghanistan, he returned to East Africa, organized Al Qaida cells in various countries in that region and served as commander of the organization's attacks in this area.

Many activists like al Fazul serve in the ranks of Al Qaida; these men were educated according to radical Islamic schools of thought and have linked their fates to the struggle of radical Islam against its enemies. These activists work to establish infrastructures, as well as to recruit activists and supporters for Al Qaida and similar organizations, and the poor Islamic population of East Africa serves as a resource for the recruitment and activation of volunteers into the organization's ranks.

As an expression of the revised policies of Yemen and Sudan following the U.S. declaration regarding the global war on terror, the presidents of Yemen, Sudan, and Ethiopia convened a summit meeting in Addis Ababa on December 20, 2003, in which they decided to increase cooperation in order to eradicate terror and bring about peace for the countries in the region.

Notes

1. Nahman Tal, *A Confrontation at Home—Egypt and Jordanian Handling of Radical Islam*, Tel Aviv University: Papyrus Publications, 1999, p. 154.
2. This section is based on Nahman Tal, *A Confrontation at Home—Egypt and Jordanian Handling of Radical Islam*, pp. 78-80.
3. *Ha'aretz*, June 26, 1995.
4. Ibid.
5. This chapter is based on Yoram Schweitzer and Shaul Shay, *The Globalization of Terror*, The Multidisciplinary Center, Herzliya: Mifalot Publishing, 2003, and New Brunswick, NJ: Transaction Publishers, 2003.
6. Yosef Bodansky, *Bin Laden—The Man Who Declared War on America*, New York: Forum, 2001, p. 263.

7.   Ibid.
8.   Ibid., p. 223.
9.   Peter L. Bergen, *Holy War Inc.—Inside the Secret World of Osama Bin Laden*, London: Weidenfeld & Nicolson, 2001, p. 118.
10.   Ibid., p. 119.
11.   This section is based on articles in the *Ha'aretz*, *Yediot Aharonot*, and *Ma'ariv* newspapers between the dates November 29 and December 5, 2002.
12.   *Ha'aretz*, December 3, 2002.
13.   *Yediot Aharonot*, December 2, 2002, quoting Minister of Defense Shaul Mofaz.
14.   *Ha'aretz*, December 3, 2002.
15.   AP Nairobi, July 8, 2003.
16.   Reported by CNN from Nairobi, June 22, 2003.
17.   Ibid.

Part V

Theoretical Analysis and Conclusions

7

The Islamic Terror Triangle—Comparative Aspects

A comparative view of the three countries—Sudan, Somalia, and Yemen—that are the focus of this study indicates several similar geopolitical and social components, along with evident disparities between the various countries. Following is a description of the similar elements from the geopolitical and social points of view:

Islam

In all three countries, the majority of the population is Muslim, but in Sudan a significant Christian minority exists in the south, which is embroiled in perpetual conflict with the country's Muslim majority. In Sudan and Yemen, the Sharia constitutes state law. In Somalia, due to the absence of an effective central government ("a failing state"), this is not clearly indicated, but in circles with Islamic orientation, the Sharia serves as the legal basis together with the secular laws and legal system, on the one hand, and tribal laws on the other.

Yemen, situated in the southern part of the Arabian Peninsula, and due to its proximity to the cradle of Islam, was the first of the three countries to adopt Islam. The Sudanese population adopted Islam because of the influence of its neighbors in the Arabian Peninsula and Egypt; but the spread of Islam was blocked in the southern area of Sudan due to the fact that the local population embraced Christianity, which had subsisted under the patronage of the colonial powers. The Somali population was the last to accept Islam.

In the course of history these three countries (or more precisely, the areas in which these countries were founded) were located at the edges of the Muslim empire and were far from its religious centers. Yemen was always overshadowed by its "big sister" Saudi Arabia, which had the unique historical role of serving as the cradle of Islam and guardian of the holy sites; thus, the spreading of Islam in Yemen was affected by developments in the Arabian Peninsula, rather than vice versa. Sudan was the only one of the three countries to aspire historically to become a guiding and influential factor in the dissemination of Islam. The era of the revolution and the Mahdi monarchy in Sudan constituted a historical milestone and a central formative factor in the development of Islam in this country. The Mahdi and, subsequently, Hassan al Turabi were Sudan's most prominent religious leaders and they have been granted significant importance in the Muslim world. The Mahdi's monarchy and the success of his struggle against the colonial powers (despite its temporary nature) have served as a source of inspiration and a model for emulation throughout history for many Islamic leaders and philosophers.

Sudan regarded itself as a bridge between the Arab world and Africa, and as a basis for disseminating Islam on this continent. Hassan al Turabi was the most prominent standard-bearer representing this approach. Thus, Sudan was actively involved in the dissemination of Islam, and these actions constituted the background for some of Sudan's conflicts with its close neighbors and more distant states, as well as the civil war raging in that country between the Muslim north and the Christian south.

Somalia's history testifies to the relatively low significance of the Islamic religious factor in the equation of power and the country's political development. Islam is admittedly one of the few factors that represent a common denominator for the majority of this country's population, but this shared determinant cannot suffice to unite and consolidate it into an effective state-oriented entity.

Foreign (Colonial) Rule

Sudan, Somalia, and Yemen were granted complete independence in the 1950s and 1960s. In the course of history, the areas where these states were founded were placed under the control of global and regional powers. Those years of foreign rule, and particularly the struggle against it, left their stamp on the historical narrative of these countries, and sometimes became the determining experience in the formation of national identity. The most salient example of this phenomenon is Sudan and the struggle of the Mahdi against the British colonial rule.

The encounter with the "controlling, exploitative and more powerful" Western culture generated feelings of hostility, frustration, and
hatred, which found political expression in the form of national liberation movements and religious organizations presenting Islam as
a solution and the proper alternative to replace Western culture, whose
most conspicuous colonial representative in the region was Britain
(Sudan—British rule; Yemen—British rule; Somalia—British and Italian rule under British dominance).

The colonial rule did not contribute to the development of institutions and government mechanisms according to the format of Western democracies, nor did it create an effective administrative infrastructure. Therefore, a short time after achieving independence,
these three countries became embroiled in political, social, and
economic crises as well as perpetual political instability. The end
of colonialism and the formation of a bi-polar world characterized by the struggle between the communist and democratic-
Western ideologies also left their mark on these countries. The various regimes in the three countries alternately adopted these rival
ideologies and accordingly shifted their internal and external political leanings:

- *Sudan*—An (unstable) democratic government in its first years, Al
  Numeiri's socialist regime in the beginning of his career, a pro-Western regime subsequently followed by Islamic rule, and an Islamic regime during the terms of al Beshir and al Turabi.
- *Yemen*—Two states were founded in the beginning of the 1960s, one a
  conservative monarchy and the other with socialist leanings, and the
  adversity between them evolved into a civil war with the external
  involvement of Egypt, Saudi Arabia, and other countries.
- *Somalia*—Ziad Barre's tyrannical regime, initially with pro-Soviet
  leanings, followed by Western leanings.

The transition from one ideological concept to another was accompanied by attempts to introduce political, economical and social
reforms, which deepened the internal rifts and schisms within the
societies in these countries.

As a result of these processes one may observe the development
of unstable political systems, in which the rules of the game were
usually established forcefully (coup d'états, brutal suppression of
the opposition, civil wars). When temporary stability was achieved
(albeit sometimes over a prolonged period), it was always obtained
by a tyrannical regime, even when it attempted to present itself as a

democratic government (I refer you to the regimes of Abud, al Numeiri and al Beshir in Sudan, Salah's regime in Yemen, and Ziad Barre's regime in Somalia.)

Civil War

The colonial inheritance of countries with a heterogeneous population involved in historical and contemporary rivalry; the lack of governmental institutions and effective, legitimate bureaucratic systems in the eyes of the population; and the violent means that the various regimes utilized in their attempts to contend with the fundamental problems in their countries were factors that led to the outbreak of civil wars in the three countries.

- *Sudan*—The civil war between the Muslim north and the Christian south which aspired to achieve independence or at least autonomy;
- *Yemen*—The civil war between the monarchial north and the socialist south in the 1960s, and an additional war in the beginning of the 1990s due to the south's attempt to secede from the north;
- *Somalia*—The civil war since the beginning of the 1990s after the collapse of Ziad Barre's regime.

In each of the three countries the civil wars yielded different results:

- *In Sudan*—The civil war has raged from the time of this country's establishment to date (although negotiations are currently underway and some agreements have been signed to achieve a resolution), and this has affected the government's stability. However, despite the prolonged war, an effective regime exists in Khartoum, which controls most of the state's area, albeit with certain restrictions.
- *In Yemen*—The civil war ended in the 1990s with the north's victory, and the country remained united under the central government of President Salah;
- *In Somalia*—The civil war destroyed the political and governmental frameworks; currently there is no effective central government in Somalia and it is defined as a "failing state."

Admittedly, only in Somalia did the political machine collapse as the result of the civil war; however, in the south of Sudan and also in Yemen there are areas that are not under full governmental control, which can be included in the category of "UGRs" (Ungovernable Regions).

Legitimization of Terror

In each of these countries, state legitimization of terror activity on its soil is indicated. The ties and links with terror organizations have changed throughout history according to the ideological and political leanings of the regime.

- *Sudan*—In the 1960s and the 1970s, Sudan supported Palestinian terror organizations and national liberation movements on the African continent. Since 1989, with the ascent of the Islamic regime in Sudan, the country has supported Islamic terror organizations.
- *Yemen*—In the 1960s, terror and guerrilla organizations, mainly in southern Yemen, fought the British presence. After South Yemen won its independence and adopted Marxist leanings, it hosted terror organizations with left-wing leanings as well as Palestinian terror organizations. After Yemen's consolidation, Islamic terror entities were supported by radical Islamic circles in the country, with the government turning a blind eye to their presence and activities.
- *Somalia*—In the 1960s and 1970s, Somalia aided terror organizations and national liberation movements that were involved in clashes with its neighbors, particularly the struggle against Ethiopia over control of Ogaden. After the collapse of Ziad Barre's government and the outbreak of the civil war, ties and links were generated between the rival factions and the terror organizations. Particularly prominent was the link between the Islamic terror organizations, including Al Qaida, and Aidid's camp.

In all three countries attempts were made to cooperate with terror organizations and to activate them in order to promote the interests of the country. Sudan appears to be the most noteworthy in this area, as both in the past and in the present it has used Islamic terror organizations to export the Islamic revolution. Since the time of the unification of its government, Yemen was not involved in the encouragement or initiation of terror activities, but it also did not take steps to prevent them, thus turning into a haven and a stopover for terror activists, particularly from the ranks of the Islamic organizations. The United States' declaration of its war against terror and the fears of the Yemenite government that it might be vulnerable to attack motivated it to cooperate with the United States. Somalia made relatively minimal use of terror organizations, mainly in connection with its struggle over the control of Ogaden. After the collapse of the Barre regime and the outbreak of the civil war, Somalia, lacking a central government, became a "failing state," thus becoming a host for various terror organizations, which have gained the protection of the various rival powerbrokers in the country.

Conflict and Controversy with Neighboring States

Each of the three countries in this study is embroiled in controversy and confrontations with its neighbors:

- *Sudan*—A border dispute with Egypt over the Hala'ib-Shalatin region, which has plentiful amounts of oil, and tension due to Sudan's support of Islamic terror organizations acting against the administration in Cairo (the climax in this regard was the assassination attempt against President Mubarak in Addis Ababa);

    —A dispute with Ethiopia, Uganda, and Eritrea against the background of their support for the Christian rebels in the south.

- *Yemen*—A border dispute with Saudi Arabia and controversy related to the Saudi monarchy's pro-Western approach (during the first Gulf War, Yemen supported Iraq, but as noted previously, today the former has adopted a more pro-Western position);

    —A border conflict with Eritrea over the control of several islands at Bab-al Mandeb (this dispute is currently in arbitration at the International Court at the Hague);

- *Somalia*—A border conflict with Ethiopia, which flared into an all out war (the Ogaden War), and currently a conflict related to Ethiopia's involvement in internal disputes in Somalia between rival actions.

    —Conflicts with Kenya and Djibouti due to their involvement in internal conflicts in Somalia.

Summary

In this chapter we reviewed the similar processes that shaped the development of the three countries at the heart of this study. In summary, it is possible to indicate five central issues that influenced the development of their approach towards the issue of terror:

1. Islam (radical)
2. A history of colonial suppression and the struggle against it
3. Civil wars
4. Legitimizing the use of terror
5. Conflicts and confrontations with neighboring countries.

As a result of the combination of these components, and because of the political and social circumstances in each of these countries, they became a source of anxiety for the West due to the fact that they served as a focus for activities of the radical Islamic terror organizations, and particularly for Al Qaida. The potential and real threat presented by these countries as a characterized group and as separate units calls for an attempt to study the phenomenon on the conceptual level and from the comprehensive point of view; these matters will be addressed in the following section.

Figure 7.1
Common Characteristics in the "Terror Triangle" States

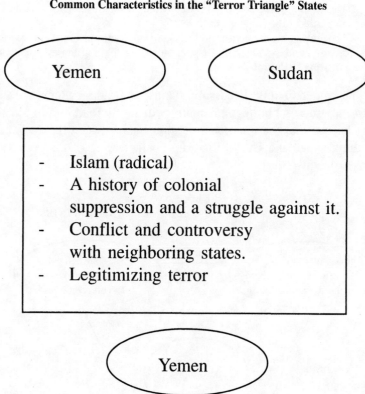

Intercultural Conflicts, "Failing States" and Al Qaida—Reciprocal Links

This section assesses the joint characteristics that arose from the analysis of the philosophical and conceptual aspects the three countries. The objective of this study is to explore the links and reciprocal relationships between the three phenomena or processes specified below:

1.   The intercultural conflict between the state-oriented culture and the nomadic culture;
2.   The intercultural conflict between radical Islam and other cultures, particularly the Western culture;
3.   The link and connection between the intercultural conflicts and the creation and existence of the phenomena of "Failing States" and "Ungovernable Regions" (UGRs).

At the center of this discussion stands Al Qaida—which according, to the study's claim, represents both the nomadic culture and radical Islam—and the reciprocal relationships between the Al Qaida and failing states and UGRs (that are characteristic of the countries discussed in this study).

Figure 7.2
Reciprocal Links between Al Qaida, Failing States, and UGRs

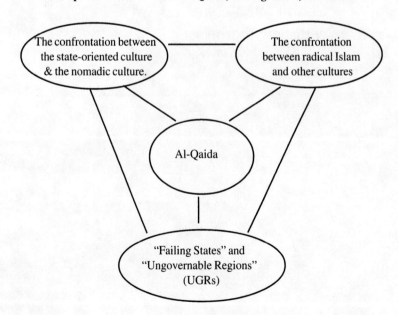

Failing States and Ungovernable Regions (UGRs)

Failing states and ungovernable regions have become a current issue on the agendas of politicians, military personnel, and academia in the West, due the crystallization of the understanding that these states and regions have turned into significant threats to the security and interests of the West. Two central threats have positioned these phenomena at the center of international interest:

- International terror
- International crime

The reality of the twenty-first century has taught us that these two non state-oriented elements—international terror and crime—have turned the failing states and the UGRs into havens and activity bases from which they can promote their interests in regional and global spaces.

During the years of the hegemony of the national-countries, states developed political, military, and economic patterns, which were relevant and effective for contact between states and state blocs in the international framework. However, the international terror organizations and the criminal organizations posed new challenges to the national-countries and served as a provocation against the main component of the state-oriented entity—the monopoly over the use of force. International terror and crime act as networks with global dispersion, while the failing states and UGRs constitute the main infrastructure's focal points and bases for action. Due to the lack of an effective central government in these places, the organizations' activities are unrestricted and they also receive support and protection from powerbrokers and local interested parties with whom they form alliances and ties.

International terror and criminal organizations do not view territory as an asset of moral significance, but rather as a basis which may be temporary and can be swapped with other territories according to evolving circumstances. To a large extent, it is possible to define these organizations as entities with a "nomadic" worldview that clearly challenges the state-oriented entity and its values. As stated earlier, the area of the failing state or the UGR serves as a refuge for criminal and terror organizations; however, sometimes it also serves as an arena of confrontation and rivalry vis-à-vis "alien" state-oriented entities acting in the same arena or as a base for attacking neighboring countries. In order for Western Countries to provide solutions to these challenges confrontation is necessary on two levels:

1.   Confronting the terror or criminal organization;
2.   Confronting the regime or powerbrokers that offer refuge to these entities.

Providing an adequate response necessitates the handling of both levels simultaneously as well as preparation for confronting the regional and global alignment of these organizations, which exceeds the boundaries of the failing state or of the UGR.

Failing States

Failing states stem from the collapse of the governmental and political structure in the country and the state's inability to enforce law and order. The process is initiated and accompanied by manifestations of anarchy and forms of violence. Former secretary-general of the UN Butrus Ghali described this phenomenon as follows:[1]

> A feature of such conflicts is the collapse of state institutions, especially the police and the judiciary, with resulting paralysis of governance, a breakdown of law and order, and general banditry and chaos. Not only are the functions of the government suspended, but its assets are destroyed or looted and experienced officials are killed or flee the country. This is rarely the case in inter-state wars. It means that international intervention must extend beyond military and humanitarian tasks and must include the reestablishment of effective government.

The state not only lacks an effective government; the situation includes the collapse of the systems that comprise the state entity. Therefore, the term "failing states" actually refers to countries that have disintegrated. The term failing state addresses a relatively wide range of situations and serves as the starting point for various interpretations vis-à-vis the phenomenon (legal, political, sociological, etc.). The main political and judicial aspects characteristic of a failing state are:

•   The collapse of the government systems, i.e., disintegration of the central government and the other mechanisms that comprise the state institutions (the judicial system, law enforcement authorities, the economic system, and more), and disintegration processes according to segmentation and cross-sectioning that characterize the society and its political system (interest groups, ethnic and religious groups, etc.), that generate internal conflicts within the country's territorial boundaries;

- The collapse of lawful government, meaning not only disintegration processes, but also the disobeying of laws and the lack of ability to enforce them;
- Loss of the ability to represent the state as a uniform entity within the international system for the purpose of presenting its positions and negotiating with external states and entities.

From the sociological aspect, the failing state is characterized by what sociologist Max Weber calls "loss of the monopoly over power."[2] In this type of reality, the legal system, the police, and other entities that serve in the role of maintaining law and order stop functioning or cease to exist. These entities may join various armed groups or criminal elements that take over the state infrastructures and resources for their own needs and establish a "government" of their own within various regions and populations in the state. This process may be described as a kind of "privatization" of the state, or in certain cases—as criminalization. In this type of situation the state ceases to exist and society reverts to a status of pre-state chaos.

Another central sociological characteristic of a failing state is the brutality and the intensity of violence within the society. To quote Arnold Gehlen:

> The immediate effect is that the persons concerned become profoundly insecure. The moral and spiritual centers are disoriented because, there too, the certainty of self-evident has foundered. Thus, penetrating to the very core of their being, insecurity forces people to improvise, compelling them to make decisions contre coeur or to plunge blindfolded into the realms of uncertainty, perhaps seeking at any price fundamentals to cling to and give them a sense of purpose. In practice, moreover, insecurity is manifested in the form of fear, defiance or volatility. The effect is to place a heavy burden of control and decision-making on those layers of the personality where life should be lived problem-free amidst the self-evident and the given if people are to be capable of dealing with more demanding situations. In other words, displacement that people suffer due to the shattering of their institutions is expressed as primitivization."[3]

From a legal point of view it is possible to claim that a failing state is an entity defined as a "state" but in practical terms lacks the ability to function as a state entity. A central component of this phenomenon is the lack of a functionary capable of signing agreements with external factors or of actually implementing them.

Examination of a failing state indicates a similarity in its historical development:

- Colonial occupation that destroyed the traditional social and political structures but failed to incorporate an effective structural and political alternative according to the Western model.

- The Cold War inspired the superpowers to support and reinforce corrupt and ineffective regimes due to considerations related to loyalty within the inter-bloc struggle. After the collapse of the Soviet Union and the end of the Cold War, many of these regimes crumbled, leaving political and social chaos in their wake.
- Modernization processes that encouraged geopolitical and social mobility but were not balanced by the building processes of the nation and the nation-state.

Although today the number of failing states is relatively low, some of the countries that were granted independence after the collapse of the Soviet Union are gradually joining this category, so there is a fear that this is not simply a marginal phenomenon but rather a "pathological" trend of a changing environment and international system.

Robert Bunker[4] points out a cyclical process in human history of order and chaos that alternate with each other. He claims that the process of institutionalizing nation-states and enhancing law and order in Western states began with the Westphalia peace compact (in 1648), while the current era is characterized by a change in direction from order to chaos, an era that challenges the nation-state as a regulator of social order.

Historical experience indicates that when the internal violence in a nation-state, which can be described as criminal activity or "a private war," grows to a level that threatens the population of the nation-state, this entity may collapse if it does not succeed in suppressing the anarchy.[5] The international reality in the current century points to a decline in the status of the nation-state's status as an entity that regulates and organizes social and political systems in parts of Africa, South America, Asia and areas that were part of the Soviet Union.[6] Bunker maintains that the threat against the nation state will rise from non-state actors:[7] "The challenge to the legitimacy of the nation state will come from armed non-state actors intent on legitimizing forms of behavior that current societies consider to be criminally or morally corrupt." Based on historical experience, Bunker claims that entities currently defined as criminal and non-legitimate elements according to our normative standards may triumph in the struggle with the state entity and form political entities which in time will constitute a substitute for today's normative systems and ultimately replace them and gain legitimacy.[8] As the result of the social and political processes described above, the nature of the confrontation also changes. The declared wars between the military forces of the nation state steadily decrease, and we witness the development of new forms of war.

In his article "Privatization of War in the Twenty-First Century," Herfried Muenkler argues that in the 1950s and 1960s many new nations joined the international system that did not succeed in obtaining control when managing war and imposing peace, as European states have achieved since the seventeenth century. Thus, internal conflict (civil wars) became a characteristic trait of countries that were established on the ruins of colonial powers, not only in the Third World but also in Europe itself (the Balkans).

Thus, it is possible to infer that war is no longer waged between countries and armies, but rather there are more and more conflicts in which sections of the population defined socially, ethnically or religiously fight against one another. In this situation, partisans or gangs, warlords as well as groups of international mercenaries, are the main players. The result of this development is the loss of the state's monopoly and a process of "privatization of war." This concept indicates that in the future there will be war between competitive groups on a social and cultural basis, and less on the basis of state interests.[9] This type of reality currently typifies failing states, but Bunker points out the inherent threat in the development of violent groups in the United States and the West, such as terror groups or gangs that deal in criminal activity. Based on the assumption that the future threat against the nation-state will stem from the generation of alternative organizations that will undermine the state's monopoly on strength, the latter must formulate organizational frames and operational patterns that will enable adequate defense against internal and external rivals.

Ungovernable Regions

The term "ungovernable region" is an amorphous term that generally refers to a region where there is no established government enforcing law and order or if a government exists it substantially differs from the governmental and administrative structure customary in the international system (from the "Western point of view"). In contrast to the term failing state, which relates to a state entity, the UGR may exist within a state where an effective government prevails in most of its territory, with the exception of a region or regions that are uncontrollable.

In recent years "remote" or undeveloped areas with a weak and ineffective central government have become a focal point for the West and the international system. Up to the twentieth century these areas, called UGRs, aroused only minimal interest in the international system, but today the combination of UGRs and the development of the media and modern technologies have turned these regions into major threats against the West and the international system because they have become a haven for international terror and criminal elements and a source that undermines the stability in the vicinity of their own boundaries as well as overseas.

These regions can be characterized as having:

- he lack of a central power capable of enforcing law and order throughout the country or at least in a significant part of its area;
- A backward economic and technological infrastructure;
- The lack of an effective administrative system;
- External powerbrokers acting within the state directly or through internal proxies;[10]
- Internal powerbrokers (proxies) generally involved in ongoing conflicts;
- Complex reciprocal links between the exogenic (external) and endogenic (internal) powerbrokers, which decrease the possibility of forming an integrative and stable government;[11]
- The state or the UGR itself involved in conflict with some of the neighboring countries;

As stated earlier, the UGR constitutes a confrontation arena for internal and external actors. The internal actors can be classified in several main categories:

- Violent powerbrokers fighting each other for control of the territory, the population, and the resources;
- Terror organizations exploiting the UGR's area for the construction of an infrastructure and terror activity outside of their territory;
- Terror organizations that make use of the territory and resources mainly for the purpose of activities in external markets;
- Ethnic, political, religious, tribal and other groups struggling for the distribution of the political power and resources in the UGR.

These actors maintain a reciprocal relationship based on the interests of the various sides, while forming coalitions and alliances that struggle against each other. These endogenic actors create external threats against both their immediate and distant environments, in matters related to international crime, drugs and terror.

The terms failing state and ungovernable region both refer to situations in which the governmental structure ceases to function in the entire state or part of it. The term failing state usually refers to a complete deterioration of the state and its institutions, while the term ungovernable region refers to a region within the state territory in which the central government has lost control but no new state substitute has been formed and a chaotic state prevails. Thus, it is possible to state that the UGR constitutes part of the disintegration process of the nation state. There are historical examples of UGRs that did not spread and the parallel existence of the nation-state functioning in other areas remained feasible, but in most cases the creation of the UGR constitutes an expression of a disintegration process that causes the ultimate deterioration of the country into the chaotic status of a failing state.

This study is focusing on three countries (Sudan, Yemen, and Somalia) which in various stages of their history (after receiving independence) had the status of a failing state or various areas of their territories became UGRs. The most salient example of a failing state is Somalia since the ousting of Ziad Barre in 1991. In contrast, both Yemen and Sudan show indications of UGRs; however, both states currently have relatively stable although weak governments.

"Islam and the Rest of the World"—The Conflict between Radical Islam and Western Cultures

Samuel Huntington claims that the source of the conflicts in the world at the end of the twentieth century and at the beginning of the twenty-first century is not ideological or economic, but first and foremost cultural. Huntington claims that up until the end of the Cold War the modern world was under the dominance of Western culture, and most of the significant clashes took place in the framework of this culture, or as he terms it "western civil wars."[12]

With the end of the Cold War, the international political system liberated itself of Western dominance, and the center of gravity shifted to reciprocal ties and conflicts between the West and non-Western cultures and between non-Western cultures among themselves. From this stage onwards the peoples and countries associated with Western civilizations ceased to be influenced upshots and victims of Western colonialism, and they became active and dominant partners in the propulsion and formation of history. During the Cold War it was acceptable to categorize the world according to the political systems and the technological/economical development of the countries (developed countries, undeveloped countries, first-world, second-world, third-world, etc.). Huntington believes that today countries must be classified in terms of civilizations or cultures, while defining civilization as follows:[13]

> A civilization is the highest cultural grouping of people and the broadest level of cultural identity people have short of that which distinguishes humans from others.

Civilization is defined via objective components such as language, history, religion, customs, and institutions, as well as subjective components such as self-definition or identification of the individual and the group; thus, it is possible to state that the civilization with which the individual identifies is the one that for him constitutes the widest and deepest level of solidarity.

Huntington counts eight central civilizations in the modern world: Western, Selb, Chinese-Confucian, Japanese, Hindu, Latino-American, Islamic, and African. Huntington argues that the Islamic civilization is the most militant among the various civilizations in our era, and that it is involved in an inherent conflict with Western culture as well as other cultures. He also points out the conflict's historic roots starting from the period of the crusades, through the Ottoman Empire and Western colonialism, up to the liberation wars of Muslim states.

A quick glance at the map of conflicts worldwide provides convincing support for Huntington's claims, as from Africa to the islands of the Pacific Ocean, Islam is involved in violent conflicts at contact or friction points with other civilizations (known as "fault line wars"). Despite the fact that political reality appears to bear out Huntington's general concept, it is still advisable to criticize and qualify some of his arguments. Huntington takes a comprehensive and sweeping approach when presenting all of the Muslim states as an Islamic cultural bloc pitting itself against Western and other cultures. However, a closer examination of the regimes in the majority of Muslim countries indicates that most of them are secular regimes or administrations with pragmatic and moderate Islamic orientation. These countries are not involved in conflict with the West. On the contrary, they have adopted the "bandwagon" approach and have joined the "modernization convoy" by adopting Western technologies, values, and lifestyles. Huntington does not differentiate between this central trend in the Muslim world and Fundamentalist Islamic trends. These movements have admittedly adopted the battle cry of the struggle against Western civilization, but they still constitute a minority in the Muslim world, albeit a militant one.

Consequently, the Muslim world is involved in a profound and harsh internal cultural conflict vis-à-vis the nature and direction of Muslim society; the results of this internal struggle currently dictate and will subsequently dictate the nature of the connections between Islamic culture and Western as well as other cultures. Regimes in many Muslim states have not only adopted the patterns of Western culture, but also rely on military, political, and economic aid from the West in order to sustain their existence.

The radical Islamic trends exist and operate in varying degrees of intensity and violence in all Muslim states as well as in some other countries identified with different cultures (China, the Philippines, Serbia, India, and more), in which they act to achieve independence for Muslim minorities. The objective of these entities is to establish religious Islamic states in Muslim countries while replacing secular regimes, and to achieve independence for Muslim communities in countries where they constitute a minority in order to establish new Islamic states.

Thus, radical Islam is involved in struggles against foreign cultures on four levels:

1. The replacement of secular regimes with Islamic regimes in Muslim countries;
2. The struggle of Muslim minorities to achieve independence and establish independent Islamic states;
3. The struggle against ethnic/cultural minorities demanding autonomy or independence from Muslim countries;
4. The struggle against alien foreign cultures, mainly against Western culture, at the fault lines and contact points with Islamic culture.

This reality is consistent with the basic concepts of Islam which regards the world as divided between the area of Islam (Dar al-Islam) and the area of war (Dar al-Harb); the aim of Islam is to bring the true faith to all of human civilization. Islamic Fundamentalism makes use of a range of means and tools in order to achieve its objectives starting from education, propaganda, economic aid and spiritual welfare, through political dissension and culminating in terror and war.

An analysis of conflict focal points indicates that their efforts are directed primarily towards a revision of the political reality inside the Muslim world, and to a lesser extent against other cultures. The new geopolitical reality in the post-Cold War era is perceived by radical Islamic circles as an expression of their success, which places Islam at the front of the confrontation vis-à-vis the Western culture headed by the only superpower, the United States.

One of the prominent phenomena characteristic of the previous millennium and also the beginning of the current millennium, which saliently reflect Huntington's concept regarding the cultural conflict, is the trend of the Afghan alumni who constitute the vanguard in radical Islam's confrontation with rival cultures. Osama Bin Laden and Al Qaida constitute the most outstanding expression of the Afghan alumni and of the cultural and philosophical concept at the root of this phenomenon.

The Conflict between Cultures: The Nomadic Culture versus the State-Oriented Culture

The end of the twentieth century and the beginning of the twenty-first century are characterized by the "conflict between cultures." As mentioned above, one of the fathers of this concept, Samuel Huntington, argues that after the end of the Cold War era the source of conflicts in the world is cultural. As stated earlier, he counts eight main cultures in the modern world and names Islam as the most militant of all.

"The conflict between the cultures" can also be conceptualized and examined from another point of view that divides cultures into two categories; the state-oriented, institutional, and territorial culture as opposed to the nomadic culture. Gilles Deleuze and Felix Gautteri discussed extensively various aspects of the conflict between the nomadic culture and the state-oriented territorial culture. This section will focus on their definitions of the terms "conflict," "war" and "war machine" in the context of the confrontation between the nomadic and state-oriented cultures.

The roots of the confrontation between the wanderer (nomad) and the farmer lie in the conflict between Cain and Abel as related in the *Book of Genesis*. The expulsion from the Garden of Eden propelled man from a state of plenty into a reality plagued by scarcity, competitiveness, force, and a battle for survival. The fourth chapter of

Genesis recounts the dramatic confrontation between Cain and Abel, which culminates in Abel's death and the decree that Cain was to become a nomad—"a wanderer you shall be in the land" (*Genesis*, 4, 12). This is the first testimony and primary mythological explanation for nomadism and for the inherent conflict between the nomad and the permanent dweller, and between the nomadic culture and the state-oriented, territorial culture.

Jacques Derrida, Deleuze, Guaterri and other philosophers regard nomadism as a philosophical concept that evolved in perpetual conflict against the state-oriented, tyranical philosophy, as they choose to define it. The nomadic society and the nomadic "war machine" are in constant movement from the conceptual point of view, although sometimes this does not involve actual physical movement. The nomadic concept opposes "domination" that the state-oriented perception enforces in all matters related to organization, space, and time.

The philosophical, state-oriented discourse always relates to the law, institutions, and contracts that jointly embody the concept of the state's sovereignty. It is this aspect that the nomadic concept views as dominating or tyrannical, or to quote Deleuze: "Even in the Greek polis (city-state), (which is perceived as the epitome of democracy), the philosophical discourse relates to tyranny and conceptual force, or at the very least it existed in the shadow of this tyranny."[14] Nietzsche was one of the first to bring up this complex issue for discussion. He argued that philosophical thought and discourse must be nomadic and free of the bureaucratic and procedural discourse. Thus Nietzsche, claims Deleuze, turned thought into a war machine and a battering ram reflecting a counter-philosophy that constantly challenges the state-oriented philosophy.[15]

Deleuze and Guaterri indicate several substantial differences between the state-oriented and nomadic approaches:[16]

- The state-oriented approach, which is founded on the definition of the state's sovereignty, is constructed in the form of a *(graded) vertical hierarchy*. The philosophical and constructive logic are based on this concept of structural and logical dependency arranged layer upon layer. By its very nature, the vertical structure creates a dictatorial pattern, since without the enforcement of conceptual and structural order the vertical structure will collapse. The nomadic approach does not accept the vertical structure and logic. The nomadic system is a *horizontal system*; on the philosophical and structural level there is no clear hierarchy, and the structural links are amorphous and less structured.

- *The territory*—The concept of "territory"—the permanence and the context of place—constitute the basic foundations of the state entity, which defines itself through the delineation of boundaries. Boundaries represent a basis not only for the physical definition of the state entity, but also address the conceptual dimensions of this entity. The nomadic outlook negates the notion of "boundaries" as well as the concept of "state." Nomadism signifies conceptual and physical deterritorization, which expresses itself in constant movement. The state does its best to settle its components, and to establish and conrol their movement and organization. However, the nomadic concept interprets this attempt in terms of compulsion and tyranny on the part of the state entity, and expresses the essence of its existence by opposing any attempt to settle or regulate it.

  Nevertheless, Deleuze and Guaterri point out that there is no "quintessential nomadism," and a paradox exists in the very fact that nomadism defines itself as different than the state entity. Moreover, there is the danger that if the nomadic perception emerges victorious, then it will also turn into a state entity.

- *The concept of time*—The concept of time is perceived differently in the state-oriented entity than in the nomadic culture. In the state-oriented culture, the perception of time is also contingent upon conceptual boundaries of the entity and represents part of the definition of the boundaries. The nomadic culture is in constant flow, in both dimensions of space and time. In the nomadic perception, the concept of time does not serve to delineate boundaries, but rather exists as a point of reference and orientation in the course of history. In the following sentences Deleuze and Guatteri encapsulate the nature of the difference between the state and nomadic entities:[17] "As a non-disciplinary force, the Nomadic war machine names an anarchic presence on the far horizon of the state's field of order."

Deleuze and Guatteri point out two types of war; the first, "the real war," and the second, the pure idea of war.[18] They perceive the pure idea of war as[19] "a war machine that does not have war as its object and that only entertains a potential or supplementary synthetic relation with war." The war itself logically contradicts the existence of the state-oriented entity and constitutes a form of antagonism directed against all forms of sovereignty. The nomadic movement is also based on fundamental antagonism, which opposes any regulated form or flow related to normalization and order. To illustrate, the two elements can be compared to the quiet and regular flow of water in a river as opposed to the turbulent churning of water in whirlpools, thus creating a swirling disorder.

It is possible to identify historical confrontations between nomadic entities and state-oriented entities in the three countries at the heart of this study. These confrontations occurred not only between powerbrokers within the state-oriented territory, but were also integrated into struggles waged against external powerbrokers, particularly colonial forces that attempted to implement state-oriented order in spaces characterized by nomadic cultures. The consequence of these confrontations was the formation of an unstable space whose components are located at different levels of intercultural confrontation. Somalia represents the most prominent example of the victory of nomadic forces and the actual dismantling of the state-oriented framework, while Sudan and Yemen are involved at different levels of the conflict, the result being that these regimes are constantly being challenged by the nomadic components that strive to dismantle them.

Areas involved in cultural confrontation constitute a preferred action arena for nomadic power entities; their very presence and activity in the arena contribute to the intensification of the confrontation between the nomadic and state-oriented cultures. The confrontation between the nomadic culture and the state-oriented culture may lead to the creation of ungovernable areas (UGRs) and failing states, which serve as hothouses for nomadic entities. Failing states pose a threat and cause instability to their immediate vicinity and beyond it, thus creating a "Catch 22" situation. This can be described as a vicious cycle in which nomadic forces confront state-oriented forces and cause the undermining and collapse of the failing state; the next step is the development of a local nomadic entity that also attracts external nomadic entities. This presence prevents the rehabilitation or construction of a new state-oriented identity, and the space becomes an area from which the nomadic entity threatens to continue spreading towards nearby state-oriented entities as well as more distant ones.

Al Qaida as an Expression of the Merging of Radical Islam and Nomadic Culture[20]

Osama Bin Laden moved from Saudi Arabia to Pakistan and from there to the Afghan front. In the city of Pashwar in Pakistan he established an organization that dealt with the recruitment, absorption, and training of Muslim fighters from all over the world who had volunteered to participate in the Jihad against the Soviet Union in Afghanistan. Already at the beginning of his career, Osama Bin Laden had adopted radical Islamic views that regarded Islam as involved in an existential struggle against the more powerful forces of the superpowers as well as against secular and corrupt Arab regimes acting according to the interests of their powerful patrons. According to Bin Laden's tenets, radical Islam is involved in a struggle to banish the corrupt leaders from the Muslim world and to found a utopian community of Islamic believers—the Umma.

Bin Laden claims that Islam has no boundaries and that the Muslim national states are the artificial creations of colonialism and imperialism, whose goal was to cause a fake separation within the Muslim world, thus perpetuating the control and involvement of the Western powers. Therefore, radical Islam represents a nomadic concept that negates the state-oriented entity and regards it as an expression of the physical and conceptual tyranny of the Western culture, which represents the state-oriented culture.

Bin Laden adopted the slogan, "not east, not west," which is accepted by those faithful to radical Islam. In 1979 he first focused his struggle upon the Soviet Union, and accepted aid from the United States, Saudi Arabia, and other "corrupt" Arab regimes to achieve his objective, but even then he never concealed his opinion that after victory in this struggle, the West's turn would come.

The war in Afghanistan saliently reflects the conflict between the state-oriented concept and "war machine" and the nomadic concept and "war machine." The Soviet Union and the Communist regime in Kabul expressed the vertical, graded state-oriented concept, on philosophical, conceptual, and practical levels, while the Afghan mujahidin, assisted by the "internacionale" of volunteers from all over the Muslim world, like Bin Laden, expressed the concept of the nomadic "war machine." This machine was built horizontally and was composed of scores of organizations and groups lacking a regulated or permanent structure and without defined procedures of cooperation, whose only loose link was the joint goal—defeat of the communist regime and banishment of the Soviet Union's forces from Afghanistan.

The nomadic war machine of the mujahidin is in perpetual movement on various levels:

•   Operating a chaotic campaign without a clear delineation of boundaries outside of Afghanistan, within Afghanistan in the areas outside of Soviet control, inside Afghanistan behind the Soviet lines, and even inside the government centers in Kabul and other cities. The operation of this type of chaotic campaign is meant to undermine the operative, structured, and institutionalized rationale of the state-oriented order.

- Creating a perpetual motion and flow of concepts and ideas all designated to jointly undermine the graded and state-oriented ideology and doctrines prevalent in Kabul, while simultaneously creating new subversive concepts (mostly Islamic).

The mujahidin movements were the most characteristic model of the nomadic war machine: They were in constant motion with the aim of undermining the physical and conceptual boundaries of the Afghan state; they generated ideas and concepts that were free of the state-oriented, tyrannical rationale; they fought a chaotic campaign that neutralized the advantages of the state-oriented superpower and gave the nomadic machine superiority. And indeed, in 1990, the nomadic war machine defeated the Soviet Union, which pulled its forces out of Afghanistan, and two years later the communist regime fell in Kabul leaving control in the hands of the mujahidin.

Deleuze and Gautteri foretold of the inherent paradox when a nomadic system turns into a state-oriented one. The Afghan case constitutes an interesting example of the opposite phenomenon: Even after their victory over the communist regime and the Soviet Union, the mujahidin movements continued their nomadic modus operandi. Thus, in the years 1992-1996, Afghanistan remained in a chaotic state, and the attempt to found a vertical, graded system that would result in a state-oriented government failed. In actual fact, Afghanistan was "controlled" by a nomadic war machine that perpetuated itself via a complex system of powerbrokers that fought each other, thus preserving the chaotic and non-institutionalized reality that characterizes the nomadic system as a non-state-oriented system.

The rise to power of the Taliban regime in Afghanistan during the years 1996-2001 wrought only slight change within the system's structure, because the internal power struggles in the arena persevered. Moreover, during these years two parallel systems existed that were constantly at loggerheads with each other: One system, a semi-state-oriented system of the Taliban regime; and a nomadic system that fought it in the form of the coalition of the "northern alliance."

At the end of the war an even more salient nomadic war machine was created in the form of the Afghan alumni, whose most prominent representative is Osama Bin Laden. The Afghan alumni are not identified with any particular state or movement, but rather express a radical religious-cultural trend that believes in the relentless struggle of Islam against heretic Muslim regimes and adverse cultures. One can indicate four main channels of activity adopted by the Afghan alumni:

1. Incorporation in the activities of radical Islamic organizations in their native countries (Egypt, the Magreb countries, Jordan, and others) and the leadership of these organizations;
2. Establishing new terror organizations, such as Al Qaida under Bin Laden's leadership;
3. Establishing "independent" terror cells without a defined organizational link or affiliation while sustaining cooperation with other Islamic terror organizations;
4. Joining areas of conflict involving Muslim populations, for example, the Balkan, Chechnya, Kashmir, Tajikistan, and more.

As stated earlier, Al Qaida and its leader, Osama Bin Laden, are the most prominent examples of the nomadic concept both from the aspect of its physical dimension and from its conceptual dimension. At the end of the war in Afghanistan, Bin Laden decided to continue the Jihad against the enemies of Islam, and he positioned the United States as a central target of this campaign. During the years 1992-2001, he "wandered" between Afghanistan, Saudi Arabia, and Sudan until his "disappearance" following the American offensive in Afghanistan at the end of 2001. Bin Laden represents the nomadic concept of the wanderer who does not settle down nor does he establish himself within a state-oriented system, but rather he is perpetually on the move. From his point of view, territory expresses only a functional and temporary need; in other words, it is essential to his ability to further his goals, but he does not form a permanent link with any particular territory.

Al Qaida was designed according to the nomadic concept as an organization without a clear, graded structure. It is composed of cells and groups spread all over the world and sustains conceptual and organizational links with countries that support terror (such as Sudan, Iran, and more), as well as Islamic organizations that hold similar worldviews.

The organization's goal is to fight an uncompromising battle against the United States, the West, and Zionism, all of which can also be defined as entities that reflect the state-oriented concept. The organization openly contests Western cultural concepts in every area; on the ideological-religious level it calls for the destruction of the Western rival and the establishment of an Islamic culture in its stead; on the economic level, it exploits the economic establishment of the Western world for its own purposes and acts through it to demolish this infrastructure, based on the understanding that most of the power of the Western culture is drawn from its economy; on the military level it established a nomadic war machine that confronts the superior power of the Western state-oriented war machine by posing challenges that render it vulnerable and irrelevant. The organization functions according to the nomadic concept, at any place and at any time, and creates disarray that undermines the foundations of the state-oriented rationale. The flexibility, agility and independence of the various components of the nomadic war machine constitute an acute problem for the state-oriented war machine of the West, which functions within the framework of the restrictions and limits that the graded state-oriented order forces upon itself.

A study of Al Qaida's areas of activity indicates some of its main characteristics:

- The organization prefers to position its central headquarters and organizational infrastructure inside the territory of a Muslim state governed by a sympathetic radical Islamic regime that supports the organization and its chosen direction, such as the Taliban in Afghanistan and the Sudanese regime headed by Hassan al Turabi.
- The organization bases its infrastructure in countries that are steeped in internal and external power struggles as well as economic woes, as this enables the development of mutual dependency between the organization and the authorities; the authorities offer the organization refuge and support in establishing the organizational infrastructure, and in exchange the organization offers the government economic and operational aid in its struggles against its adversaries. This was the case in Afghanistan and, subsequently, in Sudan.
- Due to the nature of its ties with the government in the host state and as a result of its worldview, the organization acts in external arenas of confrontation, sometimes in cooperation with the country where it claims refuge or in its name. This was particularly obvious in Al Qaida's activity in Sudan, when the organization helped Sudan and its ally Iran in their struggle against the U.S. presence in Somalia; and also in Afghanistan when the organization acted as the emissary of the Taliban regime and its patrons in Pakistan against Indian forces in the disputed Kashmir region.

- The organization does not conduct terror activity within the boundaries of the host country, but generally acts outside of the country, in order to refrain from embarrassing its "hosts" vis-à-vis attack victims.

- Despite the attempt to draw a clear line between the organization's responsibility and its host's, there have been cases where the victim country has pointed an accusatory finger at both the organization and the host country and has taken a toll from both. A prime example of this would be the cruise-missile attack perpetrated by U.S. forces against Al Qaida targets in Afghanistan and Sudan following the attacks at the American embassies in Kenya and Tanzania.

- The extent of the willingness of host countries to pay the price for their support of the organization varies from country to country, and even changes inside each country when the political and military circumstances fluctuate. Thus, due to heavy American-Egyptian-Saudi pressure, the regime in Sudan preferred to ask Bin Laden to leave the country, while the Taliban regime in Afghanistan remained loyal to the organization and paid the price by losing its government as a result of the U.S. offensive in the war against terror.

- Failing states and UGR's constitute areas of activity for Al Qaida. The organization acts in these regions to reinforce infrastructures and perpetrate attacks against its adversaries, while exploiting the lack of governmental control or the weakness of the central government, and relying on radical Islamic entities that support the organization. Examples of this phenomenon can be seen in the Al Qaida attacks in Yemen; the attacks at the end of 1992 perpetrated in connection with the U.S. involvement in Somalia, the attack against the *USS Cole* in 2000, and more. In Somalia, the organization aided Aidid's forces in their anti-U.S. activities in this country.

Al Qaida also recruits collaborators and terrorists into its ranks from among the residents of the failing state or the UGRs, and they act from within the organization's ranks and represent it in various arenas worldwide.

The nomadic character of Al Qaida prevents the creation of total and irreversible dependency between the organization and any specific state-oriented territory, and, thus, if the organization should lose its infrastructure in a certain region, it can rehabilitate and rebuild itself in another region.

- From the philosophical point of view, radical Islamic states constitute the preferred location of activity for Al Qaida because their ideology matches the organization's worldview. Nevertheless, due to the inherent nature of these countries, they embody a contradiction and conflict of interest between the nomadic entity and the state-oriented entity. This is reflected, for example, in the Sudanese decision to give in to the pressures to banish Bin Laden. This example indicates that

the state-oriented system placed the governmental, state-oriented interest (the government's survival) at the head of its priorities and sac-
rificed the conceptual-ideological component in the process.

In contrast to the Sudanese case, which represents a salient state-
oriented system (albeit a shaky one), for the most part the Taliban
regime maintained its nomadic nature and remained uncompromising
from the ideological aspect. Its relentless support for Al Qaida ultimately
led to its destruction in the confrontation with the Western state-oriented war machine. The American threat against the regime in Yemen
caused a reversal in the policy of President Salah, who preferred to
cooperate with the United States in the struggle against the organization and protect his regime, although Al Qaida still enjoys the patronage of tribal leaders and radical Islamic leaders in UGRs in Yemen.

The September 11 terror campaign prominently reflects both the
confrontation between the nomadic war machine and the state-oriented war machine, as well as the cultural conflict between Islam
and Western culture.

On September 11, 2001 four passenger planes were hijacked in
the United States; two of the planes crashed into the Twin Towers of
the World Trade Center in New York, causing their collapse, and a
third hijacked plane crashed into the Pentagon complex in Washington. A fourth airplane crashed in a wooded area in Pennsylvania, but
it is believed that its target was the Capitol building or the White
House in Washington. The targets of the terror campaign, which
were chosen carefully, are prominent symbols of Western culture in
general, and of the United States, in particular—which leads and
represents this culture. The Twin Towers were the symbol of financial power (World Trade Center), while the Pentagon is the symbol
of the military power of the United States and the West. This terror
attack expressed the profound cultural and conceptual asymmetry
between the United States, which represents the state-oriented concept, and Bin Laden, who represents the nomadic concept.

The attack was perpetrated by several small groups of terrorists
(nomads) who came from various Muslim countries (Saudi Arabia,
Egypt, and others). These hijackers took over the planes without
firearms and in some cases even without any weapons, and turned
the airplanes themselves into attack weapons. The use of an aero-
nautical mode of transportation to destroy the symbols of the state-
oriented war machine is symbolic because it represents the ultimate

form of mobility. As stated earlier, the Twin Towers and the Pentagon are both architectural monuments that represent the achievements of the Western state-oriented culture. These two stationary monuments, which constituted the embodiment of state-oriented "tyranny" in the eyes of the nomadic Islam, were destroyed with instruments that were also created by the modern West, but reflect the movement and dynamics that are particularly characteristic of the nomadic culture.

The terror attack of September 2001 exposed the weakness and vulnerability of the state-oriented system despite its absolute power, which significantly exceeds that of the nomadic war machine. The "war against terror" declared by the United States following that terror campaign also constitutes convincing testimony regarding the problematic issues inherent to the confrontation between the nomadic and state-oriented systems. The United States declared Al Qaida and the Taliban regime in Afghanistan (which had provided refuge to Bin Laden) the primary goals in its war against terror. The state-oriented war machine of the United States defeated the state-oriented war machine of the Taliban and the components of Al Qaida within it, with ease. Al Qaida's infrastructure in Afghanistan was destroyed and some of its commanders and fighters were either killed or taken prisoner. However, Bin Laden and most of the organization's leaders have so far evaded the Americans, and what is more to the point, Al Qaida's "horizontal" and decentralized organizational infrastructure was almost unaffected.

This experience teaches us that the infrastructure of the state-oriented war machine, like that of the Taliban, can be destroyed through the use of the equipment, technology, and doctrine that are at the disposal of the Western war machine, but the nomadic infrastructure necessitates completely different handling and confrontation. The nomadic culture's concepts of time and space, as well as its organizational narrative, pose a threat to the state-oriented logic and act to undermine its foundations through their very existence, even before the operational capabilities of the nomadic terror infrastructure have been translated into attacks. Thus, the definition of the confrontation as a "war against terror" addresses only a limited conceptual dimension of a far deeper and wider confrontation between the cultures. The component of terror constitutes only a single symptom, albeit an important one, of a confrontation with far greater implications.

The Campaign against Global Islamic Terror[21]

The Al Qaida attacks in the United States on September 11, 2001 were like an earthquake that provoked the United States into declaring a relentless war against terror. Threats of Islamic terror against the United States and the West were nothing new, and contending with challenges posed by Al Qaida and other radical Islamic organizations hadalready begun in the early nineties, but only the September 11 attacks illustrated the full power and gravity of the threat to the United States and the entire world, and necessitated a substantial change in the world's attitude towards the problem of terror.

The war against terror is directed against two central targets: (1) terror organizations, and (2) states involved in terror. When combined, these two aspects create international terror, which can be defined as follows:[22] The use or threat to use violence for political gain by an individual or group acting for or against an existing regime. The act is aimed at influencing a wider target population than the direct victims of the action, while the victims, the perpetrators or their contacts are unrestricted by geographical boundaries.

The various forms of countries' involvement in terror have been unified under the concepts "terrorist states" or "state-sponsored terror." These concepts create a rough generalization of the various levels of involvement of countries in terror, thus a more focused distinction is required that classifies the involvement of countries in terror according to the following categories:[23]

- *States supporting terrorism*—This category includes states that support terror organizations via financial, ideological, military and operational aid;
- *States operating terrorism*—Countries that initiate, direct, and execute terror attacks via patron organizations, while avoiding direct government involvement in the terror;
- *States perpetrating terrorism*—States that perpetrate terror throughout the world via the country's security systems (security and intelligence mechanisms).

A fourth category can be added to these three categories: the failing state which turns into a "hothouse" for terror organizations as the result of the lack of an effective government.

Paul Wilkinson defined the various types of state terror as "direct or indirect involvement of a government, via formal or informal groups, in the creation of psychological and physical violence against political or physical targets or another country in order to achieve tactical and objective targets that it is interested in."[24] State-oriented terror is characterized by an ambivalent approach to international law and order. On the one hand, states that utilize terror are willing to deviate from the international norms and from the "rules of the game" in order to inflict damage on the enemy and achieve their own goals (a prominent example of this can be observed in the "students'" occupation of the U.S. Embassy in Iran and the holding of U.S. diplomats as hostages in 1979). On the other hand, a country that utilizes terror endeavors not to reveal its involvement in this activity in order to prevent retaliatory measures against it.

Cooperation between a country and a terror organization is usually sustained on the basis of religious, ideological, or political solidarity, and on the basis of joint interests. The extent of control that the "patron" maintains over the terror organization varies according to the basis for cooperation and the level of the organization's dependence on the patron.

As mentioned earlier, the country's involvement in terror may be either direct or indirect and exist on different levels of aid and cooperation (political, economic, operational). In most cases, the ties between the patron state and the terror organization are of a clandestine nature; by using citizens of other countries a country can shirk responsibility when the activity is exposed and avoid criticism and sanctions by the international community.

Terror may be an additional or alternative tool to activating military force in order to achieve the country's objectives, while the state supports an act of terror against another state with which it is involved in conflict, but this may also apply to a situation in which the countries are not officially involved in hostile confrontation. Terror may be effective for the achievement of goals when there is doubt whether they are achievable through direct military confrontation, such as undermining the political stability in the target state or incurring damage to that country's diplomatic and economic ties with other countries.

It is possible to indicate three stages in the global campaign against terror declared by the United States:

1.   Stage 1—Destruction of Al Qaida's infrastructure in Afghanistan and removal of the Taliban regime that sponsored the organization;
2.   Stage 2—The campaign against Iraq and against Al Qaida affiliated terror cells;

3.   Stage 3—The campaign against additional countries that support terror and the continued struggle against Al Qaida terror cells and other
terror organizations worldwide.

In the first stage of the war against terror, the "coalition against
terror" headed by the United States launched its offensive against Al
Qaida in Afghanistan and the Taliban regime that served as sponsor
to Bin Laden and his organization. The coalition acted in Afghanistan, a country that clearly had all of the characteristics of a failing
state, while utilizing the Taliban regime's enemies, members of the
"Northern Alliance," in order to eradicate the Taliban regime and
destroy Al Qaida's infrastructure in this country. The combination of
American air superiority, the ongoing activation of special forces,
and the aid provided to the Northern Alliance, which carried out the
main offensive on land, led to the rapid collapse of the Taliban regime and the Al Qaida activists. Although Taliban leader Mullah
Muhammad Omar and Bin Laden, along with his organization's senior leaders did succeed in fleeing, the Taliban regime collapsed;
and even more importantly—the infrastructure of the Al Qaida organization in Afghanistan was eradicated and hundreds of organization members, including senior activists, fell into the hands of the
U.S. coalition. The American message during the first stage of the
war against terror was unequivocal:

- The United States will fight a relentless war against Al Qaida and all
  other terror organizations, and will act to eradicate them.
- Any regime offering patronage to terror organizations will pay a heavy
  price for this policy.

The eradication of the Taliban regime in Afghanistan signaled a
warning to various countries that had cooperated in one way or another with Al Qaida and other Islamic terror organizations. The fate
of the Taliban regime must have loomed strongly before the Sudanese
and Yemenite rulers as they rushed to deny any involvement in terror and even declared their willingness to cooperate with the United
States in its battle against terror.

When attempting to calculate Al Qaida's profit/loss reckoning following the U.S. terror campaign, one might say that it was a tactical
victory but a strategic loss. The tactical victory stems from Al Qaida's
success in surprising the United States, killing thousands of its citizens in its government and economic centers, and inflicting huge
damage upon its economy. The terror campaign granted Al Qaida

unprecedented media coverage, which helped to nurture the powerful image of the "Islamic front" headed by Bin Laden, thus presenting them with a significant achievement from the point of view of morale. On the other hand, Bin Laden failed to achieve his main goal, which was to provoke the United States into taking massive and aggressive retaliatory steps against the Muslim world, in the hope of inciting a frontal confrontation between Islam and the West. Not only did this type of confrontation never take place, but rather a wide international coalition formed, with the backing of Muslim countries, that granted the United States support in the military campaign fought against the Taliban regime. This campaign led to the removal of the Taliban regime in Afghanistan and to the inflicting of severe damage upon Al Qaida's infrastructure in Afghanistan. Its bases and training camps were eradicated, and the thousands of confiscated documents exposed the plans and modi operandi of the organization. The organization sustained heavy losses among its leadership, some of whom were either killed or caught, and thousands of its fighters were killed or taken prisoner. Thus, Al Qaida lost (at least temporarily) its operational bases in Afghanistan, which had constituted an essential component in its global terror infrastructure. In addition, the organization sustained a heavy blow to its prestige as a result of the successful military campaign that the United States waged against it in Afghanistan, and the "unbeaten" image that the Afghan mujahidin (with Bin Laden at its head) so carefully nurtured following its victory over the forces of the former Soviet Union was suddenly distorted.

It is important to emphasize that the campaign against Al Qaida and the Afghan alumni (with Bin Laden as their leader) is still in its initial stages, and its results depend first and foremost upon the West's determination to continue the struggle and upon its capability to provide a suitable and effective response to the threat of global Islamic terror. Failure to deal with this response to the threat may enable Bin Laden and his men to recover and rehabilitate the organization's infrastructure, and cause even graver damage than they have already. The West must comprehend that the heavy blow sustained by Al Qaida did not diminish its force, and it particularly did not lessen the strength of the terror cells supported by Al Qaida, which are linked to it and are currently waiting in many countries worldwide to continue to promote the agenda of the Global Jihad. These cells are made up of trained and determined fighters who mainly thirst for revenge. The nomadic character of Bin Laden's terror network, including all of its branches, enables it to sustain these blows but continue to operate. The survival of its senior commanders, with Bin Laden at its head, as well as his deputy Aiman al-Zawahiri and several other senior activists, and the escape of hundreds of Al Qaida members from Afghanistan via Iran and Pakistan, to countries that allow them to function—with their full knowledge or as a result of the absence of an effective central government—enable the organization to renew its preparations for continued terror activity.

For more than a decade, and with greater intensity since 1996, hundreds of young Muslims have arrived in Afghanistan from all over the Muslim world, as well as other countries worldwide—including Western Europe, Eastern Europe, Asia, North America, Australia, and Africa—and, having undergone training in guerrilla warfare and terror, were then sent back to their own countries. Thus, a pool of trained terrorists loyal to the concept of Global Jihad was created. These terrorists were assembled in terror cells, with each cell composed of a small number of activists "programmed" to perpetrate terror attacks against Islamic foes. The exposure of terror cells in Europe (Britain, France, Italy, Spain, Germany), in Asia (the Philippines, Malaysia, Indonesia, Singapore, and India), in the Middle East (Jordan, Egypt, Lebanon, Israel), and in North America (United States, Canada)—before and after September 11, 2001—serves as concrete evidence of their modus operandi, intentions, targets and the inherent danger that they pose.

Despite widespread effort to thwart the terrorist activity of the organization and its supporters worldwide, since September 11, Al Qaida has succeeded in perpetrating a series of grave attacks at various global targets, with the assistance of other radical Islamic organizations: the synagogue at Djerba Tunisia, a nightclub in Bali, Indonesia, the French oil tanker in Yemen, the Paradise Hotel in Mombassa, Kenya, targets in Riyadh, Saudi Arabia, and in Casablanca, the Moroccan capital. Moreover, a year after the collapse of the Taliban regime, resistance to the government of Khamid Kharzai and the presence of U.S. and coalition forces in Afghanistan was steadily increasing. The Taliban movement, Al Qaida and the radical Islamic organization of Khytmatiar seek gradually to re-establish their power and influence in the country, and continue to conduct guerrilla warfare—which they define as Jihad—against Kharzai's "puppet government and the American invasion forces."

Parallel to the continued fighting in Afghanistan and the global struggle against Al Qaida infrastructures worldwide, the United States extended the front of the war against global terror and toppled Saddam Hussein's regime in Iraq in 2003. President George Bush defined three of the countries that support terror as extremely dangerous and labeled them "the axis of evil." These three countries were Iraq, Iran and North Korea. The United States accused these countries of involvement in terror and of attempts to develop and acquire weapons for mass destruction. The combination of an "irresponsible and aggressive" regime, alongside a policy supporting terror and non-conventional weapons is justifiably perceived by the United States as an intolerable threat against peace in the free world. Of the three countries that make up the axis of evil, the United States chose to contend first with the Iraqi regime. While the campaign in Afghanistan was conducted with the full backing of the UN and the international community, prior to the offensive in Iraq the United States encountered difficulties in recruiting world support, and many countries—including U.S. allies in NATO—expressed reservations concerning a U.S. offensive in Iraq. Nevertheless, even without international support, the United States initiated a campaign in Iraq at the head of a small coalition, and within less than a month defeated Saddam Hussein's regime and took over Iraq.

The offensive in Iraq made it clear to states that support terror that the United States is determined and unwavering in its war against terror, and that any country that continues to support terror is risking a confrontation with the superpower and its fate may be similar to that of Afghanistan and Iraq.

The invasion of Afghanistan and Iraq by the U.S.-led coalition brought about the encirclement of Iran—another of the axis of evil countries—and the world "leader" in wielding terror for the promotion of its goals. The United States is currently presenting the Iranians with two demands: (1) cease the use of terror, and (2) cease the development of weapons for mass destruction. If Iran refuses to meet these demands, it might find itself on a collision course with the United States and its allies.

The importance of activating military force has been understood since the dawn of history. The activation of military strength in Afghanistan and in Iraq in the war against terror confirmed the necessity to use force from time to time. Nevertheless, in the framework of the campaign against states that support terror it is also possible to apply a combination of pressures as well as economic and political sanctions, which may well be no less effective than the use of military force. Confirmation of the latter can be found, for example, in the international sanctions imposed on Libya following the exposure of its involvement in the explosion of the Pan American airplane over Lockerbie at the end of 1988. The effective set of sanctions imposed on Libya by the Security Council (resolution 748, March 1991) ultimately changed Libya from a country that actively supported terror—which included some of the most brutal attacks in the history of international terror—to a country that is passive and cautious in its support of terror.

In light of this development, it is likely that the United States will first strive to persuade Iran to cooperate and accept U.S. demands, but if Iran does not acquiesce, the United States will activate various types of leverage, saving the military option as a last resort.

The intensity of the terror campaign in the United States and the damages it inflicted caused major upheaval in the consciousness of the public at large and among decision-makers all over the globe, and also caused shifts in international relationships both from the bilateral and multilateral aspects. However, the American experience vis-à-vis the Iraqi campaign has proven that, notwithstanding, it cannot expect automatic support for its steps within the framework of the war against terror, and that various countries will act according to their own basic interests, which do not necessarily correspond with those of the United States. Thus, in the matter of the offensive in Afghanistan, unprecedented cooperation was formed between the United States and Russia, which enabled military cooperation between CIS countries like Georgia and Uzbekistan, with Russia's consent. These states permitted U.S. military forces to deploy bases in their territories for the attack of targets in Afghanistan and in exchange the United States granted them economic aid. The cooperation between the United States and Russia ultimately led to the signing of a historical cooperation agreement between Russia and the NATO countries (which was originally established to counterbalance the strength of the Communist bloc made up of the Soviet Union and its satellite countries) in the matter of combating terror. However, in the matter of the offensive in Iraq, Russia was one of the primary opponents to the U.S. military campaign, and it still maintains that the United States erred when it set out on this campaign.

The relationship between the United States and China has also undergone changes as a result of the September 2001 events. The relationship between these countries has been shadowed by the competition between the two powers, which have different and sometimes opposing interests; in addition, the relationship was further strained due to the incident of the American intelligence plane caught in China. Nevertheless, the two achieved cooperation in light of the shared threat posed by Islamic terror. China, which faces the threat of Islamic terror in its Xinjiang region, also supported the international coalition against Islamic terror. However, similar to Russia, China was also adamantly opposed to the U.S. military campaign in Iraq, and claimed—on the basis of its own considerations—that the United States should not be granted legitimization to unilaterally demand the replacement of regimes and act forcefully against them.

In an interim summary of the war against terror to date (December 2003) the following results are to be noted:

- The United States has proved twice (in Afghanistan and in Iraq) that terror-supporting regimes pay the highest price—the loss of their power.
- U.S. military and technological superiority enables it to defeat political adversaries like the Taliban regime in Afghanistan and Saddam Hussein's regime in Iraq in a fairly short period of time and with a minimal death toll.
- The toppling of regimes that support terror does not ensure the establishment of a stable and democratic alternative administration; in this area the United States has achieved only limited success to date (if at all).
- The experience accumulated in Afghanistan and Iraq indicates that the ousting of a regime that supports terror is in itself insufficient; the long-term presence of forces and the investment of significant financial resources are prerequisites for the foundation of a new and stable administration that will prohibit the growth of terror in the country.
- The handling of the regimes in Afghanistan and Iraq constitutes a warning signal to states that support terror, most of which actually joined the coalition against terror in an attempt to avoid becoming a target of a U.S. offensive in the future.
- The war against states that support terror has encountered political difficulties due to a conflict of interest on the part of countries that are ostensibly members of the counter-terror coalition. This fact is clearly reflected in the lack of support for the U.S. offensive in Iraq, and this trend is expected to reoccur and even intensify in future campaigns against countries such as Iran.
- The lack of consensus and cooperation leaves the United States to bear the brunt of the burden of the counter-terror campaign. In the absence of operative cooperation and the investment of input by the international community, even the United States will find it difficult

to sustain a large number of campaigns in various confrontational arenas.

- The destruction of the terror infrastructures in Afghanistan and Iraq inflicted damage on Al Qaida but it did not significantly impair the organization's operational capabilities and infrastructures worldwide.
- Al Qaida has a world-encompassing infrastructure (globalization of terror), consisting of autonomous cells capable of perpetrating attacks and expanding the organization's covert infrastructures.
- Al Qaida has an impressive capacity to renew and rehabilitate itself, so that the apprehension of senior commanders and fighters does not leave a vacuum in the organization, and its ranks replenish themselves.
- The global war against terror, which began with the annihilation of terror infrastructures in Afghanistan and which includes various thwarting measures all over the world (freezing funds, arrests and more), has somewhat diminished the operational capabilities of the organization's cells, and these are "satisfied" with less spectacular and complex attacks than those of September 11 (although they are painful enough).
- There is effective, world-encompassing cooperation among Islamic terror organizations that assist each other in the perpetration of attacks and in the ongoing struggle against the U.S.-led coalition.
- In contrast to the effective cooperation among the terror organizations, the free world has encountered difficulties in uniting its ranks and enhancing joint cooperation in the war against terror.
- The U.S. and international presence in Afghanistan and in Iraq is perceived by large sections of the populations and certainly by entities hostile to the West as "occupation." Thus, guerrilla and terror combat are gradually developing in these arenas against the foreign presence and against the governments regarded as "puppet regimes," which are acting under the sponsorship of the foreign powers.
- This reality makes it difficult to cope with terror and forms processes that make the ability to defeat and eradicate terror seem remote and far removed from realization.

The Failing State and Its Rehabilitation as a Component of the War against Global Terror

Failing states endanger the stability of the international structure because national states constitute the foundations of world order. Global security is based on states whose role it is to prevent internal chaos and reduce the spread of domestic anarchy beyond its borders. The state serves as the intermediary between internal social, economic, and political systems and the external global system. The phenomenon of the failing state began to develop and spread at the end of World War I, due to the crumbling of the Austro-Hungarian and Ottoman Empires. This phenomenon persevered with the collapse of Western colonialism after World War II, and the dismantling of the Soviet Union at the end of the 1990s. In 1914, the number of recognized states in the international system was fifty-five. In 1960, this figure rose to ninety, and with the end of the Cold War and the disintegration of the Soviet Union, the number grew to 192. The states were not created equal, and they vary in population, resources, and governments. A modern state must grapple with far more complex demands and challenges than those faced by countries in the past. Today, the modern state is expected to supply its population with proper government, security, and economic prosperity, as well as education, health, and welfare services. Moreover, it is expected to inspire a feeling of unity and national pride, but primarily the state must provide collective and individual security and public order.

In reality, many of the newly created states are too "weak and fragile" to survive as national states, and they face risks and difficulties that may cause their decline to the status of failing states. This deterioration from the status of a standard state to a failing state involves processes that can be identified and provide advance warning as they transpire.

- *The economic aspect*—A rapid decline in the standard of living while the economic elite is comprised of favored sector-related groups (family, tribe, etc.); a severe shortage of foreign currency, which leads to a scarcity of basic food products and gasoline; a sharp decline in the government's ability to provide basic services in the areas of health, education, transportation, and such; a corrupt bureaucracy and government that take over the limited resources and transfer funds to private accounts outside of the country.
- *The political aspect*—The government is in the hands of a minority or a single ruler; sections of society feel that they are not represented by the government and are discriminated against in comparison to the elite that is identified with the administration; the government, which in the past was perceived as an entity acting on behalf of the general good, is currently perceived to represent the interests of certain sectors. Thus, polarization is created in society and the government sustains its power through control and subjugation; the freedom of speech and personal security of the individual are impaired; and the state's dwindling resources are invested in the ruler's safety.

When a stop is not put to the political and economic decline, the state reaches a decisive stage in the loss of governmental legitimacy, public order becomes uncontrollable, and the government loses its monopoly of power to halt the process of collapse; in this sort of scenario a preventive policy must be implemented, crisis management and handling must be initiated, and sometimes there arises a need for external intervention. Robert Rotberg claims that the process whereby a state becomes a failing state is reversible, that is, it is possible to put a stop to the deterioration processes in a country, rehabilitate it, and restore its status as a functioning state, even after its systems have collapsed and it has become a failing state.[25] He claims that it is possible to prevent the decline of a state to a failing state mainly through external intervention. Saving the state from the collapse processes entails two basic conditions:

- The signs attesting to the state's collapse are identified at a relatively early stage.
- he existence of an external entity willing to invest the necessary input for the prevention of state collapse.

External intervention may be reflected in the following ways:

- The involvement of a superpower that undertakes the state's rescue and rehabilitation;
- The intervention of a regional organization willing to undertake this mission;
- UN intervention.

Sometimes there is also the possibility of the incorporation and cooperation of several external entities in the rescue and rehabilitation processes preventing state collapse, starting from economic and/or military aid through the prevention of the establishment of a dictatorial regime that may induce collapse, and culminating in military intervention aimed at restoring public order and stability. A prime example of the latter is obviously Somalia, where the 1993 attempt by the United States and the UN to initiate rehabilitation failed dismally.

It is possible to indicate several central processes in the rehabilitation of a failing state:

- Cessation of violence—bringing the rival parties to a ceasefire and initiating negotiations as well as preservation of the ceasefire through an external, neutral force.
- Humanitarian aid—via state aid and international humanitarian organizations.

- Establishing a temporary government—which must include representatives of all of the relevant powerbrokers, act to restore a central
government capable of ruling and providing all of the population's
needs, and lay the foundation for the election of a representative government.
- Establishing security forces—establishing an army and police force
to replace the sectarian powerbrokers, which will be placed at the
disposal of the temporary government in order to enforce government
control. These security forces will be founded, trained, and supervised
by external international entities.
- Rehabilitation of the administrative system—remaking of the administration and renewal of the state's provision of services to its citizens.
- Rehabilitation of the judiciary system—reestablishing the judiciary
system which will function jointly with law enforcement entities to
restore personal and public security in the country.
- Rehabilitation of the political system—creating a democratic political system (insofar that this is possible) and establishing an administration representative of the entire population including all of its components.
- Economic aid—receiving international economic aid to rehabilitate
the local economy and develop the state's capability to become incorporated in global economy.

These processes may be implemented either gradually or concurrently, according to the unique circumstances in each country.

The "preventive" steps—those designated to prevent the creation
of failing states—and the actions to rehabilitate the failing state constitute a crucial component in the war against terror, as terror in general and Islamic terror in particular regard failing states and uncontrollable areas as optimal and fertile activity areas for the establishment of infrastructures and power focal points.

This theory is soon to be tested, in the aftermath of the two campaigns that the United States waged to topple the regimes in Afghanistan and Iraq. In both cases the United States must act to rehabilitate and rebuild these countries after the military offensive. Afghanistan was defined as a failing state even before the latest war,
after over twenty years of bloodshed that led to the destruction of
the state and to the dismantling of its economic and governmental
infrastructures. Iraq, on the other hand, was ruled for over twenty
years by a dictatorship that terrorized the population and enforced
law and order with an iron fist. The ousting of the regime caused a
"governmental vacuum" and a state of chaos. In both cases it would
appear that the United States is encountering considerable difficul-

ties in its efforts to establish stable governments that will restore the status of "normal states" and enable the states to function properly within the international system. The instability in both Afghanistan and Iraq is already leading to the formation of local opposition powerbrokers, acting via terror and guerrilla warfare against the U.S. forces and the U.S. supported local leadership, which is seen as an illegitimate governmental entity that must be ousted.

The United States and Its Confrontation with the Islamic Terror Challenge in the Red Sea Region

The U.S. declaration of war against terror included the methods it would use to confront the global problem. The general characteristics of the campaign were discussed in the two previous sections, therefore in this section we will focus on the issue of how the United States contended with the problem of Islamic terror in the particular region discussed in this study.

The global and overall aspects vis-à-vis the concept of the campaign against terror seriously impacted American policy in this geographical focal point. Following the American declaration of war against terror, the names of Sudan, Somalia, and Yemen arose alongside Afghanistan—which was the first target of the war—as countries that maintained ties with Al Qaida and which in time might become targets of the campaign to be waged by "the coalition against terror." In light of this threat, the leaders of these countries rushed to declare, each in his own way, that their countries were not linked with Al Qaida and Islamic terror, and that they were willing to cooperate with the United States in its war against terror.

At the same time as the offensive in Afghanistan, the United States initiated contacts with the governments of Sudan and Yemen and with various powerbrokers in Somalia, to actively recruit them in the war against terror. In addition to these contacts and talks, the United States sent boats, marines and special units to the Red Sea whose mission was to patrol these countries' coasts and prevent the arrival of activists from Al Qaida and other terror organizations fleeing Afghanistan. The presence of the American and Coalition forces was meant to put pressure on the rulers of the countries in the region and enable the United States to take military action in the area if necessary (although the scope of the forces deployed there would enable only limited special campaigns).

The policy adopted by the United States in regard to the countries in this region was based on the "stick and carrot" method. The rulers were promised military and economic aid in exchange for their co-operation along with the threat that if they refused, they would be risking political, economic and military action on the part of the U.S.-led coalition against their governments.

As a result of the Sudanese declaration regarding its willingness to join the war against terror, and after apparently proving this intention by taking practical steps, the economic sanctions imposed on the country due to its involvement in terror were lifted, and the United States began intensive mediation efforts in order to achieve a ceasefire and launch peace talks between the regime in Khartoum and the rebels in the south, an act which to date has been successful.

Yemenite President Salah was also promised military and economic aid in exchange for joining the war against terror. After improving its cooperation in the investigation of the attack against the *USS Cole* and following action taken against Al Qaida activists in its territory, Yemen was granted U.S. economic and military aid, including the provision of combat means and the training of Yemenite forces in counter-terror missions.

In Somalia, contact was initiated between American security entities and various powerbrokers in the country. However, due to the lack of a central, effective government the Americans were forced to initiate separate contacts with each one of these powerbrokers, all of which sought to elicit U.S. support in internal power struggles. Thus, each promised to join the U.S. war against terror and accused its domestic opponents of supporting Al Qaida and Islamic terror entities.

It would therefore appear that the concrete threat posed by the United States and the coalition to strike out at the regimes that support terror, based on the same format as the destruction of the Taliban regime in Afghanistan and Saddam Hussein's regime in Iraq, instigated a change in the approach of the governments in Sudan and Yemen. These regimes were forced to choose between their allegiance to their worldview and support of radical Islam, and the real danger to their governments' survival. For the time being, the consideration of survival has prevailed, forcing a compromise (if only a temporary one) on the ideological and cultural levels. However, this policy forces the rulers to contend with heavy domestic pressures from the direction of opposition circles and mainly from the groups identified with radical Islam. In these circumstances only intensive and ongoing U.S. and international pressure will preserve the policy that these countries have adopted, and any lessening of the pressure may modify the equation and allow these countries to continue supporting radical Islam.

In light of this situation, the United States must take cautious and balanced action in order to refrain from allowing these regimes to collapse, which could lead to the creation of chaotic situations including loss of central governments and the creation of nomadic entities. The latter are openly hostile to the West, a fact that diminishes the political and military influence wielded by the United States and the West, as has been the case in Somalia during the last decade.

The attack against the French oil tanker (October 2002) and the attacks against Israeli targets in Mombassa, Kenya (November 2002) serve as painful reminders to the United States and the rest of the world that the war against Islamic terror in this region is far from over. Thus, when claiming responsibility for the attacks in Mombassa, Al Qaida specifically referred to the struggle in the arena of the Horn of Africa (see the full version of Al Qaida's claiming of responsibility for the attacks in Mombassa in Appendix B):[26]

From the same place that the "crusader-Jewish alliance" sustained a blow four years ago, i.e., in Nairobi and in Dar a-Salaam, in the US embassies there, here again the warriors of the Jihad from the organization of Al Qaida have returned in order to strike a painful blow against this treacherous alliance...

...These two actions come and destroy all of the dreams of the "Jewish-crusader alliance" in this area, and prove the failure of the United States and its allies, which amassed their huge navies in order to surround and lay siege to the Horn of Africa so as to pursue the Jihad fighters in this area and prevent them from penetrating it or dispatching supplies, and to ensure that the attacks that struck them four years ago will not recur.

The Bush administration clearly identifies the risk inherent to the spread of Islamic terror throughout Africa in general, and in Eastern Africa in particular. Against this background, President Bush undertook an African tour in the course of which he visited five countries (Senegal, South Africa, Botswana, Uganda, and Nigeria), with the aim of delivering a message to all of the countries on the African Continent. President Bush emphasized the U.S. commitment to assisting African states in their battles against starvation and AIDS as well as in the promotion of democratic values.[27] During his visit,

President Bush also underlined his determination to persevere in the war against terror, and included Africa. It should be noted that prior to the president's African tour, a plan was prepared by the Pentagon to establish U.S. bases throughout Africa, in order to enable ongoing activity against terror organizations, in the light of U.S. intelligence information that the activities of Al Qaida and other terror organizations were on the rise on this continent.

As of September 2001, a task force of the U.S.-led coalition has been active in the region of the Horn of Africa. The commander of the U.S. force, Major-General John Stellar, stated that the force includes some 1,300 soldiers, about 900 of which are members of special units stationed at the Lemonier base in Djibouti. The force is equipped with transport planes and helicopter gunships, which will enable immediate action throughout the locality.[28] General Stellar also operates a sea task force that patrols the movement of ships in the Bab el-Mandeb Straits along the shores of the Horn of Africa. This task force has been granted the approval of the states in that region—Djibouti, Yemen, Eritrea, and Ethiopia—to act within their boundaries if the need arises. An example of American operational capabilities in this region is reflected in the termination of several Al Qaida activists in Yemen (November 5, 2002), via an UAV armed with missiles that hit the car in which they were traveling.

To date, the overall strategy implemented by the United States in the war against global terror has instigated changes in the policies of Yemen and Sudan, ostensibly turning them into U.S. allies in the war against terror. The combination of U.S. military presence in the region as well the offering of economic and political enticements constitute the main leverage preventing states that formerly supported terror from reverting to their erstwhile policies. The success of U.S. policy can also be seen in the progress in the talks between the Sudanese government and the rebel forces in the south, where recently an agreement was signed between the sides arranging the distribution of revenue from oil resources. This agreement constitutes an important step towards the resolution of controversial issues between the two sides. Another step attributable to the American policy is the agreement between Sudan, Yemen, and Ethiopia to increase cooperation in the war on terror.

Nonetheless, the huge area, teeming with a large and poverty-stricken Muslim population, constitutes an wide field of action for Islamic terror organizations, and therefore in the foreseeable future

Eastern Africa will continue to present a high potential for terror attacks and for the development of terror infrastructures that will pose a threat to the United States and to the Free World.

Notes

1. See the closing speech delivered by the former UN secretary-general Butrus Ghali at the UN conference dealing with public international law: "Towards the Twenty-first Century: International Law as a Language for International Relations," New York (March 13-17, 1995), Documents, p. 9.
2. Max Weber, *Staatssoziolgie* (ed. Johannes Winchelman), Berlin, 1996, p. 27.
3. Arnold Gehlen, in Heiner Keupp, *Lust and der Erkenn tnis: Der Menschals soziales Wesen*, Munich/Zurich, 1995, p. 105 (ICRC translation).
4. Robert S. Bunker, "Epochal Change: War over Social and Political Organization," *Parameters* (Summer 1997), p.15.
5. Ibid., p. 18.
6. Robert Kaplan, "The Coming Anarchy," *The Atlantic Monthly*, February 1994, pp. 44-766.
7. Robert S. Bunker, "Epochal Change: War over Social and Political Organization," p.17.
8. Ibid., p. 19.
9. William S. Lind, "Defending Western Culture," *Foreign Policy*, 84, (Fall 1991), pp. 40-50.
10. http://www.csis.org/press/pr02
11. Literature refers to two categories of actors: Endogenic actors (internal actors) and exogenic actors (external actors).
12. William S. Lind, cited by Samuel Huntington, *The Clash of Civilizations and the Remaking of World Order*, New York: Simon & Schuster, 1996, p. 9.
13. Ibid.
14. John Lechte, *Fifty Key Contemporary Thinkers*, New York: Routledge, 1994.
15. Gilles Deleuze, "Nomad Thought," in David B. Allison (ed.), *The New Nietzsche*, Cambridge, MA: The MIT Press, 1998, p. 149.
16. Ibid.
17. Ibid., p. 148.
18. Ibid.
19. Ibid.
20. This section is based on Yoram Schweitzer and Shaul Shay, *The Globalization of Terror*, The Multidisciplinary Center, Herzliya: Mifalot Publishing, 2003, and New Brunswick, NJ: Transaction Publishers, 2003, pp 58-63.
21. This section is based on Yoram Schweitzer and Shaul Shay, *The Globalization of Terror*, pp. 193-200.
22. Interate Project, *International Terrorism: Attributes of Terrorism Events*.
23. Boaz Ganor, *Defining Terrorism*, The Interdisciplinary Center in Herzliya, Vol. 4, August 1998, pp. 21-22.
24. Paul Wilkinson, *Terrorism and the Liberal States*, Macmillan Education Ltd., 1977, p. 182.
25. Robert I. Rotberg, "Failed States in a World of Terror," *Foreign Affairs*, (July/August 2002), pp. 283, 127-140.
26. Claiming of responsibility by Al Qaida in the Islamic website Azzaf Alratsatch.
27. *Ha'aretz*, Tel Aviv, July 7, 2003.
28. IslamOnline, January 10, 2003.

Appendices

Appendix A
The Conflict between the North and the South

Sudan, in its ethnic, religious, and cultural aspects, is split into two parts: the north's orientation is Arab and Muslim while the south is mainly African, Christian, and pagan. In 1899, Sudan was controlled by an Egyptian-British condominium, which preserved a certain status quo between the northern and southern provinces. Between 1930 and 1946, the prevailing approach among the British administration was that the southern districts must be part of an "East African federation," together with the protectorate areas of Uganda and Kenya, but this concept never reached fruition.[1] Under the pressure applied by the Arab nations, and particularly the leadership of North Sudan, Britain formally withdrew these ideas, and from 1946 onwards supported the integrity of Sudan (north and south).

Following processes related to the establishment of administrative autonomy, an initial formal attempt was made to mould Sudan's character as a future state. In 1947, a conference was held at Juba in southern Sudan, which was attended by representatives of the north and the south (under British sponsorship). A plan for the implementation of "national unity," based mainly on the incorporation of the southern delegates in the Khartoum House of Representatives and administration, was discussed as well as the provision of guarantees to maintain the south's unique character in the areas of culture, language, and religion.[2]

The governor-general of Sudan adopted the agreement issued at the Juba conference and incorporated its principles in a constitution written as the basis for the establishment of a legislative council and an executive council in 1948. Despite the inclusion of these agreements in a constitution, during the years 1947-1955, very little—if anything—was done to implement them. The representation of the south in the political power centers of Khartoum remained symbolic in nature, and most of the economic resources were diverted to the development of the northern provinces while discriminating against the south. The issue of the relationship between the north and the south became acute in 1953 due to the British-Egyptian agreement granting the Sudanese the right of self-definition and implementation of self-rule in that country.

The steps taken to initiate independence in Sudan on the one hand, and the feeling of discrimination that grew among the leadership on the other, raised questions regarding the ability to establish a united state in the spirit of the agreement achieved in Juba. Acts of protest quickly erupted in southern Sudan, and gradually grew more violent. Several months before the granting of independence on August 18, 1955, riots broke out in the southern regions. Military personnel from the north were killed in these riots and the authorities in Khartoum ruthlessly suppressed the riots. However, from this time onwards the south was embroiled in unrest and subversive activity that eventually developed into a civil war.

The problems regarding national integration and unity escalated in anticipation of the discussions regarding the decision to declare independence. In talks held on December 19, 1955, between the representatives from the north and the south, it was agreed that in exchange for the south's agreement to establish a united state, a federative regime would be established that would preserve the legitimate rights of the south.

On January 1, 1956, Sudan declared its independence as a united state, which recognized the rights of the south to establish a federative administration. However, upon the establishment of Sudan, the substantial differences between the north and the south immediately led to power struggles between the central government in Sudan (in the north) and the southern regions, which demanded the realization of the agreements to establish a federation by granting the south autonomy, allocating a larger portion of the resources and political power to this area, and allowing its residents religious freedom.

As a rule, the intensity of the conflict between the north and the south was directly proportionate to the attempts by the regime in the north to enforce Islamic law on the southern regions. Most of the parties that participated in Sudan's first government following its declaration of independence believed in "Arabization" and "Islamization" of the state, but the controversy also related to other issues such as the character of the state (secular/religious), its political orientation (socialist/democratic), etc.[3]

Abud's coup d'état in 1958 and the establishment of a military regime in Sudan led to an acceleration of the conflict between north and south and the exacerbation of the civil war. After Abud's ousting and the establishment of a liberal-democratic administration, a "round table" conference convened in 1956. Agreement was achieved at this conference regarding autonomy for the south, but this accord also never reached fruition.

An about face in the northern-southern relationship occurred after another coup d'état and the ascent of Jaafar al Numeiri (1969). Following the suppression of a failed communist conspiracy against his regime in 1971, al Numeiri formulated a new policy that included democratization of the regime and national reconciliation, as well as an attempt to resolve the dispute between the north and the south.

In November 1971, a peace conference was convened in Addis Ababa, Ethiopia, which was attended by representatives of the Sudanese government and the southern guerrilla forces. The conference's aim was to put an end to the civil war and resolve the main points of dispute between the north and the south, that is, the country's unity, granting greater autonomy to the south in the area of culture, and greater equality in the distribution of political power and economic resources between the north and the south.[4] In the security area it was decided at the conference to put a stop to the fighting and reorganize the Sudanese army, while giving the military a national character and incorporating about 1,000 southern guerrilla fighters into the ranks of the Sudanese army.[5] The issues of religion and culture were resolved in the framework of the new national constitution formulated in 1973, which recognized Islam, Christianity, and other traditional religions as the formal religions of the state. In the political and socioeconomic spheres, it was agreed to initiate steps toward a more equal distribution of the political power and resources.

In 1972-1983, there was a cessation of the civil war in the south, but in practical terms, the discrimination against the south persevered, and the incorporation of southern politicians in the Khartoum administration remained marginal. In 1983, al Numeiri's policies underwent a dramatic change; he adopted an extremist Islamic approach and decided to turn the Sharia into the state law. As a result of the change in this approach, the regime also violated the resolutions of the Addis Ababa conference.

The development by Chevron of the oilfields in the south near Benito, and the Sudanese government's resolution to establish refineries in the north at Port-Sudan and transfer the oil in pipes from the southern oilfields to refineries in the north met with sharp opposition from the south, which was aware that this step was aimed at keeping the anticipated income from the oil in the hands of the rulers in the north. The attempt to impose the laws of the Sharia and to introduce administrative changes aimed at weakening the south caused a quick renewal of the hostilities and civil war. Professor Ali Mazroi described the conflict between the two rival camps:[6]

Africa was torn between the forces of anarchy on one side, in the sense of decentralized violence, and the forces of tyranny, in the sense of orchestrated centralized repression.

In order to renew the struggle against the regime in Khartoum, the south organized itself on two levels: on the political level, a political branch was established—the SPLM (Sudan People's Liberation Movement); on the military level, a military branch called the SPLA (the Sudan People's Liberation Army) was established. The manifest of the SPLM/SPLA stated that the movement's struggle was to liberate the country from its foes—the bourgeois elitism of the north and the south, the religious (Islamic) Fundamentalism and the reactionary commanders from the south (the reference was to the Anyanya 2 commanders, who pledged allegiance to the north). During the initial period after its establishment the movement was satisfied with political-social change, but, subsequently, defined far-reaching objectives of autonomy and even independence, while severing ties with the north.

The ousting of al Numeiri in April 1986 did not put an end to the civil war in the south, but due to the establishment of a new government headed by Zadek al Mahdi the dialogue between the south and the government was renewed, at the end of which the sides announced a joint declaration of principles—the Koka Dam declaration (named for the location of the talks). In the joint declaration issued by the leaders of the liberation army and the SPLM, as well as the leaders of the main parties in the north, it was agreed to take action in anticipation of the assembly of a constitutional convention for the resolution of the main political disputes between the north and the south. Nevertheless, despite the Koka Dam declaration, the conflict continued in the south and even worsened due to the fact that the NIF (the National Islamic Front) had joined the coalition headed by Zadek al Mahdi. The controversy peaked with the ascent of Omar al Beshir to power (1989), who together with Hassan al Turabi (leader of the NIF) founded a Fundamentalist Islamic regime.

Omar al Beshir's regime approved the establishment of a militia called the PDF (Popular Defense Force) by al Turabi, which in cooperation with the Sudanese Army was to suppress subversion in the south. In contrast to the Sudanese army, most of whose power was based on unmotivated mandatory recruits (some of whom were even conscripted from the population of southern Sudan), the PDF was based on Muslim volunteers from the north who were highly motivated and regarded the war in the south as a Jihad.[7]

The SPLA/SPLM, under the leadership of John Garang, endeavored to establish effective political and military leadership that would unite all of the forces opposed to al Beshir's regime in the north. The decisions regarding the issues of managing the campaign, the lives of the population in the areas under the SPLA's control, and the political steps were all reached at the joint military-political forum, but the enforcement and implementation of the resolutions proved to be extremely difficult due to the tremendous decentralization of the forces and the warlords in the south, and the political and personal conflicts of interest among the leaders and local commanders.

During the years 1990-1993, the regime in Khartoum initiated the process of the country's Islamization and introduced a series of military steps with the aim of defeating the south. The assault initiated by the government forces fell upon the southern rebels during a period of a debilitating crisis which stemmed from the following causes:

- Conflict among the ranks of the southern military and political leadership caused it to split into three factions: the central faction led by John Garang, leader of the SPLA; an additional faction led by Garang's former deputy, Lam Akol, who left the SPLM due to personal power struggles and established his own faction; and a third faction led by Riak Machar (the Movement for the Independence of South Sudan), who broke away from the SPLM mainly due to a tribal rift.
- The economic and military aid granted to the rebel movements in south Sudan by the neighboring countries of Uganda and Ethiopia was decreased due to the ascent of new leadership in these countries.

In the spring of 1993, government forces initiated a wide-ranged offensive in the south with the logistical help and advice of Iran, and they attained a series of achievements in the battlefield that forced the leaders of the rebels in the south to agree to peace talks. The talks opened in Abudja, the capital of Nigeria, but the representatives of the south Sudan rebels arrived at the talks divided (each of the factions sent their own representatives), and at their end, the parties did not even succeed in reaching an agreement to stop the fighting in the south, let alone a permanent resolution to the dispute between the north and the south.

In January 1994, the offensive of the government forces was renewed against the rebel strongholds in the south. Initially, the assault was slow, but it gathered momentum in June 1994, when the government forces succeeded in capturing several provincial cities that had been under rebel control, including the city of Kaja Kaja near the Ugandan border, which served as the logistic base, housing the headquarters of John Garang. At the end of 1994, the offensive abated due to the shortage of combat equipment and ammunition, and also as a result of the rainy season that restricted the movement of the government forces, and the initiative passed into the hands of the rebels, who began attacking concentrations of forces and government centers in the south. In the beginning of February 1995 (as in previous years), the assault was renewed by the government forces, with the main effort concentrated on the rebel forces located in southeast Sudan near the Ethiopian border and led by Riak Machar. These skirmishes caused thousands of Sudanese refugees to flee to Ethiopia and Uganda.

Against the background of the intensified fighting in the south and the bitterness that prevailed in some of the government troops, an uprising erupted in one of the divisions issued the command to "move down south" and join the warfare. The uprising was suppressed by military forces led by the defense minister that were loyal to the regime, but this revolt reflected the bitterness that prevailed in the ranks of the Sudanese army due to the harsh conditions, the low wages, the shortage of fighting means and ammunition, and the preference for Turabi's "Popular Defense Forces" over the army. It would appear that following these incidents, Sudanese President Omar al Beshir instructed the provincial governors to raise the quota of recruitment to the Popular Defense Forces in their regions to 30,000 men from each district by June 1995. In light of the defeats in the battlefield, discussions were launched in 1995 between the rival factions among the southern rebels in an attempt to consolidate the ranks and improve their fighting capabilities against the regime in

Khartoum. At the same time, the spokesperson for the SPLA announced that its forces would cooperate with Muslim opposition entities in the north.

In March 1995, former U.S. president Jimmy Carter visited Sudan in an effort to find a resolution to the conflict between the north and the south. Both the central government in Khartoum—due to its increasing difficulties in managing the campaign, and the rebels—in consequence of their failures and the losses they had sustained in the latest round of skirmishes—responded to Carter's initiative and consented to a two-month ceasefire. However, this mediation effort failed too, much like its predecessors, and the civil war in Sudan continued.

The assassination attempt against Egyptian President Hussni Mubarak during his visit to Ethiopia in June 1995 exacerbated the tension between Egypt and Ethiopia and al Beshir's regime, which was accused of involvement in the assassination attempt and supporting terror. Consequently, Ethiopia stepped up its support of the rebel organizations in the south, and Egypt increased its political and military pressure on the al Beshir administration. The Sudanese government was facing various troubles, and the rebel movements in the south recovered and reinforced their ranks in anticipation of the continued struggle.

In the years 1996-2002, the conflict continued between the regime in Khartoum and the rebel organizations in the south, which enjoyed the support of neighboring African countries like Ethiopia, Uganda, and Eritrea that felt threatened by the Islamic regime in Khartoum. Humanitarian organizations in the West, as well as UN aid agencies, agreed to help the civilian population in the south, which was the main victim of the ongoing war, not only due to damages inflicted by the fighting but mainly because of starvation and disease that spread in consequence of the war, the destroyed economic and civil infrastructures, and years of severe drought.

The Sudanese government's political and economic isolation stemming from its support of radical Islam and terror (the assassination attempt against Mubarak, the attacks at the U.S. Embassies in Kenya and Tanzania, the activity of Bin Laden and Al Qaida on Sudanese soil) weakened its ability to contend with the challenges posed by the rebels in the south, thus creating a reality of perpetual war in which neither side could prevail or, alternatively, put an end to the violence.

Three main factors led to the attainment of a ceasefire in 2002 and to the launching of peace talks between the rival parties:

- The internal political struggle in Khartoum undermined the status and influence of Hassan al Turabi, who had adopted an extremist approach to the struggle in the south;
- The attacks on September 11 2001, the U.S. declaration of the war against terror, and al Beshir's fear that Sudan would become a target of this war combined to cause a turnabout in Sudan's policies and motivated it to cooperate with the United States, including the U.S. mediator who was acting to achieve a ceasefire in the country's civil war;
- The oil produced in the southern regions of the state could significantly change Sudan's economic plight, but is contingent upon the achievement of peace and internal stability.

The Sudanese government and the rebel organizations led by John Garang launched negotiations in July 2002 via U.S. mediation, which first took place in Switzerland and then shifted to Kenya. In October 2002, the parties reached a ceasefire agreement, and it was agreed to continue with the talks in order to put an end to the war.[8] The rebels' spokesman, Samson Kwaje, told the BBC that both parties had conceded that after a six-year period a referendum would be conducted regarding the right to self-definition of Sudan's southern provinces, as well as in the matter of the imposition of Islamic law in north Sudan only. The government's representative to the talks, Gazi Sallah a-Din, stated that the agreement included a plan that would resolve the substantial problems related to religion and state, as well as self-definition in the southern provinces. "Those were the two most difficult problems that we faced," he added.[9]

The agreement was signed following five weeks of negotiations in the city of Machkos, Kenya, and its implementation was contingent upon the cessation of all violent activity. It was signed between the government and the SPLA in addition to several other factions, but it did not cover all of the rebel groups active in the south. In mid-November 2002, the parties declared that they were extending the ceasefire agreement and continuing the peace talks until March 2003. On January 1, 2003, in a Sudanese Independence Day speech delivered by Sudanese President al Beshir in the city of Melcal in southern Sudan, he stated, "Sudan is interested in a comprehensive peace in the framework of which there will no longer be hegemony of one party in the country."[10] The president elaborated that he was referring to a just distribution of political power and resources between the government and the rebel movements in the south.

However, the peace process is fragile and has encountered considerable difficulties on the part of all the parties involved.

- Mass demonstrations organized by the leaders of radical Islamic movements in Khartoum called for the prevention of Sudan's becoming "a secular state" and demanded that a stop be put to any attempt to actively divide it into separate entities in the north and south.[11]
- The government in Khartoum claimed that some of the isolationist movements in the south were not honoring the ceasefire agreement and were continuing to attack government forces.
- Leaders of the SPLM and heads of international humanitarian organizations claim that government forces are conducting "ethnic cleansing" in southern Sudan in areas near the oilfields. According to these reports, over 200,000 citizens have abandoned their homes and have become refugees. According to certain evaluations, Sudan is attempting to establish "facts in the field" in areas of strategic economic importance prior to the signing of peace agreements that will determine the fate of these sites.[12]

On January 8, 2004, despite all of the difficulties mentioned above, the Sudanese government and the rebel forces in the country signed an agreement for the distribution of the country's resources—the first step towards the resolution of the controversial issues between the parties and the achievement of a peace agreement.

The dispute related to the distribution of revenue from the oilfields had exacerbated the friction between the parties in recent years, after the Sudanese government had attempted forcefully to take over the oil-rich areas that were located in the rebels' areas of influence. Rebels' organizations and human rights activists claimed that the government was evicting thousands of southern villagers from their homes—people who identified with the movement to liberate Sudan and resided in the areas of the oilfields.

The main issue covered by the agreement concerns the distribution of Sudan's revenue from the sale of about 250,000 barrels of oil daily, which are produced in the state's southern region. According to the agreement, the income from the oilfields will be divided equally between the sides during an interim period of six years, at the end of which discussions will be held regarding permanent arrangements in the country; at that time the possibility of dividing Sudan into two independent states will be raised for discussion.

The agreement also addresses other economic issues, the most important of which is the question of economic freedom under religion: As the central Sudanese government is based on Islam, most of the banks in the country act according to Muslim religious law, which forbids charging most kinds of interest. According to the agreement, Western banks may operate in Southern Sudan and act according to accepted standards in the Western world. In addition, a new currency will be set for the country.

Another agreement that the sides are endeavoring to achieve in anticipation of an overall peace agreement will finally determine the regional division between the north and the south. The main dispute relates to three controversial border areas, which the sides will have to divide among themselves. The Sudanese government and the rebels will also have to come to an agreement regarding the distribution of authority between the two parties, and the representation that the rebels will have in the government, the Parliament and the civil service during the transition period. At the end of this period, the residents of the south will vote in a referendum regarding whether they wish to remain part of Sudan or separate from it.

On May 26, 2004, the two sides signed a peace accord, ending a twenty-one-year war that killed 2 million people. Addressing the Sudanese nation at the 15th anniversary of the National Salvation Revolution, President al Bashir said that the realization of peace in Sudan placed before the nation a new challenge of development and rehabilitation, boosting peace and making voluntary unity the sole option for the Sudanese people. He claimed that the peace was the most important event in Sudan after the nation's independence.[13]

However, the peace accord signed on May 26, 2004, does not include a separate conflict in the western region—Drafur. In July 2004, U.S. Secretary of State Colin Powell and U.N. Secretary Kofi Annan called on al Bashir's government to rein in Arab militias blamed for attacks on African villages in Drafur, where the conflict caused the deaths of more than 30,000 people and drove more than 1 million people from their homes.[14]

It would appear that the willingness of the north to cooperate in peace talks stems mainly from American pressure applied on al Beshir's regime through the carrot and stick method; the stick is the American threat to take forceful steps against the Sudanese regime, while the carrot constitutes the lifting of sanctions imposed upon Sudan and the significant economic improvement to be anticipated upon the cessation of the civil war, which costs the country millions of dollars annually.

Appendix B
The Wording of the Claiming of Responsibility by Al Qaida for the Attacks in Mombassa, Kenya

Praise to Allah who said: "And you shall kill the collaborators wherever you shall find them, and you will take them captive and you shall set upon them every ambush" (the Surah of Repentance).

In this honored month, in its last blessed ten days, we first greet our brethren in Palestine, and then our Muslim nation. We purposely delayed these greetings, so that they would come at the same time as two actions in Mombassa Kenya against Israeli interests, so that this blessing will be meaningful in these circumstances, when the nation suffers at the hands of its crusader and Jewish foes.

From the very location where the "crusader-Jewish alliance" was struck four years ago, meaning Nairobi and Dar a-Salaam, at the U.S. Embassies there, here the mujahidin of the Al Qaida organization return again to strike a painful blow to this treacherous alliance. But this time against the Jews, in order to relay a message to them as follows: the deeds you perform—the spreading of corruption on earth, the conquest of our holy sites and the crimes against our brethren in Palestine—the slaughter of children, women and the elderly, the demolishment of homes, the uprooting of trees and the imposing of an unjustified siege—will not pass without a similar act, which surpasses it in impact. For our children your children, for our women your women, for our elderly your elderly, for our houses your strongholds, and for the siege over a slice of bread, a siege of terror and fear, where we will pursue you wherever you may be—on land, in the sea and in the air.

The mujahidin have adhered to their commitment to Allah to support His religion and fulfilled the obligation that they have undertaken upon themselves vis-à-vis their nation to boost it and remove the insult and humiliation from upon it, by striking painful blows and successful actions against the treacherous crusader-Jewish alliance, before and after they perpetrated the following actions:

1. Destruction of the American Embassy in Nairobi;
2. Destruction of the American Embassy in Dar a-Salaam;

3.   Destruction of the *USS Cole* in Aden;
4.   Destruction of the World Trade Center in New York;
5.   Destruction of the U.S. military stronghold, the Pentagon;
6.   Hijacking of an American airplane in Pennsylvania on its way to the American Congress.

The United States has gone mad because of the terror and anxiety that have struck it because of what it has seen and heard, and because it could not bear what has struck at it, undermined its entity and eradicated its prestige forever more. Therefore, it forced the whole world to join its ranks and launched a cruel offensive, the like of which never occurred in history both old and new, against the group of believers fighting the Jihad and against the young Islamic state, thinking that in this way it would succeed in extinguishing the ember of Jihad and eradicating the armies of Allah.

The entire world became an office of the American intelligence department, pursuing them at any location on earth and under the skies. They have forgotten that the Islamic faith fortifies, is fortified and puts down roots during times of trouble, distress and pressure, and the mujahidin have proved this in reality and succeeded, thanks to Allah, to deal their blows and carry out their attacks during a year of persecution and pursuit. They have attempted and perpetrated the following actions since the beginning of the crusade against Afghanistan in the middle of the month of Rajeb 1422 (according to the Hajri calendar, parallel to the beginning of October 2001) to date:

1.   The Djerba attack against a Jewish synagogue in Tunisia;
2.   The booby-trapped shoe on an American passenger plane;
3.   The attack against French soldiers in Pakistan;
4.   The attack against the huge oil tanker in al-Machla, Yemen;
5.   The killing of U.S. marines in the island of Filcha, Kuwait;
6.   The destruction of a nightclub at Bali and additional acts that accompanied it on the same day in Indonesia.
7.   Two attacks in Mombassa, Kenya against Jewish interests (the launching of two missiles against an Israeli airplane and the eradication of a hotel where Israelis were staying);
8.   Scores of attacks in Afghanistan and in other places worldwide;
9.   Additional acts that were not mentioned due to special considerations.

They emphasize that their blows will continue with Allah's help, so that the entire world will know that the crusader war against Islam and Muslims has failed, and it will never succeed or bear fruit according to the desire of those who incite it—the Jews and the crusaders—because in essence, it is the war between faith and heresy, between truth and lies, between justice and injustice, and Allah delivers victory to this religion, and supports His servants, the commanded fighters.

The two attacks in Mombassa against Israeli targets come just at this time in order to prove several important facts and special meanings including:

1.   That the mujahidin succeeded in achieving their chosen goal with superior attention, while the entire world, in the east and west, stands against them and persecutes them everywhere on earth. This proves the weakness of this campaign, its disintegration and its helplessness in the face of the successful movements and attacks of the mujahidin.

2.   Also, these two actions come and destroy all of the dreams of the "Jewish-crusader alliance" in this area, and prove the failure of the United States and its allies, which amassed their huge navies in order to surround and lay siege to the Horn of Africa so as to pursue the Jihad fighters in this area and prevent them from penetrating it or dispatching supplies, and to ensure that the attacks that struck them four years ago will not recur.

3.   These two actions are an additional slap in the face to the Israeli "Mossad," just as it was made to sustain a slap in the face when the Jewish synagogue in Djerba was attacked, and as they dealt a slap in the face to all of the American security mechanisms earlier, a slap that has put an end to its myth and image, through which it frightened the whole world due to its ability to infiltrate and reach whoever it wants. In this way they amputate the arm that Sharon declared would reach anyone who tried to harm the security of Israel internally and externally.

4.   And these two actions come to pose a thousand question marks and exclamation marks vis-à-vis countries that join this alliance, which spent billions on plans to secure flights within, and here they face the storm of the mujahidin from the outside, and where did it come from?!

5.   These two attacks also reiterate that nations that place murderers and war criminals on the throne of government, as do the Americans, the Jews and others, will bear the responsibility for their acts and aspirations, and will not evade divine vengeance delivered at the hands of His mujahidin servants. Our new proof is what happened in Bali and the developments that came as a result, which caused sleepless nights to the nation's foes in every place.

Also, these two actions proclaim to Muslims everywhere that the mujahidin identify with their brethren in Palestine and continue fearlessly in their path, determined to cast off humiliation from their nation. Thanks to Allah they continue to grasp the reins of this initiative, and they are capable of surprising the enemy and strike out at his vital organs at the appropriate place and time, and they are the ones to determine this.

And finally, these two actions are meant to declare that the nation, including its Arab and non-Arab sons, the black and the white, faced this enemy and the offensive declared against the Muslims as one man.

We call on all our dark-skinned brothers on this continent, which are the nations that suffer most from the colonialism, that stole their lands, plundered their lands, turned them into their slaves and deprived them of basic human rights, to emulate the examples of the heroes of these two actions in Mombassa and turn the land into hell under the feet of the Jewish and crusader invaders.

And in summary, we call on the Muslims in the east and west to unite, come together and abandon their dissension and disputes. We also call on them to bear full responsibility for this crusader-Jewish attack, which is primarily meant to uproot the Muslims, obliterate their faith, invade their countries and steal their resources and treasures. They must know that they are capable of acting against this enemy. The complex of "victim" that haunted us for over one hundred years has disappeared never to return, and the years of wandering and defeat that our enemy wished us to endure have with Allah's assistance turned into days of triumph, pride and ability.

The proof that your brothers have presented to you through their actions, the blood with which they paid and the money and time that they invested attest to the ability of this nation to give, to rise and stand strong for eternity.

On this blessed occasion, we remind Muslims that it is dangerous to be dragged into the error of reconciling themselves to what America and its allies are preparing for the Iraqi, Muslim people. They must rise to their brothers' aid using all means and must not allow the American invader to set foot on their land. They must oppose this in every way and manner, so that he will feel that he is on territory that will not accept him, under a sky that does not cast shade upon him, and is among hostile nations that abhor him.

Signed:
The political bureau of the Al Qaida Organization—Algihad, Monday, 27 Ramchan 1423, December 2, 2002.

Notes

1.   Francis Deng and Prosser Gifford (eds.) *The Search for Peace and Unity in Sudan*, Washington D.C.: The Wilson Center Press, 1987, p. 10.
2.   Chris O'Brien, "Islam and Power in Black Africa," in A. Cudsi, H. Dessuki, and E. Ali (eds.) *Islam and Power*, London: Croom Helm, 1981.
3.   Dustan M. Wai, *The African-Arab Conflict in the Sudan*, New York and London: African Publishing Company, 1980, chapter 6.
4.   Draft Organic Law to Organize Regional Self Government in the Southern Provinces of the Democratic Republic of the Sudan, Charter 4, Article 7.
5.   Gustavo Beanvides and M. W. Daly (eds.), *Religion and Political Power*, New York: African Publishing Company 1989, p. 83.
6.   P. M. Holt, M. W. Holt, and M. W. Daly, *The History of the Sudan*, Boulder CO: Westview Press, 1979, pp. 89-102.
7.   Randolph Martin, "Sudan's Perfect War," *Foreign Affairs*, March/April 2002.
8.   IslamOnline, October 15, 2002.
9.   IslamOnline, January 2, 2003.
10. Ibid.
11. IslamOnline, June 9, 2003.
12. According to reports of the French new service AFP from Khartoum, January 16-18, 2003.
13. *Sudan Tribune,* Khartoum, June 29, 2004.
14. *Sudan Tribune,* Khartoum, June 1, 2004.

Index